Talking Stones

TALKING STONES

The Politics of Memorialization in Post-Conflict Northern Ireland

Elisabetta Viggiani

berghahn
NEW YORK · OXFORD
www.berghahnbooks.com

Published in 2014 by
Berghahn Books
www.berghahnbooks.com

Library of Congress Cataloging-in-Publication Data
Viggiani, Elisabetta.
Talking stones: the politics of memorialization in post-conflict Northern
Ireland / Elisabetta Viggiani.
    pages cm
Includes bibliographical references and index.
ISBN 978-1-78238-407-6 (hardback) -- ISBN 978-1-78533-341-5 (paperback)
-- ISBN 978-1-78238-408-3 (ebook)
  1. Memorialization--Political aspects--Northern Ireland. 2. Collective
memory--Northern Ireland. 3. Political violence--Northern Ireland--History--
20th century. 4. Northern Ireland--Politics and government--1994- I. Title.
  DA990.U46V45 2014
  941.60824--dc23

                                                              2014014153

British Library Cataloguing in Publication Data

A catalogue record for this book is available from the British Library

ISBN 978-1-78238-407-6 (hardback)
ISBN 978-1-78533-341-5 (paperback)
ISBN 978-1-78238-408-3 (ebook)

To Professor A. Musacchio, Alvaro and my beloved grandparents, Elvia and Nino

Men make their own history, but they do not make it as they please; they do not make it under self-selected circumstances, but under circumstances existing already, given and transmitted from the past. The tradition of all dead generations weighs like a nightmare on the brains of the living. And just as they seem to be occupied with revolutionizing themselves and things, creating something that did not exist before, precisely in such epochs of revolutionary crisis they anxiously conjure up the spirits of the past to their service, borrowing from them names, battle slogans, and costumes in order to present this new scene in world history in time-honored disguise and borrowed language.

– Karl Marx, 1852

CONTENTS

FIGURES

TABLES

FOREWORD

Commemoration City:
Shared Futures through Contested Pasts

Belfast 2013. The city has changed. It is almost twenty years since the ceasefires and fifteen since the signing of the political settlement that brought widespread and violent hostilities to an end. The city streets that rioters had so often dug up to hurl at the police and military as well as at one another have once again been paved, if not with gold, then at least with expensive pavoirs. Long gone are the hollowed shells of burnt-out buildings and the toothless gape of empty bomb sites. The skyline is punctuated now by concert halls, shopping malls and iconic, landmark new builds, one of which commemorates Belfast's historic contribution to shipbuilding, a reminder that, even as it regenerates, the city has never been short of things to remember. Yet at the same time, other rents remain in the city fabric, if not of bomb site then in an explosion of debate and sometimes anger at what could or should be remembered and recalled. Belfast is now the undisputed boomtown of disputed anniversaries, a Commemoration City where the site of memory is more hotly contested than any piece of commercial real estate.

Cities transitioning from conflict like Belfast provide productive contexts for the exploration of how violent events of the past are understood and represented. Yet transitional societies often struggle with how and whether to remember the events of their recent past – and with what to include, omit or forget. This richly textured book engages with these issues of memory and the past, and moves them on through a compelling analysis of the Irish case. It argues that the void created by the absence of an official state policy on memorialization in Northern Ireland has been occupied by a broad range of groups and organizations, each with its own manner of, and reasons for, remembering: victims' and survivor groups, churches, theatrical companies, ex-prisoner organizations and residents' groups. Some of the media of remembering deployed by these groups is more visible and durable than others and includes vigils, storytelling, stained-glass windows, pop-up theatre and the construction of physical monuments. The principal focus here is on physical sites of remembrance, such as memorial gardens, plaques and murals, sites that are routinely visible to passers-by and of which the author mapped no fewer than 157 in the Belfast urban area, 79 per cent of which were built since the agreement was signed in 1998. Ironically, it is perhaps these most visible forms of recalling the recent past in Northern Ireland – gardens of remembrance and memorial plaques – that have been the least well documented, and we are indebted to the author for her comprehensive account.

This efflorescence of public and lay monumentalizing has coincided with a massive upsurge of interest in memory in the social sciences, much of it stimulated by Maurice Halbwachs, whose writings in the first half of the last century introduced the concept of 'collective memory', which stresses that individual memories are shared memories, framed by group membership, and dependent on social relations. Halbwachs's work generated widespread interest in previously disenfranchized and subordinated groups, whose memories had often been dominated, hidden or actively suppressed by the 'official' memories of the state and by other powerful institutions and elites. Memories hitherto marginalized became increasingly recognized as legitimate windows on the past which could complement, balance or challenge dominant historical accounts in a development that democratized memory and encouraged diverse voices to speak. These interpretative strands underpin the analysis in this book, which focuses on the particularly striking and singular case of what unfolds when there is no agreed, official, state-sanctioned approach to memorializing the past, despite long-standing recommendations that consideration should be given to such an approach.

Using extended case studies, the book documents how memory making and nation building – so often the jealous monopoly of the state – have flourished in Belfast in the hands of a range of non-state organizations, some of which, though bordering on legality, have the moral endorsement of sections of the population. It shows how, through memorials and murals, each of the groups (two Republican and two Loyalist) considered here imprint upon the cityscape their distinctive memories and readings of the past that contain their own exclusions, inclusions, silencings and celebrations. The outcome is a scattering of the past and a fragmentation across space and memory of the contested elements of which that past is retrospectively composed. More than just an architectural backdrop to urban life that determines the territorial boundaries to partisan and moral readings of a violent history, these permanent monuments and competing testaments to the past themselves substantiate and shape memories through their symbolic, spatial and linguistic codes.

Belfast's memorials to the conflict often have a superficial similarity irrespective of origin, and they draw in some measure on shared cultural forms of garden remembrance that include engraved stone slabs of marble or granite, lists of names and dates, floral tributes, landscaped paving, shrubs and gravel, and outdoor seating. But these superficial similarities of appearance belie starkly different political and moral readings of the past and the legitimacy or illegitimacy of the violence that took place then which are evident from a memorial's location and expressed through symbol and text. National and other flags as well as symbols associated with republicanism or loyalism – such as harp or crown, lily or poppy – as well as content of the text and contrasting use of language distinguish each side in addition to the style of the commemorative displays performed there.

It is crucial to remember that many of those who support these memorials – organizationally, financially and by providing labour and materials – consider them central to claims to justice and recognition. The memorials offer a means (and, for some, the only means) of truth telling and of dealing with the losses of the past. That the sacrifices of 'fallen comrades' during the armed struggle were commemorated in public memorials through which they achieved a wider recognition, for example, played a part in encouraging some paramilitary groups to relinquish violence. At the same time, of course, memorials materialize the city's divisions, leading some commentators to argue that they represent a continuation of ethnic division and conflict by other means, and are always at risk of being usurped for political and instrumental ends. Certainly they have been effective as settings through which to infuse contemporary political messages with the pedigree of the past. But to view the memorials only in these terms, as the work of memory entrepreneurs who choreograph the past for purely political ends, would be to over-simplify their role and how they are experienced. We learn in this book that effective memorials are synoptic in that they collapse the local and the national, the individual and collective, the past, the present and the future, not in the sense that they mean all things to all people at all times but in so far as their interpretative flexibility and adaptability are responsive to context and change. Memorials mean different things to different people and even to the same person at different times. Yet they are not open to just any interpretation. Instead, they offer a framework that encompasses interpretative possibilities while allowing for variation constrained within a set of acceptable possibilities. They therefore condense much variation, becoming reservoirs of a potential range of meanings and actions, only some parts of which are actualized at any particular moment. Even though their concrete and brick are apparently impervious to change, they are complex communicative channels that can be used to look backwards and forwards, as conduits to the past which offer credibility and legitimacy to new messages for the future that transform the message of the group in response to political contexts of transition in what could be seen as a politics – rather than a conflict – by other means.

Just as memorials ethnicize the urban environment so they also emotionalize it, evoking for some people feelings of fear, anger, revulsion, revenge, for others feelings of compassion, empathy, regret, and for yet others an ambivalent, incoherent and shifting mix of all of these. Even as emotions are obviously also susceptible to partisan readings, they also transcend political divisions and many individuals on all sides struggle with the entanglements of politics, emotion and morality that these memory narratives represent. Memorials recognize the past but they confront people with it as well, challenging them to reflect and make up their minds about events and actions in which they themselves may have been involved and about which some now feel equivocal. Belfast's many memorials to the conflict have been successful in constructing a narrative memory of the past, but there remain those who, while recognizing themselves in that collective memory, struggle even to *think* about what they did, never mind *speak* of it. Such a potent package of emotions paradoxically marks both the divisive power of memorials and their transcendent potential.

As physical structures, memorial plaques and remembrance gardens are built to endure. They concretize history and project it forwards in perpetuity, enabling possible future evocations of the events they embody. They both stand for history and stand against it, in the sense that while they represent the past they also resist the forgetting that the passing of time may bring about. Long after those with direct experience of these events have gone, the monuments are likely to remain, perhaps 'invisible' to some of those who follow and who simply pass them by, but also open to activation by others who in future find in them the potential to express new forms of grievance and hurt. Exactly how and for what purposes events and individuals marked by memorials are remembered are open to change and to being reimagined and reinvented. As well as looking back memorials project ahead, casting shadow or light depending on where and in what manner they are interpreted and reflected.

In this respect, *Talking Stones* offers grounds for optimism. At the heart of the book is a persuasive argument and vision that suggests that grassroots' versions of the past may be more effective in establishing common ground between opposing groups than all the efforts at inclusivity instituted from above. In this view, rather than contributing to the perpetuation of the conflict, the memorials and commemorations analysed here may offer a means to transform it. A reading of the past which sees its violence and suffering from an experiential perspective, through the eyes of those who were there and endured the trauma and pain, can offer an essentially human account that is blind to sectarian advantage and blame, and can provide a first step on the path from contested past to common future.

Hastings Donnan
November 2013

ACKNOWLEDGEMENTS

I wish to express my deep gratitude for the help, invaluable insight and knowledge provided by my mentors, Dr Dominic Bryan and Prof. Hastings Donnan, who have supported me throughout my journey at Queen's University Belfast; in particular, I would like to thank them for their encouragement to undertake the door-to-door survey, which resulted in one of the elements of my research that I am most proud of.

I am hugely indebted to Dr Kris Brown who followed and advised me since my first day of fieldwork in 2006. Without his extensive knowledge of the topic and the city of Belfast, his encouragement when problems arose, and his constant support, friendship and constructive criticism, this book would not have been possible. One day we will write together that famous guide on the best Ulster fry in Belfast. To my dearest colleague, office sharer and housemate, Dr Liam Kelly, goes all my affection; it has been an incredible journey and you will always be in all the best memories of my time in Belfast. Dr Gordon Gillespie and the staff of the Institute of Irish Studies, Queen's University Belfast, in particular Joan Watson and Valerie Miller, have also helped me with their support, advice and friendship.

I am most grateful to all those people of Northern Ireland who agreed to be interviewed or to participate in my survey, as without their collaboration none of this would have happened. In particular, I would like to thank Gerard Murray, who provided invaluable access to material related to the INLA/IRSP Belfast Teach na Fáilte, and Jackie McDonald, who always welcomed me when I popped down uninvited to the John McMichael Centre in Sandy Row; and I sincerely appreciated the kindness of the ladies and gentlemen who invited me to their homes for tea or supper during my fieldwork.

Belfast City Council, the Northern Ireland Housing Executive, the Northern Ireland Planning Service and the Northern Ireland Roads Service either provided information or access to archives. Special thanks go to the staffs of the Linen Hall Library, Belfast (Northern Ireland

Political Collection) and the Belfast Central Library (Newspaper Library) for their assistance.

I would like to thank the amazing team at Berghahn Books for enabling me to publish this book, in particular Adam Capitanio and Charlotte Mosedale for their patience and help in guiding me through the editing and publishing process. I would also like to thank the following people who have helped me with proofreading and the collection and display of data: Stuart Boyd, Jason Conlon, Daniela Cossu, Simone Cucchi, Matt Hunt, Karen Lane, Christopher McAtackney and Barnaly Pande. Special thanks to Eliana Bucceri for her invaluable help and skills in building my online database 'Talking Stones'.

This work was partly funded by a Department for Employment and Learning (DEL) Research Studentship and the Larmor-University Studentship.

LIST OF ABBREVIATIONS

CAIN   Conflict Archive on the INternet
CIRA   Continuity Irish Republican Army
CLMC   Combined Loyalist Military Command
DUP   Democratic Unionist Party
GAA   Gaelic Athletic Association
ICA   Irish Citizen Army
INLA   Irish National Liberation Army
IRA   Irish Republican Army
IRB   Irish Republican Brotherhood
IRSM   Irish Republican Socialist Movement
IRSP   Irish Republican Socialist Party
LPA   Loyalist Prisoners' Aid / also Loyalist Prisoners' Association
         (UDA)
MLA   Member of Legislative Assembly
NICRA   Northern Ireland Civil Rights Association
OIRA   Official Irish Republican Army
PAF   Protestant Action Force
PIRA   Provisional Irish Republican Army
PUP   Progressive Unionist Party
RHC   Red Hand Commando (UVF)
RIR   Royal Irish Regiment
RIRA   Real Irish Republican Army
RUC   Royal Ulster Constabulary
SAS   Special Air Service
SDLP   Social Democratic and Labour Party
SF   Sinn Féin
UDA   Ulster Defence Association
UDF   Ulster Defence Force (UDA)
UDP   Ulster Democratic Party
UDR   Ulster Defence Regiment
UFF   Ulster Freedom Fighters (UDA)

UPRG	Ulster Political Research Group (UDA)
UUP	Ulster Unionist Party
UVF	Ulster Volunteer Force
UYM	Ulster Young Militants (UDA)
YCV	Young Citizen Volunteers (UVF)
WDA	Woodvale Defence Association (UDA)

INTRODUCTION

Memorials as Silent Extras or Scripted Actors?

$$\ggg \bullet \lll$$

One man killed, 153 people injured and over 800 people arrested – this was the price paid in the name of memory a few years back in Tallinn, Estonia's capital, during two nights of clashes over a Soviet war monument. The bloody controversy arose after the Estonian government passed a bill that allowed the removal of a bronze statue of a Soviet soldier that had stood in the centre of the capital since 1947. Estonian nationalists – who regarded the statue as a symbol of the nearly fifty years of Soviet occupation of the country – clashed with ethnic-Russian Estonians who, in contrast, saw the statue as a symbol of the liberation of the country from the Nazis by the Red Army during the Second World War. Calm was restored after two days of rioting, looting and vandalism, with the authorities being forced to move the statue to a secret location, ultimately placing it at the military cemetery in Tallinn. The 'Bronze Night' – as it is commonly remembered – was the worst episode of civil unrest in Estonia since the Soviet reoccupation in 1944, and one of the lowest points in diplomatic relations between Estonia and Russia since the collapse of the Soviet Union and the country's independence in 1991 ('Tallinn Tense after Deadly Riots' 2007). The Estonian government allocated 4.6 million euros from its federal reserve to cover the damage caused by the riots to public properties, vehicles and private businesses, in addition to the costs for the police operation, the reburial of the bodies and the guarding of the diplomatic missions in Moscow and St Petersburg ('The "Bronze Night" Cost Estonia over 4mn Euro' 2007).

Controversies over the past, such as the Estonian case, are nothing new and many examples can be found in widely differing geographical and historical contexts throughout the world and the centuries. Rather, the interesting question is: why would governments and public authorities put their ever-shrinking budgets at memory's service, as in the case of the National September 11 Memorial and Museum in New York which has been estimated at U.S.$710 million (Cohen 2012)? Why would people be willing to incur incarceration or hospital bills, or even to lay down their lives in the name of the ephemeral concept of 'collective memory'? The answer is because memory is seldom about the past: as Nora puts it, 'through the past, we venerate above all ourselves' (Nora 1989: 16).

Firstly, what is 'collective memory'?[1] From Maurice Halbwachs's seminal work *Les Cadres Sociaux de la Mémoire* in 1925, an extensive literature on the topic has been produced, in particular since the 1980s, of which Chapter 1 presents an overview of key developments, figures and academic works. For the purpose of this book, this author accepts the definition of collective memory as 'shared social frameworks of individual recollections' of a group's past (Halbwachs 1950, in Misztal 2003: 4). A social group's collective memory is structured and articulated in a collective 'narrative', that is, 'an account, or narration, of events, stories or tales' (Misztal 2003: 160), 'a basic "story line" that is culturally constructed and provides the group members with a general notion of their shared past' (Y. Zerubavel 1995: 6). This narrative is usually constructed through a selective use of a group's past. Collective memory and the narrative(s) through which collective memory finds expression underpin a social group's identity, sense of continuity and cohesion. While we, as individuals, remember by means of an independent cognitive process, this process always takes place in the social world and it is, therefore, influenced and constrained by the social frameworks about the past shared by the group we belong to. The social nature of memory is, however, not only limited to the fact that members of the same social group share a common collective past, but it also manifests itself in the fact that this past is remembered and represented through shared cultural forms, in particular commemorative activity. In today's societies, cultural artefacts (such as monuments, statues, souvenirs and films) and cultural practices (such as commemorations, ceremonies and rituals) provide the means through which collective memory is objectified, projected and transmitted. Collective memory can, therefore, be interpreted as 'a group's representation of its past, both the past that is commonly shared and the past that is collectively commemorated, that enacts and gives substance to that group's identity, its present conditions and its vision of the future' (Misztal 2003: 158).

Since the emergence of 'nation states' in the Western world in the late eighteenth century, ruling authorities and political elites have employed memory as a 'political asset' to shape the collective identity, symbolic continuity and social cohesion of the nation's 'imagined community' (Anderson 1983). Among other forms of ritualized or commemorative activity, such as the institution of national anthems, flags, official memorial days and state/national holidays, war commemoration and memorialization, in particular, have become essential weapons in the 'symbolic arsenal' that a state can deploy to foster a nation's collective memory and to project a dominant narrative of its shared past. This hegemonic role in the process of memory making is asserted into the civic space by means of state-sponsored memorials such as cenotaphs, 'Tombs of the Unknown Soldier', and state-organized commemorations, which act not merely as historical markers, but more importantly as ideology conveyors. While generally the state or ruling authorities establish the canon of official memory in a given society, this does not exclude the possibility for parallel narratives of the collective past to be publicly articulated by other societal agencies or groups, such as war veterans, women's groups, opposing political parties, and ethnic minorities (Ashplant, Dawson and Roper 2000: 20–32). These narratives constitute what Foucault (1977) has termed 'counter-memory', that is, 'an alternative view of the past which challenges the dominant representation of the past' (Misztal 2003: 158); they can be 'sectional' or 'oppositional', depending on the degree of challenge they pose to the official state narrative in terms of public recognition and sociopolitical mobilization (Ashplant, Dawson and Roper 2000: 20–32). In the Estonian case that opens this book, both 'versions' of history remembered and supported by Estonian nationalists on one side and ethnic-Russian Estonians on the other are parallel narratives of the same collective past – coexisting or, in the case of the Bronze Night, clashing for public recognition, not only among themselves, but also oppositionally against the state-sanctioned version of that past.

In situations of civil war or ethnic conflict, narratives of the past often underpin the opposing ontological and ideological claims of the different 'battle lines' and help to sustain each group's identity and cohesion. This book investigates a fascinating scenario where the prerogative of memory making and nation building, usually reserved for the state, has been taken on by non-state organizations that, in some cases, operate on the border of legality. It uses as a case study the landscape of permanent memorialization that came about in Northern Ireland to commemorate the casualties of the Northern Irish conflict, also commonly referred to as 'the Troubles'. This conflict was a period of ethno-political violence between sections of the Unionist/Loyalist (mainly Protestant) and Nationalist/ Republican (mainly Catholic) population of Northern Ireland, conventionally dating from 1969 until the signing of the Belfast/Good Friday Agreement in 1998, which resulted in the death of over 3,700 individuals.[2] Although Unionists have always been a highly fragmented group, deriving from a wide range of social, economic, political backgrounds and religious denominations within Protestantism, at the core of Unionism is the determination that Northern Ireland must remain part of the union with Great Britain, because Unionists see themselves as historically, politically and culturally British – not Irish. The term 'Loyalist' refers, in a general sense, to a person who is loyal to the British Crown, but in a Northern Irish context it has come to signify that section of the Protestant/Unionist population which gives tacit or actual support to the use of force to defend the union with Great Britain. On the other hand, Nationalists can be seen as a more united group as they are members of one church, the Roman Catholic. The majority of Nationalists see themselves as historically, politically and culturally Irish, and believe that the partition of Ireland was unjust and that the thirty-two counties of Ireland should constitute a unified, independent political entity. Under the wider ideological umbrella of Nationalism, a major distinction has to be made between constitutional Nationalism and Republicanism: while constitutional Nationalists advocate a united Ireland being achieved through political means, Republicans see (or, at least, have seen in the past) the use of armed force as legitimate.[3]

In relation to public memorialization of the past, Northern Ireland represents an unusual, fascinating scenario. As a consequence of the 1921 Anglo-Irish Treaty, which marked the end of the Irish War of Independence, the Irish Free State was established as a self-governing dominion of the British Empire, comprising twenty-six out of the thirty-two counties of the island of Ireland. The six northern counties of Antrim, Armagh, Derry/Londonderry, Down, Fermanagh and Tyrone – whose population consisted of two-thirds Protestants and one-third Catholics – had the previous year opted out of this political solution to become Northern Ireland, one of the four states that constitute the United Kingdom. From 1921 to 1972, Northern Ireland was ruled by a series of Unionist governments, which exercised a certain degree of political, social, economic and cultural discrimination towards the Catholic population of Northern Ireland.

Since the inception of the Northern Irish state in 1921, the Unionist establishment exercised its memory-making function in relation to the two world wars and conflicts fought on foreign soil, and translated its official narrative into civic space with the erection of cenotaphs, war memorials and statues in city or town main squares and streets. In addition, state-sponsored commemorations, for instance Remembrance Sunday, were regularly held, and the Twelfth of July celebrations, organized by the Protestant Orange Order to commemorate the victory of Protestant King William III of Orange over Catholic King James II at the Battle of the Boyne in 1690, were de facto state commemorations, at least until the late 1960s (see Chapter 2).[4] With the outbreak of the Troubles in 1969 and the introduction of Direct Rule over Northern Ireland in 1972, thirty years of unstable governmental settlement ensued with the result that no official narrative of the Troubles has been promoted due to the lack of a clear political elite. To this day, the state and its organs are noticeable for their absence on civic space in Northern Ireland in relation to the memorialization of the Troubles, to the extent that an abdication of the right to 'manufacture' official memory has occurred. This public vacuum has, in fact, been promptly filled by non-state agencies that played an active role during the conflict – namely, the four main paramilitary groups and, in some cases, their respective political parties; as a result, four partisan narratives of the same past can be observed in the public arena in contemporary Northern Ireland.

Book Outline

Based on an analysis of more than 150 permanent memorials to the casualties of the Troubles on public soil in the city of Belfast, this book interrogates the spatial and temporal occurrence of forms of memorialization, the iconography and symbolism used at memorial sites and their practical and symbolic reasons to shed light on how collective memory in divided societies is used to: (a) project in the public arena 'versions' of the past that foster the national identification, symbolic continuity and social cohesion of opposing 'imagined communities'; (b) construct opposing narratives of ontological, historical and ideological legitimation, and narratives of victimhood and moral justification for the use of violence; (c) subsume individual memories within shared mnemonic frameworks due to the asymmetry of power in the production of public memory; and finally, (d) mediate new political messages and shield political leaderships from criticism in times of political transformation or ideological takeover. It aims to illustrate how memorials, although inanimate artefacts, are not mute, solidified reifications of collective memory. Memorials are not just a backdrop for the ritual action during which collective memory is moulded and transmitted, nor do they simply define its spatial boundaries, but they actively contribute to the process of creation, articulation and transmission of collective memory through their physical configuration, symbols, language and location.

The first chapter provides an overview of the book's theoretical background, briefly outlining the key developments, figures and trends in the conceptual fields of collective/social memory, material culture and the politics of memory. It will help the readers to familiarize themselves with concepts such as collective memory versus individual memory, cultural and material memory, collective narrative of the past, ritual and commemoration, war memorialization and politicized memory. A comparative dimension exists, whereby examples from other historical and geographical contexts, such as post-First World War Great Britain or contemporary Cyprus, are presented. The chapter concludes with a brief outline of the research methodology for this book.

Chapter 2 sets the historical background of this work. It gives a brief outline of the recent political history of Northern Ireland (mainly from the late 1960s) for readers who might not be familiar with it already, and introduces the main 'protagonists' of the book. It also looks at different forms of memorialization that have been used in Northern Ireland from the late 1960s, including funerary rituals, commemorations, mural painting, commemorative banners and memorial bands, memorial publications and pamphlets, oral history projects, and memorial prizes and awards. Finally, it classifies different types of permanent memorials (to paramilitary combatants, civilian casualties, security forces, and memorials in governmental buildings, party offices, workplaces, churches).

Drawing mainly on a database of over 150 memorials compiled by this author over four years – also available online (Viggiani 2013) – Chapter 3 is an exploration of permanent memorialization in relation to the spatial and temporal dimensions. Borrowing theoretical concepts and categorizations from cultural geography and sociology, what is investigated here is the impact of collective memory on the geography of urban territory and its direct relationship with patterns of residential segregation, social segmentation and sectarian division in the creation of an ethnicized space. In relation to space, it is also examined if and why memorials can act as territorial markers, can be considered sacred space and can be used as memory aids. In relation to the temporal dimension, the year 1998 (when the Good Friday/Belfast Agreement was signed, and officially considered as the end date of the conflict) is taken as a historical watershed to investigate if permanent memorialization can be deemed a sign that a conflict is over, or if it is a continuation of it through symbolic means. The hypothesis that memorials can be used as identity crutches by social groups in times of social, cultural and historical transformation and as a benchmark to measure a society's progress in its post-conflict path is also investigated in the latter part of this chapter.

Chapter 4 examines how 'memory makers' – a definition the author coined to signify agents that have a degree of control over the creation of public mnemonic artefacts due to their social, cultural, economic or political predominance in a given society – employ memorialization to construct collective narratives of ontological, historical and ideological legitimation by means of a selective use of the past. The chapter is divided into two main sections. In the first part, the interrelationship between individual memory and collective memory of an event is investigated, while proposing a theoretical framework that explains how individual 'stories' are subsumed within a collective 'history' of the past. Employing both quantitative and qualitative evidence, the second part of the chapter analyses the key symbolism, iconography and inscriptions found at memorial sites to understand how opposing public narratives of national identification, ontological, historical and ideological legitimation, victimhood, moral justification for the use of violence and stigmatization of the adversary are projected by means of careful use of imagery, symbols, language and a process of selective remembering and social amnesia. This chapter also introduces examples of how memory is used by political leaders and public figures to serve present purposes of political and ideological legitimation.

Based on 145 structured and semi-structured interviews with key stakeholders (political party representatives, paramilitary ex-combatants/ ex-prisoners, community and local authority representatives, members of the clergy, etc.) and local residents, chapters 5–8 present four case studies, one for each main paramilitary group – and, in some cases, their respective political parties – in Northern Ireland. When considered collectively, the four case studies follow the 'lifespan' of a memorial, from the formation of the memorial committee that oversees its building to the diachronic use of memorial sites during annual commemorations.

Chapter 5 is centred on the memorial activity of the Provisional Irish Republican Army (PIRA) and Sinn Féin from the late 1990s. Following the lifespan and memorial programme of the PIRA-aligned Greater Clonard Ex-Prisoners' Association, this chapter first investigates the reasons for the formation of ex-prisoners' groups in a post-conflict setting, their role in society and the importance of oral history and community-led memorial programmes. Based on interviews with ex-prisoners, local residents and access to the association's bulletins and memorial pamphlets, this chapter analyses how processes of memorialization and commemoration can act as a linchpin between the microlevel, represented both by single individuals and the local community, and the macrolevel of the social 'mnemonic collectivity' and the national imagined community. Using as a case study the memorial garden in the Republican area of Clonard in Belfast, the symbolism, iconography and language used at this site are interrogated to understand how the Provisional IRA – once one of the most violent proscribed paramilitary organizations – has succeeded in projecting a dominant narrative of historical and ideological legitimacy in the public arena. Practical aspects of memorialization – in particular, issues relating to planning permission, funding and the building process – are also documented.

Chapter 6 investigates the emergence of alternative views of the past or 'counter-memories' that challenge the dominant representation of the past. Having been granted unprecedented access to the IRSP/INLA Teach Na Fáilte Memorial Committee Belfast's minutes, members' recollections and archive, this author explores how sectional – and at times oppositional – narratives of the past are articulated and gain public recognition in coexistence and relation to dominant narratives of that past which are concurrently present in the public arena. Using the example of the 1981 Republican hunger strike, the difficult task faced by any group who wants to promote a counter-memory in society is illustrated: how to retain elements of the dominant narrative, while at the same time having to differentiate itself in terms of ontological and ideological legitimacy. Also in this chapter, the key elements, symbols and purposes of the periodic commemorations that take place in and around memorial sites are analysed.

Drawing from Smith's (1997) definition of 'Golden Age' and its significance in shaping a group's collective memory, the first half of Chapter 7 examines how a proscribed organization such as the Ulster Volunteer Force (UVF) has succeeded in 'borrowing' the myth of the Somme and appropriating its 'commemorative density' to project a narrative of historical and ideological legitimation, both as a specification of and in opposition to the history and symbolism of the First World War and the Battle of the Somme in the wider society. Using the annual paramilitary commemorations at three UVF murals in the Woodvale district of Belfast as a case study, the second half of the chapter shows how memory is used for present political and ideological purposes. Memorial orations given by the leadership and other public figures at these memorial sites from the early 1990s to the present day are analysed to show how the ritual action, with its immutable and traditional form, allows for claims of ontological legitimacy and a sense of continuity with the past to remain constant, while accounting for the adaptation of political and ideological messages to shifting historico-political contexts by means of the ritual's ever-changing meaning.

Chapter 8 focuses on the symbolic struggles that memory makers can face in the process of constructing credible narratives of historical legitimacy: using the example of the Ulster Defence Association (UDA), the first part of this chapter investigates different forms of symbolic conflict that can be detected in a society where different groups compete for the appropriation of so-called 'symbolic capital' and sift through the confusion of the past to establish original genealogies, credible myths of origin and golden ages that differentiate them from their competitors in the public arena of memory making. The second part of the chapter uses as a case study the Remembrance Sunday service held at the UDA memorial garden in the area of Sandy Row in Belfast to illustrate how both micro- and macropolitics are played out during commemorative services. In particular, it is investigated how memorials can act as a gateway to a symbolic, ideological national identity and the macrolevel of state politics, while still pertaining to a microlevel form of memorialization and being inextricably linked to the dimension of local or community politics.

Based upon a door-to-door survey and interviews conducted with local residents in Belfast, Chapter 9 sheds light on the other end of the spectrum of collective narratives about the past: those 'communities' who periodically witness memorials being built a few yards away from their homes, and parades passing through their streets, and who are therefore 'memory receivers' – a term this author coined to signify those individuals or groups who do not exert any degree of decisional power over what is commemorated in the public arena but are the intended recipients or 'end users' of these constructed narrations of the past. Using the analytical distinction posited by Scott (1990) between 'public' and 'hidden transcript', the aim of this chapter is to investigate the complex relationship between 'memory makers' and 'memory receivers', and to uncover the 'hidden transcript' of power relations over memory, focusing on the extent to which the 'memory receivers' accept and 'buy into' the memory makers' collective narratives about the past. Here, local communities' attitudes towards memory and memorialization are analysed, while exposing the varied and internal tensions, idiosyncratic differences and interpretative discrepancies that are 'glossed over' by power holders when presenting a consistent and uniformed collective view of a group's past to the outside world.

Chapter 10 draws conclusions on how collective memory and war memorialization are used in contemporary society to promote present political and ideological strategies. In relation to post-conflict settings, in particular, it advances an interesting hypothesis whereby bottom-up partisan narratives of the past can be considered perhaps more effective in the process of seeking a common ground between opposing groups than top-down cross-community, inclusive narratives of the past lowered onto society by governments and conflict-resolution bodies.

Notes

1. Although the terms 'collective memory' and 'social memory' were theorized by different scholars and present some conceptual differences (see Chapter 1), they are often used as synonymous in the literature and will be so used in this book.
2. In the course of this book, the term 'post-conflict' is used to refer to any event, social trend, political development, etc. that occurred after 1998. It is important to note here that there are still significant speculations within contemporary Northern Irish society as to whether the conflict has really come to an end – perhaps refuelled in recent years by the violent events in Belfast and Derry/Londonderry during the 2010 marching season and the most recent Union flag dispute in late 2012/early 2013. Since the people interviewed seemed to be divided on this issue, both positions have been accounted for throughout the course of this book, without taking a personal stance. The term 'post-conflict' is, nonetheless, used to indicate the indisputable societal move that occurred in Northern Ireland since the mid-1990s, from violence as the dominant mechanism of engagement to the sphere of politics.
3. On the Northern Irish conflict and the difference between Unionism, Loyalism, Nationalism and Republicanism, see Tonge (2002).
4. Founded in 1796, the Orange Order is a Protestant fraternal organization that acts as a wider umbrella for the Protestant tradition, drawing its members from a variety of social, political and economic backgrounds. Historically, it has had close links to the Unionist political establishment in Northern Ireland.

Chapter 1

COLLECTIVE MEMORY AND THE POLITICS OF MEMORIALIZATION

A Theoretical Overview

≥•≤

> The complex of practices and means by which the past invests the present is memory: memory is the present past.
>
> – Terdiman 1993: 8

From antiquity, the process of remembering has fascinated humankind because it is central to our ability to conceive reality and to our cognition of the world we inhabit with its physical and logical relations. In the Western world, memory is fundamental to the formation of our identity as a person and to the perception of our uniqueness and difference from others, to the extent that 'a really successful dissociation of the self from memory would be a total loss of the self – and thus of all activities to which a sense of one's identity is important' (Nussbaum 2001: 177). Since Sigmund Freud postulated in the early twentieth century the existence of an archive of memories in the unconscious of the individual psyche, processes of memory have been analysed by psychologists exclusively as acts performed by individuals in the secluded recesses of their minds. From the 1980s onwards, however, processes of remembering and forgetting have been ascribed to the social sphere and increasingly investigated from a variety of disciplines' points of view, with literature on the topic flourishing in sociology, social psychology, anthropology, history and political science; a theoretical distinction has generally been postulated between active remembering (or performative memory), embodied in the concepts of tradition, ritual action and commemoration, and mental process, with its cognitive and emotional attributes.

Memory in the Social World: Collectiveness versus Individuality

The French sociologist Maurice Halbwachs (1925, 1941, 1950, 1980, 1992) was the first to investigate mnemonic processes as primarily social practices, coining the term 'collective memory'. A disciple of Émile Durkheim, Halbwachs (1992: 182) asserts that memory is structured by group identities and is, therefore, always 'socially framed'. Individual memory, both autobiographical and historical, results from 'the inter-section of collective influences' (Halbwachs [1926] 1950: 44), in the sense that it is the unique combination of one's collective memories as a member of different groups, such as family, local community or political party. Individual memories cannot exist in isolation but must be communicated and shared in order to find confirmation in other group members' remembrances. Collective memory, thus, amounts to 'shared social frameworks of individual recollections, as we share our memories with some people and not others' and is central to the social identity and cohesion of a group (Misztal 2003: 12). While individual memories change as an individual's affiliations vary throughout the course of life, collective memory provides the group with a shared image of itself and its past, which is part of the group's common (self-)consciousness and ensures its sense of unity and continuity (Halbwachs [1926] 1950). This is particularly significant in Northern Ireland where shared, yet oppos-ing, images of the same past are central to the creation and maintenance of different groups' collective identities and their sense of historical continuity.

Halbwachs' original theorization – and more recent republication in English of his work *La Mémoire Collective* in 1980 – has opened up debate into the complex relationship between individual and collective memory.[1] Fentress and Wickham (1992) challenge Halbwachs' emphasis on the collective nature of social consciousness, advocating for a more active role for the individual in the process of remembering. They intro-duce the term 'social memory' to distinguish between memory as 'repre-sentation' and memory as 'action': the individual retains ownership of the initial private cognitive process and network of ideas, but the memories he/she deems relevant become then social when communicated to others through 'commemoration', intended as 'the action of speaking or writing about memories' (ibid.: x). This book demonstrates how, while individuals retain personal memories of people and events related to the Northern Irish conflict, these memories are subsumed within shared social frameworks of remembrance that underpin the collective identity of the two opposing 'imagined communities' (Anderson 1983) in Northern Ireland, the Catholic/Nationalist/Republican and Protestant/Unionist/Loyalist communities.[2]

In contrast to the idea of a total subordination of the individual to a collectivity, the intersubjectivist sociology of memory (Funkenstein 1993; Schudson 1997; E. Zerubavel 1997; Prager 1998; Sherman 1999) asserts that while it is the individual who remembers by means of an independent mental act, 'his or her memory exists, and is shaped by, their relation with what has been shared with others . . . it is . . . a past lived in relation to other people' (Misztal 2003: 6). A group's collective memory is, therefore, 'quite different from the sum total of the personal recollections of its various individual members, as it includes only those that are *commonly shared* by all of them' (E. Zerubavel 1997: 96).

A second area of theoretical contention opened up by the republication of Halbwachs's work is the significance of the present and the past in the formation of social remembering.

The Shaping of Collective Memory: Present versus Past

The role and relevance of the past and its influence in shaping collective memory can be broadly summarized in three main theories. One theory argues that collective memory is fluid and flexible, dictated by contemporary attitudes and historical occurrences, and can therefore be readapted or reconstructed (Halbwachs 1941). Several recent studies have accounted for changes in attitudes to the past (and its memory), for example in post-communist countries after the collapse of the USSR (Greenblatt, Rev and Starn 1995; Rosenberg 1995; Borneman 1997; Szacka 1997; Argenbright 1999; Verdery 1999; Foote, Tóth and Árvay 2000) and in relation to the memory of the Holocaust in Germany and other countries (Maier 1988; Hartman 1994; Koonz 1999). A second theory proposes that it is, instead, the past that shapes our understanding of the present (Shils 1981). Tradition, with its constant re-enactment and reaffirmation of the past and past beliefs, addresses the need of social groups to feel a sense of historical and cultural continuity, outliving changes in society. The third theory proposes that both change and continuity play a role in shaping collective memory. Based on an analysis of how the memory of George Washington developed in the American consciousness before and after the Civil War, Schwartz (1991) suggests that collective memories change as a consequence of shifting values, beliefs and circumstances, but that old beliefs and images are concurrently preserved and coexist with the new, reflecting dialectical tendencies universal in society to embrace and reject aspects both of its past and present. This study finds that Northern Ireland's collective memory is heavily influenced by contemporary historical and political circumstances, and that the process of selective remembering helps to sustain different groups' present claims of historical legitimacy and collective identification.

Lieux de Mémoire as Conveyors of Social Memory

According to Nora (1989: 8), living memory and milieux de mémoire (real environments of memory) characteristic of so-called primitive or archaic societies have been substituted in today's Western societies by 'sifted and sorted historical traces', by memory 'institutionalized through cultural means' (Assmann 1995, in Misztal 2003: 130–31). Such 'cultural memory' is embodied in lieux de mémoire (places of memory), 'objectifications that store meaning in a concentrated manner' (Heller 2001: 1031), including artefacts (monuments, statues, films) and practices (commemorations, ceremonies, festivals and rites), that assume a central role as conveyors of collective memory. It is precisely through commemorative ceremonies and ritual bodily activity that social groups convey and sustain their collective memory (Connerton 1989). Commemorations become the elected social occasions where shared representations of the past are transmitted from old to young members of the group, and where all gather together to express and reaffirm a common sense of social identification and to legitimize present social institutions and practices.

In relation to Northern Ireland, considerable academic attention has been directed both to the commemorative practices of the Protestant/Unionist/Loyalist and Catholic/Nationalist/Republican communities and to the more 'static' form of remembrance of mural painting.[3] Permanent memorials to the casualties of the Troubles have, however, been somewhat conspicuous by their absence in academic literature, if we exclude a brief report commissioned by the Northern Ireland Community Relations Council (Leonard 1997b) and some recent academic articles (Graham and Whelan 2007; McDowell 2007, 2008a, 2008b; Switzer and McDowell 2009).[4] Through a combination of qualitative and quantitative research, this book aims to fill that gap, beginning with a survey of permanent forms of memorialization to the victims of the Northern Irish conflict in the city of Belfast.[5]

Politicized Remembering: The Nexus between Memory and Power

The growing weight of ethnic minorities in Western Europe and the United States as a result of immigration, the fragmentation of the Soviet bloc along ethnic lines and the upsurge of many intragroup conflicts throughout the world have given new momentum to studies on collective memory, particularly to the exploration of the nexus between memory and power in relation to ethnicity and national identity (see Ashplant, Dawson and Roper 2000; Müller 2002). Memory becomes a crucial factor in the construction and preservation of nation states, intended as communities of memory, in the sense that their members not only share similar traits such as ethnicity, culture and language, but are bound together by a common understanding and representation of a shared past that underpins their collective identity. Smith (1996), for instance, postulates that shared 'ethno myths' are one of the foundational elements of a nation state and must be taken into account along with economic and political circumstances in any analysis of modern nationalism. Similarly, Anderson (1983) indicates how 'ghostly national imaginings' are conjured up from the national past in order to make the present generation feel a connection with the dead who belonged to the same 'imagined community', thus securing and reinforcing the nation's imagined continuity and transcendence beyond time and mortality. Although Northern Ireland cannot be considered a nation state as such, as its very ontological existence is contested between the two opposing ethnic communities who live within its official boundaries, it is possible to talk about two *projected* symbolic national identities – Irish and British – with which the Catholic and Protestant population of Northern Ireland can respectively identify. This book investigates how collective memory helps to shape and reinforce these two opposing projected symbolic national identities.

The Politics of War Memory and Commemoration

Since the invention of the 'nation state' in the late eighteenth century, the 'political demands' on memory have intensified, with ruling authorities in most Western European countries introducing a series of ritual practices which were 'deliberately designed to symbolize national unity, to ensure state legitimacy and build political consensus' (Misztal 2003: 38). Hobsbawm and Ranger (1983) have famously coined the term 'invented traditions' to account for the sudden proliferation of national celebrations in Western Europe since the industrial revolution, and have classified them into three overlapping categories: 'those establishing or symbolizing social cohesion or the membership of groups, real or artificial communities; those establishing or legitimizing institutions, status or relations of authority; and those whose main purpose was socialization, the inculcation of beliefs, value systems and conventions of behaviour' (Hobsbawm and Ranger 1983: 9). Invented traditions, despite being newly created, tend to use old models and materials for new purposes, in an attempt to establish continuity – in many instances, fictitious – with a suitable past. In Northern Ireland, for instance, the modern-day Loyalist paramilitary group Ulster Volunteer Force has successfully appropriated the name and symbols of the homonymous organization that fought in the Battle of the Somme in 1916.

War commemoration and memorialization have long been recognized by political elites as a crucial symbolic weapon to bind a nation's citizens into a collective national identity and to enhance authority over them. From the French Revolution (1792–99) and the German Wars of Liberation against Napoleon (1813–14), mercenary armies are substituted by citizen armies; wars are no longer dynastic struggles between monarchs, but are fought for the abstraction of 'the people' by volunteers who enrolled in the name of the 'motherland' or 'fatherland' of the nation (Mosse 1990: 18). From the First World War, the 'Myth of the War Experience' and the 'cult of the fallen soldier' (ibid.: 7) become 'a centrepiece of the religion of nationalism after the war', ensuring that 'the memory of the war [is] refashioned into a sacred experience which [provides] the nation with a new depth of religious feeling, putting at its disposal ever-present saints and martyrs, places of worship and a heritage to emulate', thus justifying the nation in whose name blood had been sacrificed.[6] As Anderson (1983) points out, the remembrance of those who gave their lives in the name of the nation assumes a key role in the perpetuation of a nation's appeal to die for it, in that it binds the living generation to an ideal of citizenship that commands allegiance to the nation's imagined community and a willingness to make the supreme sacrifice for the common good: compelled by a sense of indebtedness and gratitude towards past citizens who fulfilled the patriotic 'oath' of loyalty, the present citizens are, thus, morally committed to follow their noble example, should necessity require it (King 1998: 195–97). For both Republican and Loyalist groups in contemporary Northern Ireland, the symbolic construction of a direct lineage from 'martyrs' and 'heroes' of wars past is paramount in the projection of claims of historical and ideological legitimacy, such that modern day volunteers are depicted as the rightful inheritors of past volunteers' valour and willingness to pay the ultimate sacrifice in the name of opposing 'nations'.

Two main theoretical approaches seem to underlie studies of war memory: on one hand, the interpretation of processes of war commemoration as fundamentally political; on the other, their significance on a psychological and emotional level. Hobsbawm, Ranger, Mosse and Anderson belong to the first approach and examine how the state or hegemonic political elites construct and promote selective versions of the past in order to legitimize their authority and maintain social cohesion. From this perspective, war memorials and commemorations are 'political symbols' used to 'monetize' what Bourdieu (1990) has termed the 'symbolic capital' available to a social entity, becoming politically significant strategic assets for the ruling establishment (Harrison 1995: 269–70).[7] In contrast, Winter and Sivan (Winter 1995; Winter and Sivan 1999) argue for a more private and 'existential' function of war commemoration and, although the public/political dimension is not altogether excluded, they attempt to refocus attention on the individual's process of remembrance. In his study on First World War commemorations, Winter (1995) introduces the figures of the 'melancholic' and the 'mourner': whereas the former is pathologically 'trapped' in mourning, thus never achieving detachment from the lost object, the latter embarks in a healthy teleological process of grieving that terminates with disengagement from the lost object, closure and healing. From this perspective, war memorials and the rituals that unfold around them function as a way of translating individual grief into shared public mourning, in an attempt to address the universal human need for psychological reparation of loss. Similarly, Hamber and Wilson (2003) suggest how memorials – together with truth commissions and public apologies – can play a 'therapeutic' role. These so-called symbolic acts of reparation, however, do not possess healing power per se: it is not their deliverance, but the process that takes place around them that can bring final closure for bereaved individuals.

In situations of ethnic conflict or civil war such as Northern Ireland, war memorials and commemorations become a powerful political tool to project and sustain narratives of legitimation and victimhood against the other faction's claims and versions of the past (Cairns and Roe 2003). As Longley (2001: 231) has pointed out in relation to Northern Ireland, one must add 'a preposition to the verb "remember" – remembering *at*', so that, when the past is recalled, attention must be given not only to which group remembers and for what purpose, but also against whom.[8] In addition, in societies that undergo a crucial period of transition after decades-long internal conflicts, where a selective and partisan use of the past has helped to perpetuate communal divisions and hatred over the years, the study of how this past is remembered and commemorated acquires further relevance in light of present circumstances and future develop-ments. In Northern Ireland, since the signing of the Good Friday/Belfast Agreement in 1998, which marked a shift from violence to politics as the dominant mechanism of engagement, conflict-related memorialization has assumed an increasing significance.[9] Here, memorialization can be interpreted not merely as 'the sad coda of individual loss after the cacoph-ony of war, or no more than the capstone lowered onto the completed edifice of a restructured and peaceful society', but it has become an active and evolving practice that reflects developments in the political process of peace making, shapes political developments, and has a transformative power in present society (Brown 2006: 1).

The Memory Makers and the Projection of Narratives about the Past

According to Ashplant, Dawson and Roper (2000: 16), the politics of war memory and commemoration consists precisely in 'the struggle of differ-ent groups to give public articulation to, and hence gain recognition for, certain memories and the narratives within which they are structured'. In societies throughout the world, the nation state or ruling establish-ment is central to the politics of war commemoration, in that they set the official 'canon' for memory, constructing dominant or hegemonic (master) narratives of the national past that underpin the nation's social unity and shared identity. The state attempts to assert full control over official processes of war memory and commemoration, such as permanent memorials and a calendar of annual or anniversary ceremonies, select-ing and reworking pre-existing war narratives, which provide 'a national repertoire of useable images, plots and figures' from the national past (ibid.: 22). Although hegemonic, official memory can come under pres-sure from the projection of 'counter-memories' (Foucault 1977) articu-lated by different components of civic society or social groups who feel excluded or alienated from the hegemonic version of the past; depending on the degree of public articulation and socio-political support that these counter-memories achieve, 'sectional' or 'oppositional' narratives of war can enter the public arena and run parallel, be incorporated by or openly challenge the dominant narrative.

In Northern Ireland, the lack of an obvious political elite as the result of an unstable governmental settlement for over thirty years has brought about a state of affairs where the local government has carefully selected its involvement in commemorative practices, thus, in part, abdicating its right to manufacture official memory and the role of nation building that comes with it. While the casualties of the two world wars and other conflicts fought on foreign lands such as the Korean War are officially commemorated (for instance, in the grounds of Belfast City Hall), minimal state-sponsored acts of remembrance related to the Troubles occur in public spaces in Northern Ireland. In fact, the only official site of memory related to the Troubles is located outside Northern Ireland: the Ulster Ash Grove, a section of the National Memorial Arboretum near Lichfield in Staffordshire, England, is sponsored by the Northern Ireland Office and commemorates 'the men and women of the Royal Ulster Constabulary G.C., the Armed Forces and other organizations in the service of the Crown who laid down their lives in the cause of peace in Northern Ireland, 1969–2001' (RUC GC Foundation 2004: 6–7).[10] Graham and Whelan (2007: 491–92) point to a process of 'distancing' whereby the state is willing to sponsor 'a distant and geographically obscure form of commemoration . . . in a curiously contextless and placeless surroundings' in an attempt to deny its role as an active participant in the conflict, creating 'less a site of memory than, in Foote's typology (1997), a site of obliteration where the evidence of death and tragedy is effaced and removed from view so as not to impede the desire to forget'.[11] For Bell (2003: 114, 1097), the lack of a state canon for memory is due to the fact that the 'Belfast Agreement was fashioned so as to avoid the need for a societal narrative [about the Troubles]' and contained 'no mechanism for dealing with past abuses, or "truth-telling"'. In a similar fashion, the British state has been reticent to engage with the memory of the Troubles on Northern Irish soil, also cognisant that the few memorials to British Army casualties existing in the public arena have been repeatedly vandalized, as in the case of the plaque in memory of eighteen soldiers killed by a Provisional IRA bomb in Warrenpoint, Co. Down in 1979 ('Massacre Memorial Vandalised' 2004).

Brown (2009) and Cavanaugh (1997) have suggested that the lack of national state legitimacy in Northern Ireland has resulted in the creation of a space for paramilitarism, in terms of use of violence, communal defence and social control. Similarly, the absence of an official state-sponsored narrative of the Troubles has created a public vacuum in the memorialization and interpretation of the Troubles, available to be claimed by other non-state agencies of articulation. As mentioned earlier, it is the four main paramilitary groups – and, in some cases, their respective political parties – who have stepped in to fill this void in the production of 'official' memory by projecting their different narratives of the war in the public arena and, as a consequence, their opposing narratives of national identification and political legitimation.

Methodological Framework

Since the study of war memory and commemoration is a vast and multi-layered field, four delimiting parameters were applied for the purpose of this book. Firstly, the analysis of public rather than private permanent physical forms of memorialization – namely, gardens of remembrance, memorial monuments and stones, commemorative murals and plaques (both stand-alone and applied to new or pre-existing murals). As a result, memorials located on private premises and accessible by invite or pre-booking only (such as inside governmental buildings, party offices, Orange Order halls, churches and police barracks) were not taken into consideration; however, memorials in graveyards, or *outside* governmental buildings, party offices, Orange Order halls, churches and police barracks, or within the grounds of private clubs but freely accessible to the public, have been included in the analysis. Occasional or annual commemorations taking place at and around these sites of memory, particularly when occurring in case study locations, were also included in the analysis. Geographical locale defined the second parameter of this research. Data was primarily collected in the Belfast Urban Area, although data related to permanent memorials throughout Northern Ireland is also included in order to acquire a general picture of the culture of commemoration in the province. A third temporal parameter limited research to Troubles-related processes of memorialization – in other words, to commemorative sites (and events) in memory of individuals who lost their lives as a direct result of the Northern Irish conflict from 1969 (conventionally taken as its starting date) to the present day. However, both Republican and Loyalist modes of memory encourage references to pre-Troubles iconic events such as the 1916 Easter Rising or the Battle of the Somme, therefore memorials commemorating pre-1969 historical figures, groups or events have been included since they were commissioned alongside Troubles-related forms of memorialization by the same associations or groups in an attempt to draw an ideological unbroken line between past and present in the construction of narratives of historical continuity and legitimation (Appendix A). A fourth and final parameter focused the research on commemorative forms relating to Republican and Loyalist paramilitary culture through direct contact with individuals who played an active role during the Troubles, enabling an investigation of paramilitary ideology 'at the source'.

This book is the result of a combination of quantitative and qualitative research elements based upon four main activities of investigation: (a) a database of Troubles-related permanent forms of memorialization in Belfast (quantitative); (b) a survey of local residents' views on these

Table 1.1 Memorials' distribution across the sectarian divide

Group	Memorials	Murals	Plaques	Total (per group)
Protestant/Unionist/Loyalist	23	17	12	**52**
Catholic/Nationalist/Republican	43	19	43	**105**
Total (per type)	**66**	**36**	**55**	**157**

Source: Viggiani 2013

memorials (quantitative/qualitative); (c) a series of interviews with key stakeholders (qualitative); and (d) participant observation in numerous commemorative events throughout the city (qualitative).

Database of Memorials

The database of permanent memorials is the result of fieldwork conducted through the streets of Belfast between September 2005 and August 2009, and comprises 157 entries (see Table 1.1), also featured in an online version (Viggiani 2013).

Survey of Local Population

Between 28 May and 18 June 2008, one hundred local residents were surveyed by door-to-door questionnaire in order to ascertain their views and feelings regarding their local memorials (see Tables 1.2, 1.3 and 1.4). Four areas of Belfast were selected for the survey: Clonard (C), Turf Lodge (TL) and Woodvale (W), all situated in the west of the city, and Sandy Row (SR), located between the city centre and the university area in the south.[12] All four are working-class areas and are among the hundred most deprived areas in Northern Ireland in terms of income, employment, health and disability, education and training, geographical access, social environment and housing (NISRA 2005: 38–64). Clonard is a predominantly Catholic and staunchly Republican area, sitting within the Lower Falls electoral ward, a Sinn Féin bastion. Situated between the Lower Falls and the Andersonstown area, Turf Lodge is also part of the Catholic/ Republican 'bloc' in West Belfast. Wedged between the Republican Falls and Ardoyne areas, Woodvale represents, together with the Shankill, the staunchly Protestant/Loyalist side of West Belfast, avowing politi- cal support for the Democratic Unionist Party and, in the Shankill, for the Progressive Unionist Party. Finally, Sandy Row is a predominantly Protestant Loyalist area, although part of the politically and socially

Table 1.2 Respondents' religious affiliation

Religious Affiliation	C	SR	TL	W	Total
Roman Catholic (RC)	27	0	23	0	**50**
Protestant (P)	0	24	0	24	**48**
Other	0	0	0	1	**1**
No Religion	0	1	0	0	**1**

Source: Viggiani 2013

Table 1.3 Respondents' gender distribution

Gender	C	SR	TL	W	RC Subtotal	P Subtotal	Total
Male	13	14	14	11	27	25	**52**
Female	14	11	9	14	23	25	**48**

Source: Viggiani 2013

Table 1.4 Respondents' age distribution

Age	C	SR	TL	W	RC Subtotal	P Subtotal	Total
< 18	0	1	1	1	1	2	**3**
18–24	3	0	2	2	5	2	**7**
25–44	7	6	6	3	13	9	**22**
45–60	8	6	8	3	16	9	**25**
> 60	9	12	6	16	15	28	**43**

Source: Viggiani 2013

varied Shaftesbury ward.[13] It is important to note that, when talking about the Republican and Loyalist communities in Northern Ireland, there exists a vast section of the population who hold different political views and who do not support paramilitarism.

Confino (1997: 1395) laments how 'many studies of memory are content to describe the representation of the past [and] tend to ignore the issue of reception', which is 'a necessary one to avoid an arbitrary choice and interpretation of evidence'. Similarly, many local residents that took part in this survey commented with a tinge of disbelief how previous studies on visual displays of identity tended to infer the meaning of such displays among local communities solely by an external observation of their occurrence. This study is the first of its kind to ascertain *in loco* the local residents' ideas and opinions in relation to visual displays of identity.

Interviews

A series of forty-five semi-structured interviews were conducted between January 2007 and July 2008, in order to gain access to the views and opinions of key stakeholders and community representatives in relation to memorialization in Northern Ireland. In addition, various conversations were had in less formalized settings, such as receptions, dinners and informal visits. While it is important to note that there are crossovers, each interviewee was assigned to a single category based on their official position stated prior to the interview. These categories are summarized in Tables 1.5, 1.6 and 1.7.

Interviews were conducted using the approach variously termed 'informal ethnographic interviews' (Agar 1980), 'non-standardized interviews' (Ellen 1984) or 'semi-structured interviews'. In comparison with questionnaire-type interviews, with this method questions are more open-ended and to a certain degree improvised and 'informants can criticize

Table 1.5 Interviewees' category affiliation

Category	No. of interviewees
Political party representative	7
Paramilitary ex-combatant, ex-prisoner and/or activist	21
Community representative	8
Police force	1
Public local authority	1
Orange Order	2
Clergy	1
Local resident	4
Total	45

Note: See Tables 1.6 and 1.7, respectively, for a breakdown of the interviewees' political and paramilitary affiliation.
Source: Viggiani 2013

Table 1.6 Interviewees' political party affiliation

Political party represented	No. of interviewees
Sinn Féin	2
SDLP	1
UUP	1
DUP	1
PUP	1
Alliance Party	1
Total	7

Source: Viggiani 2013

Table 1.7 Interviewees' paramilitary affiliation

Paramilitary group represented	No. of interviewees
PIRA/SF ex-combatant, ex-prisoner and/or activist	7
INLA/IRSP ex-combatant, ex-prisoner and/or activist	4
UVF/PUP ex-combatant, ex-prisoner and/or activist	3
UDA/UDP/UPRG ex-combatant, ex-prisoner and/or activist	7
Total	21

Source: Viggiani 2013

a question, correct it, point out that it is sensitive, or answer in any way they want to' (Agar 1980: 90). The interviews were based on a series of 'loose' questions divided into four main categories: history of memorialization and community relations in the area; practical information about memorials and commemorations; the symbolism and politics of memory; and the relationship between local communities and commemorative practices. However, a more structured approach was adopted, especially during later stages once the research had become more directed and focused, or when a particular issue had to be investigated in depth or in technical detail.

Commemorations

From January 2006 to August 2009, commemorative parades and ceremonies held at memorial sites (both Republican and Loyalist) were recorded by means of participant observation. Where possible, photographic and audio records were taken, otherwise field notes and supporting press coverage were collected as soon as possible after the event. Documents produced by the various groups and other archival documentation also supported the analysis.

Notes

1. For the different critiques of Halbwachs' theoretical approach, see Misztal (2003: 54–56).
2. See Chapter 4 for a further analysis of how this author interprets the Catholic/Nationalist/Republican and Protestant/Unionist/Loyalist communities to be two 'imagined communities'.

3. For the Protestant/Unionist/Loyalist community, see Jarman (1997, 1999), Bryan (2000) and Kennaway (2006) in relation to the Twelfth of July Orange celebrations; see Longley (1994), Jarman (1999), Officer (2001) and Brown (2007) for the commemorative activity around the 1916 Battle of the Somme. For the Catholic/Nationalist/Republican community, see O'Keefe (1992), Johnson (1994), Walker (2000), Beiner (2000) and Collins (2004) on the commemoration of the 1798 United Irishmen rebellion; see Longley (1994), Jarman (1999), Daly and O'Callaghan (2007) and Doherty and Keogh (2007) for the commemoration of the 1916 Easter Rising. On the tradition of mural painting in working-class areas of Northern Ireland, especially in the cities of Belfast and Derry/Londonderry, see Rolston (1991, 1998b, 2003b), Jarman (1992, 1993, 1996a, 1996b, 1998) and Sluka (1992, 1996), who all provide a comprehensive history of political/paramilitary murals from their first occurrence at the beginning of the twentieth century to contemporary post-conflict Northern Ireland; a great collection of images is offered by Rolston (1992, 1998a, 2003a), McCormick (1996–2013) and the Bogside artists (Kelly 2001).

4. More extensive studies on memorials in Northern Ireland have been conducted in relation to First World War memorials (Switzer 2007) and civic statuary in Belfast (McIntosh 2006). Kerr (2008) provides an overview of Republican memorials in West Belfast.

5. An early version of the database of memorials to the casualties of the Northern Ireland conflict in Belfast compiled by this author was published on the CAIN website in 2006. Subsequently, CAIN's online digital archive of memorials 'Victims, Survivors and Commemoration', the result of a two-year project funded by the Arts and Humanities Research Council (AHRC), was launched in June 2009.

6. For the role of warfare in the formation of ethnic communities and nations, see also Smith (1981a, 1981b, 2003) and Hutchinson (2007).

7. Specific examples of the political significance of war commemoration – and, in many instances, social amnesia – in the process of national identity formation come from Australia (Thomson 1994); France (Lebovics 1994); Germany (Mosse 1990; Koshar 1994); the United Kingdom (King 1998); and Israel (Y. Zerubavel 1995; Azaryahu and Kellerman 1999).

8. On the significance of memory in 'divided societies', see Papadakis (1994) on Cyprus; Bar-Tal (2003) on Israel; Kgalema (1999), Naidu (2004) and Southern African Reconciliation Project (2005) on South Africa; Bet-El (2002) on the former Yugoslavia; Di Lellio and Schwandner-Sievers (2006a, 2006b) on Kosovo.

9. See Chapter 3 for an analysis of the temporal significance of the appearance of memorials since 1998.

10. See 'Memorial for "Troubles" Victims' (2003) and 'Tribute to Murdered Officers' (2003). This observation excludes mention of security forces who died 'in subsequent conflicts' on some pre-existing memorials to the two world wars or memorials on private premises, such as the RUC Memorial Garden in Belfast (see also Chapter 2).

11. A similar process can be observed in the Republic of Ireland in relation to the Irish National War Memorial in Islandbridge. In an attempt to 'forget' that almost fifty thousand Irishmen died in the Great War fighting on the side of Britain, the memorial park was firstly designed for various central locations and then relegated to Islandbridge, a peripheral area of Dublin, near Phoenix Park. Completed in 1939, the memorial park was never officially opened, with the Irish government refusing an invitation to attend the first Armistice Day ceremonies held there in 1937, and

was left to fall into a state of disrepair until major restoration works were carried out in the late 1980s. Reopened in 1988 with government representatives missing from the opening ceremony, the park was eventually given an official government opening in 1995, fifty-six years after its completion (Leonard 1997a: 66–67; Whelan 2003: 185–90).

12. In the case of the INLA, the plaque in memory of Ronnie Bunting and Noel Little in Turf Lodge was taken as an example/exemplification of their commemorative activity in Belfast.

13. In the 2011 Belfast City Council local elections (Belfast City Council Elections 1993–2011), the Lower Falls and Upper Falls electoral wards (which include, respectively, the Clonard and Turf Lodge areas) both returned four Sinn Féin councillors and one Social Democratic Labour Party (SDLP) councillor; the Court electoral ward (Woodvale) returned three Democratic Unionist Party (DUP) councillors, one Progressive Unionist Party (PUP) and one Independent councillor; the Laganbank electoral ward (Sandy Row) two SDLP councillors, one Sinn Féin, one DUP and one Alliance Party councillor.

Chapter 2

THE ARMALITE AND THE PAINTBRUSH

A Brief History of Memorialization of the Troubles in Northern Ireland

$\Longrightarrow \bullet \Longleftarrow$

'In proud and loving memory of Francie (Pól Beag) McCloskey. First person to die in the Troubles. Murdered by the R.U.C. at this spot on 14th July 1969. Ar dheis dé go raibh a anam (May his soul be on God's right side)'. In this way, the town of Dungiven in County Derry/Londonderry lays claim to the grim primacy of the first victim of the Troubles, showcasing this bleak fact in a plaque encased in the pavement of its main street near where Francis McCloskey was fatally injured in a police baton charge during disturbances following an Orange Order march. In Belfast, a relative of John Patrick Scullion, who died on 11 June 1966, two weeks after being shot near his home in Oranmore Street in the Clonard area by UVF members, stated in the pages of *The Irish News* that 'we [the family] feel that he has been forgotten. When the record of the story of the troubles comes out he will never be mentioned. We know for a fact that he was the first victim of the troubles' (McKittrick et al. 2007: 26). The controversy over who should be recognized as the first victim of the Troubles reflects the heightened sensibilities and explosive frustration that mounted among the Catholic population in Northern Ireland in the mid-1960s, for reasons explained below, and resulted in intercommunity violence which, as few would have predicted at the time, was just the start of a thirty-year-long permanent state of conflict in the province.[1]

With the approach of the fiftieth anniversary of the Easter Rising in April 1966, intercommunal tension rose significantly in Northern

Ireland. In addition, in the following year the Northern Ireland Civil Rights Association (NICRA) was formed to campaign for the civil rights of Catholics in Northern Ireland, against whom a degree of discrimination was exercised since the partition of the island in 1921.[2] Following these events, a period of increasing civil unrest ensued, with violent clashes between civil rights activists and the police force of Northern Ireland, the Royal Ulster Constabulary (RUC) – most notably in Burntollet in October 1968. On 12 August 1969 in the aftermath of an Apprentice Boys of Derry parade, fierce rioting erupted between the local Catholic population and the RUC (and Protestant crowds) in the Bogside area of Derry/Londonderry, which lasted for almost two days with the erection of makeshift barricades which made the Bogside a de facto 'no-go area'. The insurgency soon spread to other areas of Northern Ireland, in particular Belfast, where major clashes occurred in the west and north of the city on 14 and 15 August, until the British Army was deployed on the streets to restore calm. What started as a four-day stint of civil unrest was to extend to thirty years of ethno-sectarian conflict in the province, a conflict which would claim the lives of 3,720 individuals (McKittrick et al. 2007: 1552):[3] of these, the majority were Catholic and Protestant civilians – with, respectively, 1,259 and 727 casualties – followed by members of the British Army (503 casualties), Republican paramilitary groups (395 casualties), the RUC (303 casualties, including its Reserve), the Ulster Defence Regiment/Royal Irish Regiment (206 casualties), Loyalist paramilitary groups (167 casualties), and 160 other people who died in Troubles-related accidents such as heart attacks (ibid.).

A look at the breakdown of the agencies responsible for these deaths (McKittrick et al. 2007: 1553) gives a clear picture of the main 'protagonists' of the Northern Irish conflict. After 1969, the RUC, the local police force established in 1921 at the origin of the Northern Irish state, was supported by a permanent military detachment of the British Army in Northern Ireland and by the Ulster Defence Regiment (renamed the Royal Irish Regiment in 1992), a regiment of the British Army formed in 1970 as a result of the security emergency in the province and made up of members recruited exclusively in Northern Ireland. Composed mainly of Protestant members and granted unprecedented policing powers with the 1922 Special Powers Act (HMSO 1922), the RUC was traditionally perceived by the Catholic/Nationalist/Republican population as a sectarian and partisan force;[4] with the outbreak of the Troubles, this perception was reinforced by the force's harassing behaviour towards Catholics with unwarranted house and body searches and alleged collusion with Loyalist paramilitary groups. Welcomed by the Catholic population in the early days of its deployment on the streets of Northern Ireland, the British

Army was also soon to be perceived by the Catholic population as lacking neutrality and as the armed manifestation of an hostile and alien 'imperial' power.

In addition, from the 1960s a series of militia that would play an active role in the conflict in the forthcoming decades were formed. With discontent mounting among Protestants during the years of the O'Neill government, which was seen to be kowtowing to nationalist requests, in March 1966 elements within the Protestant population, rallied by the fervent oratory of Ian Paisley, organized themselves into what would constitute the nucleus of the Ulster Volunteer Force to 'defend' British loyal Northern Ireland in the wake of the Easter Rising Republican celebrations (Hennessey 2005: 49–59). Although named after the organization that fought during the First World War and that subsequently helped Northern Ireland come into existence, 'the UVF [of the beginnings] . . . was a far cry from the original body of that name. It was instead made up of at most a couple of dozen men who met in backstreet pubs, many in the Shankill Road district, to discuss over drinks means of combating the practically non-existent IRA' (McKittrick and McVea 2001: 35). Soon becoming the second largest Loyalist paramilitary group, the UVF has been responsible for the death of 569 individuals (including killings committed by the smaller UVF-aligned Red Hand Commando). As a result of the heightened intercommunal tension in Belfast between 1968 and 1970, a second Loyalist paramilitary group, the Ulster Defence Association (UDA), was established in 1971 as a centrally coordinated organization for the local vigilante groups springing up across the North to defend Protestant areas from IRA attacks (McDonald and Cusack 2004: 17–20); it soon developed a military arm, the Ulster Freedom Fighters (UFF). The UDA/UFF was to become the largest of the Loyalist paramilitary groups, claiming the lives of 431 individuals.

As for the Republican side, in the aftermath of the Battle of the Bogside and the rioting in Belfast in August 1969, internal tensions grew within the IRA, with a nucleus of volunteers dissatisfied with the organization's ineffective reaction in the North and advocating a return to more traditional methods and approaches to military action. The IRA had been established in Dublin in 1913 and had been the protagonist of the 1916 Easter Rising and the Irish War of Independence against Britain; but after the partition of the island in 1921, it had progressively lost support and, in the wake of the outbreak of the Troubles, was militarily disorganized and structurally ineffective. On 18 December 1969, a group of twenty-six IRA breakaway members met in Belfast to found a new IRA, the Provisional IRA, committed to the 'fundamental republican position: a thirty-two-county Irish republic to be brought about by military means' (English 2003: 104–8). The Provisional IRA was to become one of the most sophisticated non-state paramilitary groups the world would ever know, responsible for the death of 1,768 individuals. Among a plethora of minor groups that were established throughout the years both on the Republican and Loyalist side, another Republican paramilitary organization played a central part in the conflict. The Irish National Liberation Army (INLA) was established in December 1974 out of the main body of the IRA, which assumed the name of Official IRA in order to differentiate itself from the Provisional IRA or 'Provisionals'; the INLA advocated that the war for national liberation of the six Northern counties could not be rescinded from the socialist class struggle throughout the island of Ireland (Holland and McDonald 1994: 30–38). Smaller and less organized than the other three groups, the INLA would nonetheless be responsible for the deaths of 151 individuals – including killings committed by the Irish People's Liberation Organization (IPLO), a group formed in 1986 after an internal schism within the organization.[5] These four paramilitary groups have also developed, to differing degrees, successful manifestations in the political arena. Most notably, the Provisional IRA has strong links with Sinn Féin: founded in 1905, the party mirrored the internal split in the IRA, dividing in 1970 into Provisional and Official Sinn Féin. Led by Gerry Adams, Provisional Sinn Féin is now the second main party in Northern Ireland, participating in a power-sharing government with the Democratic Unionist Party. The INLA's political expression can be found in the Irish Republican Socialist Party (IRSP): founded by Seamus Costello in 1974, it is inspired by the socialist revolutionary Irish Socialist Republican Party of James Connolly. The UVF is linked to the small left-wing Progressive Unionist Party, founded in 1979. Finally, the UDA had links with the now defunct Ulster Democratic Party.[6]

Sectarian tensions and violence escalated in Northern Ireland in the late 1960s/early 1970s, to the extent that, after a dramatic incident in Derry/Londonderry on 30 November 1972 that brought Northern Ireland close to an outright civil war – famously remembered as 'Bloody Sunday' – when thirteen civilians were shot dead by the British Army during a civil rights march, the British government disbanded the (Unionist) Stormont parliament and reintroduced Direct Rule over the province. Thirty years of armed conflict between Republican paramilitary groups on one side and the security forces and Loyalist paramilitaries on the other were to ensue. Although the vast majority of combatants' energy was channelled towards military action, commemorative activity always ran parallel, even during the darkest years of the Troubles.

Commemorating during the Troubles

Funerals and Communal Burials

Since the funeral of the iconic nineteenth-century figure of Irish Nationalism, Charles Stewart Parnell, in 1891, when tens of thousands lined the streets of Dublin, the funerary ritual has played a pivotal role in the history of Irish Republican commemoration.[7] Rooted in the Roman Catholic religious tradition, the wake and the funeral have been identified by Arensberg (1968) as the most important ceremony of rural Ireland and the chief expression of traditional social life (Metress and Metress 1993: 3). In times of emergency legislation and political censorship, funerals were often 'the only public occasion on which dissident and "subversive" views could be put forward without fear of instantaneous arrest; that usually followed the moment the orator set foot outside the cemetery' (Doherty and Keogh 1998: 186). Similar to apartheid South Africa, funerals during the Northern Irish conflict represented the main social occasion when the Republican community could gather together, as Republican commemorations were often banned.[8] Unsurprisingly these events assumed a clear political meaning, especially on the occasion of the death of an IRA volunteer. Republican funerals followed a conventional format during the conflict: after the customary wake, the coffin, draped with the Irish flag and usually bearing the gloves and beret of the fallen volunteer, was flanked by a uniformed IRA honour guard and taken by public procession, first to the church for the funeral service and ultimately to the cemetery. Preceded by a lone piper, the funeral procession could be attended by hundreds of thousands of mourners, as in the case of Bobby Sands' funeral in May 1981, whose body was accompanied by over a hundred thousand people (Metress and Metress 1993: 2). At the graveside, a customary oration was followed by the recitation of a decade of the rosary in Gaelic and the folding of the Irish tricolour, which was presented to the family of the deceased along with his/her gloves and beret. The ceremony traditionally closed with the uniformed IRA unit firing a volley of shots over the grave which was accompanied by military commands in Gaelic (ibid.: 3), although it is worth mentioning that both the RUC and British Army sometimes went to elaborate ends to try to stop this practice. In post-conflict Northern Ireland, Republican funerals still attract thousands of mourners to the streets and follow a similar format, with the exclusion in recent years of paramilitary emblems and shows of strength such as the volley of shots.[9]

With the UVF and the UDA declared illegal organizations in 1966 and 1992 respectively, Loyalist funerals were also a common occurrence during the Troubles. Drawing from the British Army military funerary service, they followed nonetheless a similar format to Republican funerals, the only differences being that the coffin would be draped in a Union flag, and paramilitary insignia linked to the Loyalist groups would be displayed instead. It also became common to see Orangemen, often belonging to the same lodge as the deceased, accompanying the coffin wearing their official Order bannerettes.[10]

Republican volunteers were usually buried in Catholic cemeteries, such as Milltown Cemetery in Belfast, either in individual/family graves or in communal plots with their comrades. As the erection of new and the replacement of existing Republican monuments were forbidden after partition (Leonard 1998–99), Republican communal plots in Catholic cemeteries remained throughout the conflict the only form of permanent memorialization available to the Republican community. Target of recurring attacks carried out by loyalists or the B-Specials – the UDR's predecessors – most Republican plots, some of which predated the conflict, have had to be repaired or entirely replaced over the past thirty years (ibid.). In order 'to restore where necessary, and to maintain fittingly, the graves of all those who died for Irish freedom' (NGA 1985: 7), the National Graves Association, Belfast (*Cumann Uaigheann na Laocradh Gaedheal, Béal Feirste*) was founded in the mid-1930s.[11] A separate organization from the homonymous organization founded in Dublin in 1926, the Belfast Association has, since 1946, regularly erected, restored and maintained monuments and graves to Republicans buried in Belfast, including the Provisional IRA plot and the County Antrim Memorial plot in Milltown Cemetery. Conversely, Loyalist volunteers were interred in individual or family graves in Protestant cemeteries, such as Roselawn Cemetery in Belfast, whereas communal plots were rare, or non-existent. Although prisoners' associations have often maintained graves, a central organization equivalent to the National Graves Association does not exist on the Loyalist side.

Annual Commemorations

Despite heightened concern over security, public commemorations were regularly held during the Troubles. The Orange Twelfth celebrations, commemorating the victory of Protestant William III of Orange over Catholic James II at the Battle of the Boyne in 1690, have been an annual occurrence since the end of the eighteenth century and remained the major event in the Orange/Loyalist calendar during the conflict. However, whereas the Twelfth was to all intents and purposes a state ritual during the so-called Stormont years (1921–72), after 1972 it became more a site for political struggle, reflecting the gradual decrease of the political hegemony of Orangeism and the Orange Order since the mid-1960s (Bryan 2000: 78–96). Other public commemorations for the Protestant community included events in June/July in memory of the Battle of the Somme, Remembrance Sunday in November and the commemoration of the siege of Derry/Londonderry in December.[12] Although parading was not a practice central to the Catholic culture in Northern Ireland, the Ancient Order of Hibernians had held Nationalist parades in Northern Ireland since the 1890s on St Patrick's Day (17 March) and Lady's Day (15 August).[13] Easter commemorations (in memory of the 1916 Easter Rising in Dublin, which led to the War of Independence from Britain) remained the major public event for the Republican movement, with regular parades being held in Belfast, Derry/Londonderry and Newry (Jarman and Bryan 2000: 95).

While the police ensured that Orange parades were able to march undisturbed wherever they chose, at least until the mid-1980s, the power given to the authority to ban gatherings and manifestations was often exercised in trying to stop or ban Republican Easter Sunday processions and meetings long before the beginning of the Troubles, resulting in violent clashes and arrests (Jarman and Bryan 2000: 98).[14] During the Troubles, Easter commemorations were confined to Catholic areas where the display of Republican symbols and the flying of the Irish tricolour were tolerated, even if not legal, with de facto illegal (following the 1970 Public Order Bill) parades organized by the various Republican paramilitary groups. In Belfast, three distinct marches – organized by the Provisional IRA, the Official IRA and the INLA – were held from the Falls district to Milltown Cemetery. Exacerbating the perception of unequal treatment of the two traditions by the authorities, Orange parades were allowed to walk down Catholic areas, whereas 'green' parades were banned from city centres until 1993 when a Republican march commemorating Internment was permitted into the centre of Belfast (ibid.: 108).[15] Other Republican commemorations during the Troubles included the annual June 'pilgrimage' to the graveside of Theobald Wolfe Tone, leader of the United Irishmen rebellion, in Bodenstown, County Kildare; events commemorating major anniversaries, such as the fifth anniversary of the 1981 hunger strike and smaller local commemorations to remember the IRA Border Campaign (1956–62) and the deaths of IRA volunteers in the late 1960s/early 1970s. Public parades on the street were often echoed by smaller-scale analogous events within prison walls, with both Loyalist and Republican prisoners gathering in jails' courtyards for a brief service on the occasion of Remembrance Sunday and Easter Sunday, respectively.

The Mural Painting Tradition in Northern Ireland

The Early Years

Featured in the background of most media reports of local and international news crews during the Troubles, murals became a significant and dynamic facet of the political and cultural life of Northern Ireland and, since the early 1980s, dominated the public scene as the most popular form of visual display of identity and political expression during the conflict. Over the years both communities, through murals, have expressed their changing political strategies and ideological aspirations, their most celebrated achievements and their deepest-seated fears. However, as Jarman (1992: 149–55) has argued, it would be incorrect to interpret murals as a form of communication between the two communities or as a way of shifting the otherwise impossible dialogue from the political arena to the symbolic level of 'visual statements'. Although Loyalist and Republican murals have developed along parallel paths and many similarities in themes and images can be detected between them, they must be read as the expression of two largely separate and independent internal discourses, as part of the ongoing 'debate concerning power and the meaning of traditional symbols' within each community; it is only the 'shared socio-political environment' that has generated correspondence (ibid.).

Dating from the beginning of the twentieth century, mural painting was originally an exclusively Protestant tradition linked to the Twelfth of July celebrations, with the murals of the early years depicting 'historical events of loyalist relevance . . . flags, shields and other heraldic imagery' (Rolston 1996: 192): painted in 1908 on the Beersbridge Road, East Belfast, the first mural ever to appear on the walls of Belfast portrayed William III of Orange – King Billy, as he is affectionately known – at the Battle of the Boyne. This practice tended to decline in the late 1960s and early 1970s with the end of the political and cultural hegemony of Unionism, but experienced a 'revival' in the early 1980s, during the 1981 Republican hunger strike, when ten Republican prisoners in the Maze prison – popularly known as Long Kesh or the H-Blocks – starved themselves to death at the zenith of five years of protests staged inside prisons in Northern Ireland and Great Britain to see the prisoners' political status reinstated. Painted by local youths as a way of propaganda and to mobilize support for the hunger strikers, the first Republican murals featured the hunger strikers' names and portraits, excerpts from poems, quotations, slogans and both traditional and new Republican symbols, such as the Irish tricolour, the Starry Plough, the phoenix, the 'H' from

H-Blocks and the lark in barbed wire (Rolston 1992: 25–33; Sluka 1992: 197–99). As a reaction to the appearance of the first Republican murals, a new wave of Loyalist paintings of a more militaristic kind appeared from the mid-1980s.

Armed Struggle and Party-Political Murals

Many scholars (Jarman; Rolston; Sluka) have categorized the evolution of the mural tradition in Northern Ireland into different 'phases' or 'periods', with murals painted between 1983 and 1984 labelled the phase of 'armed struggle' and those from 1985 to 1990 labelled 'party-political' murals (Sluka 1992). On the Republican front, the use of murals was progressively appropriated by the political leadership: a number of trained artists were hired to work directly for Sinn Féin, whose political support would grow steadily after the hunger strike, and murals increasingly became a powerful and effective weapon to convey political and ideological messages, and to promote a revival of the Irish culture. During the armed struggle period, Republican murals depicted modern IRA volunteers, sometimes accompanied by important Republican figures from the past to give historical perspective to the present struggle, and focused on the themes of repression by the RUC and British Army and resistance to the British occupation (ibid.: 202–3). From the mid-1980s onwards, the emphasis on the political role of Sinn Féin and its electoral politics, always flanked by the armed struggle, increased dramatically, and a wider, international breadth was introduced, with numerous murals in support of other national liberation movements, such as the Palestinian or the Basque struggles (ibid.: 204–7). In contrast with the variety of themes and international references of Republican paintings, Loyalist muralists have often been accused of 'narrowness of artistic imagination and expression' (Rolston 1996: 198). Produced almost exclusively by Loyalist paramilitary organizations, Loyalist murals featured 'traditional' Unionist/ Protestant themes – King Billy, the Union flag, the Crown – together with depictions of armed, hooded figures and emblems and insignia of the different Loyalist paramilitary groups, maintaining throughout the conflict a threatening, militarist and, at times, gruesome tone. Occasionally, connections with the past were drawn, with particular reference to the 1913 UVF and the 36th Ulster Division who fought in the Somme (Sluka 1992: 207–12). It is interesting to note that murals in memory of fallen volunteers – the so-called 'memorial murals' – remained a constant feature throughout the conflict both for Republicans and Loyalists, developing from simple sketches to elaborate representations depicting life-size portraits of the individuals commemorated.

Post-Ceasefire and Peace Process Murals

With the declaration of paramilitary ceasefires in 1994 and the beginning of the peace process, new murals depicting more contemporary themes and symbolic representations eventually replaced the old murals of the 'conflict era'. In a development of what Sluka (1996: 383) termed the 'culture of resistance' stage (1991–93), which began a few years before the IRA ceasefire and saw a progressive move away from 'armed struggle' images, the dominant themes of post-ceasefire mainstream Republican murals were 'Irish cultural identity (i.e. Irish/Celtic/Gaelic language, mythology, art, music, poetry, literature) and political issues such as the peace process itself, the campaign for the release of political prisoners, disbandment of the RUC, and rerouting of sectarian Protestant Orange Order marches away from Catholic districts' (ibid.: 384). Memorial murals, murals commemorating iconic historical events of Irish Republicanism and murals in support of other international conflicts also intensified during this phase.

In contrast, Loyalist murals lacked the political, cultural and international references of their Republican counterparts, and in the post-ceasefire and peace process years became more aggressive and militaristic, acting as a reassurance to local communities that 'the Loyalist guns were still around to prevent anything which could be interpreted as a Republican victory' (Rolston 2003b: 7). This increasing militaristic tone could also be seen as a consequence of the heightened rivalry between different Loyalist paramilitary organizations. Showing something of a 'blindness' towards contemporary political developments, and expressing no clear 'national' or 'constitutional' aspiration, they nonetheless expressed support for the release of political prisoners (Rolston 2003a: x). Memorial murals and murals commemorating the Battle of the Somme (mainly commissioned by the UVF) remained a common feature during the peace process years.

From the early 1990s both Republican and Loyalist murals – particularly memorial murals – became the focal point for periodic paramilitary commemorative events in memory of fallen volunteers, with flute bands and contest prizes (more commonly on the Loyalist side) increasingly being named in honour of deceased volunteers and activists.[16]

The 1998 Agreement and the 'Boom' of Permanent Memorialization

After years of discontinuous negotiations between the major political parties in Northern Ireland, external mediation efforts from the Irish,

British and U.S. governments, and a vacillating peace process which continued to witness acts of violence from both sides, on 10 April 1998 the Good Friday/Belfast Agreement, based on the principles of consociationalism (power sharing) and consent, was endorsed by most parties in Northern Ireland (with the exception of the Democratic Unionist Party and the small U.K. Unionist Party) and the Irish and British governments.[17] Although the Northern Irish conflict was to claim the lives of over a hundred more individuals from 10 April 1998 to the end of 2006 (McKittrick et al. 2007: 1552), permanent memorialization to the casualties of the Troubles reached an unprecedented scale after 1998.

Post-Agreement Murals

Republican and Loyalist memorial murals – often adorned by commemorative plaques –appeared with greater frequency, remembering fallen volunteers either individually or collectively in the brigades, companies and battalions to which they belonged. Murals celebrating iconic historical events or figures of either Irish Republicanism or the Unionist/Loyalist tradition also became more numerous and elaborate: the 1913 UVF and the Battle of the Somme featured as the most common themes of Loyalist murals; in contrast, the 1916 Easter Rising and the 1981 hunger strike featured prominently in Republican murals.

A more recent group of memorial murals commemorates civilian victims and mass atrocities of the Troubles. In particular, some Republican murals remember specific categories of victims, such as plastic bullets victims (Islandbawn Street) and black-taxi drivers targeted by Loyalist death squads (Falls Road, Ardoyne Avenue). Republican murals addressing international issues have continued to flourish after the Agreement, with, for instance, the now famous 'International Wall' at the entrance of the Lower Falls displaying ever-changing murals on varied political and historical topics.

Finally, in an attempt to move away from militaristic images, particularly in Loyalist working-class areas, numerous governmental and private 're-imaging' or 'regeneration' funding schemes have brought about the substitution of old 'armed struggle' murals with paintings on themes of cultural and historical relevance to the wider province: for instance, depictions of Northern Irish sporting heroes such as footballer George Best can be found in Blythe Street (Sandy Row), Woodstock Road and in the Cregagh Estate, while footballer David Healy adorns a wall on the Albertbridge Road; *The Lion, The Witch and The Wardrobe* by Belfast-born writer C.S. Lewis inspired two 'Narnia' murals in Ballymacarrett Road and Dee Street, and the sinking of the Titanic features in a mural at the junction of Dee Street and the Newtownards Road. Overall, however, the practice of mural painting has decreased in post-conflict Northern Ireland, and the 'baton' of visual statement of identity has passed to alternative forms of memorialization.

Permanent Memorials

Perhaps the most significant development in the landscape of commemoration after 1998 has been the incremental proliferation of permanent forms of memorialization, most commonly the creation of outdoor memorials to remember casualties of the conflict. These range from simple commemorative crosses, plaques and memorial stones to elaborate gardens of remembrance comprising numerous permanent commemorative components (stone centrepieces, plaques, statues, fountains, benches, etc.). Outdoor memorials can be classified into different types, depending on the section of society that they commemorate.

Memorials to Paramilitary Combatants

Memorials commemorating members of paramilitary groups who lost their lives 'during active service' represent the most frequent form of permanent memorial in Northern Ireland. As discussed further in Chapter 3, the Provisional IRA on the Republican side and both the Ulster Volunteer Force and the Ulster Defence Association on the Loyalist side have been particularly active in commemorating their dead in this fashion in their respective areas of influence. To date, the Irish National Liberation Army has only erected a series of commemorative plaques in Belfast, though some permanent memorials to INLA members can be found in other parts of the province, such as Derry/Londonderry, Strabane and Dungiven.

Republican and Loyalist memorials differ in their inclusion of those commemorated. Whereas Provisional IRA memorials often commemorate Republican activists and civilian casualties (including women and children) alongside fallen volunteers, Loyalist memorials only remember members who died as a consequence of their active involvement in the military struggle, with no mention of civilian casualties.[18] Although the different paramilitary organizations usually keep their dead clearly separated, some Republican memorials remember 'all the Republicans that died in the struggle for Irish freedom' (author's emphasis) and the fact that members of different Republican paramilitary groups died for or as a result of the same wider cause at times appeases differences in political and ideological affiliation to unite all fallen in the 'garden of martyrdom' of the greater Republican community. No similar example of inclusive commemoration exists for Loyalist paramilitary casualties, with memorials stating precisely the belonging and allegiance of those they commemorate: loyalty to one's organization survives one's own death, and the volunteers' sacrifice gives lustre first to the battalion and company they served, then to the cause.

Memorials to Civilian Casualties

Civilians who lost their lives in shooting incidents by paramilitary groups or state forces and in bombing attacks by paramilitary groups are commemorated throughout Northern Ireland, either individually or collectively, especially in the case of mass killings. Memorials can take various forms: plaques, murals, memorial stones, crosses, sculptures and stained-glass windows. In Belfast there are various examples of memorials commemorating Catholic and Protestant civilian deaths. A unique example is an old lamppost placed in the Shankill Memorial Park in memory of the casualties of the 1993 bombing of Frizzell's fish shop, which entombs a casket containing the ashes of floral tributes placed on the Shankill Road following the atrocity (*Combat* July 1994: 6; Shankill Memorial Park, Viggiani 2013). In some cases tributes to civilian casualties who died during the conflict have been added to pre-existing First and Second World War memorials, as in the case of the Enniskillen War Memorial, where eleven bronze doves were added to commemorate the eleven people killed by an IRA bomb in 1987 during a Remembrance Sunday service (Leonard 1997b: 17–18; 'Enniskillen Bomb Memorial' 2010).

Memorials to Security Forces

Outdoor memorials commemorating members of the RUC, UDR/RIR or the British Army who died during the conflict are rare on public soil in Northern Ireland. Some exceptions include a series of plaques in Ballygawley, County Tyrone, in memory of eight British Army soldiers killed in a coach explosion in 1988, and a plaque in Caledon, County Tyrone, remembering three policemen and a nun killed by an IRA bomb in 1990. In Belfast the only public plaque, that commemorates 'deceased members of the Security Forces in the Greater Shankill Area', can be found in Bray Street, Woodvale, and was commissioned by the Orange Order in 1996. UDR memorial plaques can be also found in rural towns such as Markethill (Donnan 2005). Memorials to the British Army and police casualties are usually situated on private grounds, inside army barracks, police stations and (Protestant) churches. In Belfast, two large memorials to the security forces exist: the memorial garden in the grounds of Palace Barracks, Holywood, dedicated to the men and women of the Army, Royal Navy and Royal Air Force who lost their lives in various conflicts including Northern Ireland; and the Royal Ulster Constabulary George Cross Garden in the grounds of the Police Service of Northern Ireland headquarters on Knock Road, Brooklyn, opened in September 2003 in memory of RUC officers who died in Northern Ireland from 1922 to 2001. Both gardens are built on private premises and public access is strictly limited.[19] A controversial issue over the years has been the addition of security force casualties who died during the Troubles to pre-existent memorials of the world wars (Leonard 1997b: 16–19). As a general rule, only servicemen killed in the two world wars could be recorded on these memorials and, under legislation, names could be added only if the conflict involved a formal British declaration of war (which was not the case in Northern Ireland); on occasions, however, these guidelines were ignored, and following a ruling by a district council in 1993, the recording on local cenotaphs of British servicemen killed in Northern Ireland is now permitted (ibid.: 17; Leonard 1998–99).

Memorials in Government Buildings, Party Offices, Workplaces and Churches

A few memorials can be found in local government buildings, the most striking being a stained-glass window inside the Derry/Londonderry Guildhall in memory of the 'innocent people killed during the Troubles in the Derry area' (Leonard 1997b: 21). As part of the refurbishment work recently carried out in the grounds of Belfast City Hall, a memorial fountain to all Belfast City Council employees who were killed during the conflict was unveiled in the rear courtyard in 2009. It is also common to find paramilitary and civilian memorials inside Sinn Féin and PUP party branches or community and ex-prisoners centres, where ex-combatants now carry out their new role of community workers – an example of this is the framed memorial picture commemorating Trevor King in the PUP office on the Shankill Road. Other memorials have been erected by firms and companies in their workplaces to commemorate members of staff who died during the conflict, such as the ceramic panel in Belfast's Laganside Bus Station in memory of twelve deceased employees of Citybus and Ulsterbus. Plaques, stained-glass windows or other similar commemorative features dedicated to members of the security forces can be found in Protestant churches (ibid.: 22), though there do not appear to be similar memorials inside Catholic churches. Some memorials have been erected in the precincts of Catholic churches, such as the commemorative cross 'dedicated to the memory of all the deceased members from St Matthew's Parish especially those who died as a result of the conflict in our country' beside St Matthew's Church in the Short Strand area of Belfast (St Matthew's Chapel, Viggiani 2013).

Commemorative Banners and Memorial Bands

In addition to being commemorated on memorials in their organizations' grounds and on plaques inside halls, deceased members of the Orange Order, the Royal Black Institution and the Apprentice Boys of Derry have also been commemorated on banners and drums used during the Twelfth of July celebrations (Leonard 1997b: 23). In more recent years, Loyalist paramilitary groups have reproduced this tradition, naming flute bands in memory of deceased members or commemorating them on banners carried during parades. Although the display of paramilitary insignia is officially banned by the Orange Order, some instances have been recorded where banners portraying members of Loyalist paramilitary groups have been displayed, for example during the Orange parade on the Springfield Road on 28 June 2003 when a bannerette of Old Boyne Island Heroes LOL (Loyal Orange Lodge) 633 portraying UVF member Brian Robinson was carried by an Orange-sash-clad Eddie McIlwaine, sentenced for his part in the Shankill Butchers' campaign of terror in the 1970s (Cox 2003: 4–5; McKernon 2003: 4; *Sunday Life* 20 July 2003: 6; Kennaway 2006: 52, 261–62). In comparison, banners carried by Sinn Féin *cumainn* (party branches) commonly portray members of the IRA or Republican activists killed during the Troubles, and the same *cumainn* are sometimes named after them.[20] Similar to their Loyalist counterparts, Republican bands are sometimes named in memory of deceased Republicans. In addition, there is a long tradition of composing ballads and tunes in memory of Republican casualties (Leonard 1997b: 24).

In 2004, the East Belfast Historical and Cultural Society produced historical lamppost-mounted plastic bannerettes in order to counter the use of paramilitary flags. These bannerettes are now a common occurrence in Belfast during the marching season, sponsored by Orange lodges, local businesses and politicians. Similar bannerettes commemorating members of both Loyalist and Republican paramilitary groups have since appeared, especially in west and north Belfast: for example, in 2006 images of the ten hunger strikers were featured on bannerettes in some Republican areas of Belfast to commemorate the twenty-fifth anniversary of the event (Bryan et al. 2010: 8–9).

Memorial Publications, Commemorative Pamphlets and Oral History Projects

Since 1998, a series of local memorial projects have been carried out by memorial committees, ex-prisoners' groups and historical associations in different areas of the province (mostly Republican), which have usually resulted in the publication of (sectional) commemorative pamphlets or booklets that recall the tragic events that took place in the different areas during the conflict and which recite the Roll of Honour of local casualties. A comprehensive memorial book titled *Tírghrá* ('Love of Country', 'Patriotism') in memory of the 364 Republicans whose names are on the IRA Roll of Honour was produced in 2002 and presented to each family together with a sculpture of an Easter lily during a high profile event in the City West hotel in Dublin on 13 April 2002 (Spain 2002; Lane 2002). Among cross-community memorial publications, the 'greatest act of remembrance that has yet emerged' – as Fintan O'Toole commented on the pages of *The Irish Times*[21] – is the book *Lost Lives*, published in its first edition in 1999, which is a chronicle of the 3,720 people who lost their lives as a result of the Northern Irish conflict from 1966 to 2006. Some oral history projects such as the work of *An Crann/The Tree* or the Falls Community Council's *Dúchas* ('Heritage') Living History project have combined storytelling initiatives, workshops, artefacts and photographic exhibitions to document personal testimonies and individual experiences of the Troubles.

Memorial Prizes, Awards and Trophies

Finally, memorialization is not limited to physical forms but can assume non-tangible expressions, such as the naming of sporting events, grounds and trophies after individuals killed during the conflict. Since traditional Republican commemorations were banned by the Stormont government, some Gaelic Athletic Association teams, grounds, tournaments and trophies have been named after iconic figures of Irish Republicanism, as in the case of the GAA stadium in Belfast named after Irish revolutionary Roger Casement. There are also a few examples of GAA teams, grounds, tournaments and trophies named after IRA and INLA volunteers who lost their lives during the Troubles, such as the Kevin Lynch Hurling Club in Dungiven, the McDonnell/Doherty Park in West Belfast (home ground of St Teresa's Gaelic Football Club) and the Michael McVerry Cup in Cullyhanna, Co. Armagh.[22] Policemen and soldiers have been, instead, commemorated through the naming of some angling, soccer, rugby and golf trophies (Leonard 1997b: 24).[23] Educational prizes, grants, annual lectures, research trusts and study exchanges provide other examples of this form of memorialization (ibid.: 25, 31).

Post-Conflict Commemorations

The 'memory boom' witnessed after 1998 was also observed in the sphere of public commemoration. Traditional annual events, such as the Twelfth of July and Remembrance Sunday, or Easter Sunday and the various anniversaries of the deaths of the hunger strikers, are now complemented by a myriad of smaller, more local commemorations. Both Republican and Loyalist paramilitary groups have developed an intensive calendar of commemorations, with almost every urban district and most rural areas featuring a series of commemorative parades, processions, and candle vigils marking the anniversary of individual casualties related to the Troubles.

Peace or Cross-Community Memorials

In his report *We Will Remember Them*, Sir Kenneth Bloomfield recommended that 'at the appropriate time, consideration should be given to a Northern Ireland Memorial in the form of a beautiful and useful building within a peaceful and harmonious garden' (Bloomfield 1998: 51). To date, however, there have been no permanent cross-community memorials that honour all casualties of the Troubles through the same artefact. The few existing peace memorials, in particular abstract sculptures, have been conceived spontaneously by individual artists. Some attempts were made to commemorate all of the victims of the Troubles, but these were all temporary installations (Leonard 1997b: 26–28). During Easter 2006, for example, Hilary Gilligan, a University of Ulster art student, wrote the names of more than 3,300 individuals killed during the conflict in chalk on the pavement of Royal Avenue in Belfast city centre.

In summary, memorialization has been a common feature of Northern Irish society since the inception of the state in 1921: while Unionist commemorations were considered de facto state rituals, and were preserved and facilitated by the security forces, Republican commemorations were, conversely, considered subversive and often banned. Although the energies of active combatants were directed elsewhere during the Troubles, the practice of commemoration remained significant throughout the years of the conflict, in particular paramilitary funerals and mural painting. After 1998, a significant increase in permanent memorials has been witnessed in Northern Ireland, together with the emergence of smaller scale commemorations to local paramilitary dead. The following chapter investigates in more depth the temporal and spatial dimensions of permanent memorialization through which paramilitary narratives about the conflict are projected in contemporary Northern Ireland.

Notes

1. For the history of the Northern Irish Troubles, see Stewart (1967, 1989); Buckland (1981); Hennessey (1997, 2005); Bew and Gillespie (1999); McKittrick and McVea (2001).
2. On discrimination against the Catholic population in Northern Ireland, see Hewitt (1981); Whyte (1983, 1990: 58–66); Elliott (2000: 383–94); Mulholland (2004); Hennessey (2005: 67–106).
3. On the ethno-sectarian nature of the Northern Irish conflict, see Ruane and Todd (1996). Many studies have been conducted on the nature and interpretation of the Northern Irish conflict. Among the most significant are: Whyte (1990); McGarry and O'Leary (1995); Darby (1997); Bew, Gibbon and Patterson (2002).
4. From now on, when talking about the 'Catholic population' and the 'Protestant population' in Northern Ireland, it is inferred that this refers to the Catholic/Nationalist/Republican population and the Protestant/Unionist/Loyalist population, respectively.
5. For a history of the Ulster Volunteer Force, see Boulton (1973); Dillon (1989); Cusack and McDonald (1997). For a history of the Ulster Defence Association, see McDonald and Cusack (2004); Wood (2006). For a history of the Provisional Irish Republican Army, see Taylor (1997); O'Doherty (1998); Harnden (1999); Coogan (2002); Moloney (2002); English (2003, 2006); Bowyer Bell (2003). For a history of the Irish National Liberation Army, see Holland and McDonald (1994).
6. On Sinn Féin, see Taylor (1997), Feeney (2003), Maillot (2004) and Bean (2007). On the IRSP, Holland and McDonald (1994). On the PUP, Cusack and McDonald (1997). On the UDP, Wood (2006).
7. For an analysis of Nationalist/Republican funerals in post-1916 Ireland (Free State/Republic of), see Doherty and Keogh (1998). For an analysis of Republican funerals in Northern Ireland, see Metress and Metress (1993).
8. According to the 1951 Public Order Act (Northern Ireland), a 48-hour notice for any public procession was to be given to the Royal Ulster Constabulary, with the exception of funeral processions and 'public processions which are customarily held along a particular route'. With the outbreak of the Northern Irish Troubles, the Act was amended in 1970 to ban the formation of paramilitary associations, their illegal meetings and processions, and the carrying or display of weapons in public places.
9. Although mainstream Republican funerals do not feature paramilitary displays anymore, these manifestations occur sporadically to the present day during dissident Republican funerals, an example of which happened during the funeral of John Brady in October 2009, when four men wearing balaclavas and paramilitary uniform

fired a volley of shots in the air over his coffin in Strabane, Co. Tyrone ('Shots Fired at Cell Death Funeral' 2009).

10. A public controversy arose, for instance, in 1989 after UVF member Brian Robinson was killed by the British Army. Death notices from his Orange lodge – the 'Old Boyne Island Heroes' LOL 633 – appeared in the local press (*Belfast Telegraph* 4 September 1989: 2) and lodge members wearing full Orange regalia flanked his coffin at his funeral (*Belfast Telegraph* 5 September 1989: 1). Following a letter of complaint to *The Belfast Telegraph*, the then County Grand Master of the Grand Orange Lodge of Belfast John McCrea (*Sunday Life* 24 September 1989: 31) and the then Lodge 633 secretary (*Belfast Telegraph* 6 October 1989: 6) attempted with scarce success to distance the Orange Institution from paramilitarism. On the connection between Orange Order and Loyalist paramilitarism, see Kennaway (2006: 47–52, 261–64).

11. For a history of the National Graves Association, see NGA (1985).

12. An iconic event in Ulster Protestant culture and mythology, the siege of Derry/Londonderry took place from 18 April to 28 July 1689 when the city was besieged for 105 days by the army of Catholic James II during the so-called Williamite War. Famously, a group of young apprentices – in whose memory the Orange organization, The Apprentice Boys of Derry, was named – closed the gates of the city in December 1688 as part of a previous attempt to enter the city during the war.

13. For a history of Nationalist parades in the Orange state, see Jarman and Bryan (2000).

14. In his biography, Irish Republican Joe Cahill recalls how during Easter 1942 an IRA unit staged a diversionary action to allow parades commemorating the Easter Rising to take place in West Belfast, given the government ban on Republican commemorations. An RUC officer was killed while chasing the IRA volunteers, leading to the arrest and execution of famous Irish Republican Tom Williams (Anderson 2002: chapter 3).

15. Internment without trial of IRA suspects was introduced in Northern Ireland on 9 August 1971 and resulted in the detainment of over 2,400 people in the first six months, most of who were freed after a short time in custody. The use of internment was continued for four years and attracted much condemnation of Britain, without succeeding in halting the violence in Northern Ireland or defeating the IRA (McKittrick and McVea 2001: 67–75).

16. Among the earliest examples of this practice, the Vol. Brian Robinson Memorial trophy was established in 1990 and presented to the best flute band taking part in the annual parade in his memory in the Woodvale/Shankill area of Belfast (*Combat* 31 August 1990: 13). For more information on paramilitary commemorations, see Chapters 5–8.

17. The theory of consociationalism was formulated by the political scientist Arend Lijphart (1968) to explain the democratic development in the Netherlands. It consists of a method of conflict resolution that 'advances a system of consensual multiethnic power sharing as opposed to majority rule' (Taylor 1991: 1). According to Lijphart (1977: 25–52), a 'consociational democracy' can be defined in terms of the following four characteristics: (1) government by a grand coalition of the political leaders of all significant segments of the plural society; (2) the mutual veto or 'concurrent majority' rule; (3) proportionality as the principal standard of political representation, civil service appointments and allocation of public funds; and (4) a high degree of autonomy for each segment to run its own internal affairs. In Northern Ireland, the model of consociationalism deployed contains 'cross-community power-

sharing, minority protections, community (segmental) autonomy and equality, and weighted majority decision-making on contentious issues' (O'Leary 1999, in Tonge 2002: 187); it resulted in the creation of a power-sharing executive headed conjointly by a Unionist First Minister and a Nationalist (nowadays Republican) Deputy First Minister and an Assembly whose key decisions are taken on the basis of a principle of cross-community voting system – the D'Hondt system. On consociationalism in Northern Ireland, see Taylor (2009).

18. The eleven memorials in memory of Protestant civilian casualties that are included in the database were not directly commissioned by paramilitary organizations, but by cultural or historical associations, although it is worth noting that some of these associations might have links with paramilitary groups.

19. For the Palace Barracks garden, see 'Palace Barracks Memorial Garden' (2002–10); for the RUC garden, see 'RUC GC Garden'.

20. On Orange/Loyalist and Republican banners, see Jarman (1997: 163–205; 1999).

21. As noted on the book's 2007 edition back cover.

22. Kevin Lynch was one of three INLA members who died during the 1981 hunger strike, together with IRA volunteers Joe McDonnell and Kieran Doherty. Michael McVerry was shot by British Army soldiers in 1973 and was the first IRA member to die in South Armagh during the Troubles.

23. It is worth mentioning that Leonard does not give any examples of sporting tournaments named in memory of security forces' casualties, and this author has not been able to find any additional sources corroborating the evidence of this claim.

Chapter 3

THE 'LANDSCAPE OF MEMORIALIZATION' IN BELFAST

Spatial and Temporal Reflections

⋑•⋐

> Public memory is 'the dynamic process by which groups map myths (in the anthropological sense) about themselves and their world onto a specific time and place'.
> – Till 1999: 254

Paramilitary-related memorials to the casualties of the conflict have become a common occurrence in most working-class areas of Belfast to the extent that in some estates one needs only walk a few yards before encountering some form of remembrance. An aerial overview using Google Maps displays the geographical distribution of the 157 memorials analysed in this study (Viggiani 2013). Borrowing theoretical concepts and categorizations from cultural geography and sociology, this chapter investigates the existence of these memorials in relation to the geography of the city and its patterns of residential segregation, social segmentation and sectarian division. In addition, some reflections on the temporal occurrence and historical significance of memorials to the casualties of the Troubles are presented.

'New' Cultural Geography and the Concept of Landscape as 'Text'

The late 1980s and 1990s witnessed the emergence of a novel trend within the discipline of cultural geography: if Carl Sauer and the so-called

Berkeley School interpreted landscapes merely as 'inert imprints or "containers of culture"' (Sauer 1925; Wagner and Mikesell 1962), 'new' cultural geography shifted the focus to the highly political nature of culture, conceiving landscape as 'a social and cultural production which both represents and is constitutive of past, present and future political ideologies and power relationships' (Whelan 2003: 12).[1] Landscapes came to be interpreted as 'texts' with their symbolic and semantic elements, written by agents of power and 'actively shaped and reshaped, created and destroyed' by the people who inhabit them; texts that can be read and decoded 'in order to reveal the ideas, practices, interests and contexts of the society that produced [them]' (ibid.: 12–13). The idea of landscape as text and symbol can be extended to encompass a 'reading' of landscapes as 'iconographic discourses embedded in broader cultural and political debates' (ibid.: 14), used by ruling authorities and social groups throughout the world to inscribe group identity and collective heritage onto the territory. Cultural landscapes[2] are, therefore, 'intimately related to the creation and reinforcement of official constructions of identity and power' (ibid.: 15); as a result, official public landscapes act as a 'spatialization of public memory' (Johnson 1995: 63), reifying 'specific narratives of nationhood' and 'reducing fluid histories into sanitized, concretized myths that anchor the projection of national identity onto physical territory' (Bell 1999: 186).

Selective versions of a shared past are, thus, distilled into statues, monuments, street naming and other architectural elements and history, as wished to be remembered, effectively mapped onto the geography of a place. Public monuments, in particular, are not 'merely ornamental features of the urban landscape, but rather highly symbolic signifiers that confer meaning on the city and transform neutral places into ideologically charged sites' (Whelan 2003: 18). From the mid nineteenth century, ruling authorities in Europe were 'affected' by a frenzy of monument building aimed at strengthening political support, instilling a sense of political unity and cultivating national identity (ibid.). Sites of memory however, 'not only help to legitimate structures of authority and dominance but are also used . . . to cultivate alternative narratives of identity' (ibid.: 19). In situations of conflict, as in Northern Ireland, monuments themselves become sites of contested identities and ideologies.

Belfast and the Ethnicization of Space

A brief analysis of the geography of contemporary Belfast reveals a 'patchwork city' where natural boundaries, mainly the River Lagan and Belfast

Lough, in conjunction with man-made barriers such as motorways, road and rail systems and the so-called 'peace lines' delineate what Jarman terms 'a mosaic of sectarian fragments' (Jarman 1992: 148), a succession of separated, distinct areas defined along the Catholic/Protestant ethnic division.[3] The 'neutral' commercial and administrative centre of the city stretches southward to encompass not only the university and middle-class areas along Malone Road and Stranmillis Road, but also inner city Protestant working-class areas such as Sandy Row, Donegall Pass, Donegall Road/the Village. The area to the east of the Lagan is a mix of Protestant middle-class and working-class areas, with the exception of the small Catholic enclave of Short Strand. To the west and north of the city are a succession of mainly working-class estates, inhabited by one or the other community, in many cases adjacent to one another: in the west, the Catholic/Republican 'bloc' constituted by the Andersonstown/Turf Lodge/Falls areas faces the staunchly Protestant/ Loyalist Shankill and Woodvale; in the north, the Catholic Ardoyne, New Lodge and Cliftonville areas lie side by side with the Protestant Tiger's Bay, Skegoneill and Ballysillan districts. Given that interfaces – that is, points of contact between a Protestant and a Catholic area – occur most frequently in the west and north of the city, it is here that the highest levels of sectarian violence have been experienced during the conflict, with West and North Belfast presenting the highest average of incidents and resident deaths (Fay, Morrissey and Smyth 1999: 143–45).

Although residential segregation has characterized the city of Belfast since the late eighteenth century (Jarman 1993: 109–10), it intensified and solidified significantly after the outbreak of the Troubles in 1969. Boal and Murray (1977, in Jarman 1993: 109) estimated that, between 1969 and 1976, approximately sixty thousand people in Belfast (12 per cent of the population) were forced to relocate as a result of the conflict. By 1972, 70 per cent of Catholics and 78 per cent of Protestants lived in streets where over 90 per cent of people pertained to the same religion (Boal 1982: 253). This percentage has remained largely unchanged since 1998: based on 2001 Census data, 67.3 per cent of Catholics and 73 per cent of Protestants still live in areas where at least 81 per cent of people pertain to the same religion (Shirlow and Murtagh 2006: 59–60). As a general trend, working-class areas experienced a higher level of residential segregation than middle-class areas (Breen and Devine 1998: 54–56). Throughout the conflict, segregation characterized other aspects of social life, such as education, employment, marriage, sports and nightlife (ibid.).

Patterns of social segregation and sectarian division have gradually been inscribed into the territory, and ideological differences have become a concrete and material element of the physical environment. Flags, painted kerbstones, murals and, in more recent times, memorials have all contributed to map out these patterns and differences and to make tangible the mental boundaries of what Said defines as 'imaginative geography'. Such mental boundaries designate 'a familiar space which is "ours" and an unfamiliar space beyond "ours" which is "theirs"' (Said 1978: 54–55). Place in Northern Ireland, thus, becomes 'an activated facet of the ideological struggle' (Jarman 1998: 86) between the Catholic/Nationalist/Republican and Protestant/Unionist/Loyalist communities; together with rituals, forms of memorialization serve as 'icons of identity and spatializations of memory that transform neutral spaces into sites of ideology' (Graham and Whelan 2007: 477).[4] Some initial considerations on the relationship between memorials and territory can be drawn from the observation of the geographical distribution of these identity and ideological markers in contemporary Belfast.

The Spatial Dimension of Memorialization

Some initial considerations can be made if we look at the geographical distribution of memorials in Belfast. Of all the memorials analysed, 83.5 per cent are located in West Belfast (67.5 per cent of total) and North Belfast (16 per cent of total), the two areas that present most interfaces and that have experienced the highest number of incidents and resident deaths (see Table 3.1).[5]

Like murals, memorials seem to be exclusively an occurrence of working-class areas, whereas middle-class areas and the neutral city centre do not present paramilitary-related displays of identity or ideologico-political affiliation (Jarman 1993: 120).

Memorials to the casualties of the Troubles tend to be localized in nature, to the extent that almost every working-class estate can boast its own memorial. Although larger communal gardens are built where the necessary space is available, Republican memorials often mark the

Table 3.1 Geographical distribution of memorials in Belfast

Area of Belfast	Memorials	Murals	Plaques	Total
North	14	4	7	25
East	7	5	0	12
South	8	2	4	14
West	37	25	44	106
				157

Source: Viggiani 2013

spot of death of the individual(s) commemorated, or are situated in the proximity of their family or private dwelling. Loyalist memorials, on the other hand, do not generally follow this pattern, although there are some exceptions such as the plaque in memory of the UDA brigadier John McMichael, erected in Lisburn near the spot where he was killed by an IRA car bomb in 1987 (see also Leonard 1997b: 14).

Official public memorials, commissioned by the state or the local authorities, are generally situated at the heart of civic life, in the city or town main square or street; in a mimicking exercise, the majority of paramilitary-related memorials (mainly commissioned by the paramilitary groups themselves or aligned associations) sit at the heart of the estate in which they did or still operate.[6] This has a practical as well as a symbolic rationale. On a practical level, the location of memorials in hidden side streets, far off main roads, makes them easier to be controlled and protected from external acts of vandalism. In addition, given that the Northern Ireland Roads Service can only legally remove memorials which constitute a danger to road safety (gleaned from interview with a representative of the Road Service) and that the Belfast Housing Executive and City Council are reticent to send their personnel into estates to take down paramilitary-related paraphernalia, memorials thus positioned are less likely to attract the unwanted attention of local authorities. On a symbolic level, memorials can be considered, like murals, 'objects which confirm beliefs rather than challenge those of other people' (Jarman 1993: 120). While flags and painted kerbstones are often situated at interfaces, defiantly looking outward towards the opposite community,[7] the location of memorials at the heart of the estate would suggest that they firstly cast their ontological shadow inward, towards the community whose culture, history and identity they claim to represent and whose collective memory they attempt to reify. They seem to create what Feldman (1991: 36–39) has termed a 'sanctuary space', a place of safety and security, not only from physical aggression but also from ideological and cultural attacks, providing 'visible reassurance of the certitude of one's own faith among the competing ideologies' (Jarman 1993: 127). The very fact that memorials are located *within* the communities to which they symbolically appeal, appears to call into question the hypothesis that territorial demarcation is an intended rationale behind their construction.

Memorials as Territorial Markers

Whereas flags, graffiti, painted kerbstones and, to a lesser degree, murals symbolically mark ethnic boundaries between different areas and inscribe into the territory signatures of spatial ownership that leave no doubt as to which 'side of the divide' dominates that specific place, the fact that memorials are hidden from strangers' sight has led some interviewees to declare that memorials should not be interpreted primarily as territorial markers. As a Protestant respondent affirmed in interview with the author – echoed also by Catholic respondents:

> people in Northern Ireland don't need markers to know where they live, they have lived there all their lives, they know where the boundaries are. I knew in growing up what area I didn't walk through or walk into in the early sixties; I didn't need to wait [until] the memorial went up.

That a number of memorials are located along interfaces is, according to some interviewees, inevitable given the higher levels of violence that occurred in these contact zones and the desire to mark the exact spots where such deaths took place, rather than the consequence of an explicit intention to antagonize the neighbouring community. Undoubtedly, memorials are not intended to be ethnic 'boundary markers' and, as political messages, are 'primarily directed at those broad communities of support which sustained the paramilitary groups rather than outside bodies of opinion' (Jarman 1998: 86). It is this author's opinion, however, that memorials perform some function of territorial demarcation in the sense that they constitute 'identity markers'. At a moment in history when sectarian wall paintings are being covered up or replaced with more neutral and inclusive images of cultural/historical events and sporting heroes, memorials have been passed the 'baton' as visual statements of belonging of a place to one community. Attracting less attention from public opinion and being perceived as less threatening, given their lower level of visibility and assertiveness, they nonetheless act as an equally powerful signature of spatial ownership as their earlier mural counterparts.

Like murals, memorials are generally commissioned by paramilitary groups or ex-prisoners' associations closely linked to paramilitary groups. As Jarman (1993: 127) suggests,

> [during the conflict] as the open demonstration of the paramilitary presence was increasingly restricted and they were excluded from the more powerful media of communication, it was left to the very bricks and mortar to confirm that there would be 'No Surrender' and that 'Tiochfaidh Ar La' ('Our Day Will Come').

Although all four of the main paramilitary organizations have declared that 'the war is over' and have almost fully decommissioned, memorials still represent a reminder of the dormant presence of paramilitarism in

Northern Ireland: by honouring fallen members of specific companies, battalions and brigades, they remain a tangible reminder of their role as 'community defenders' during the conflict (see Chapter 9) and, for some interviewees, simultaneously act as an ominous 'promise' that military protection will resume should the need arise again in the future.[8] In reference to the transition from murals to more permanent memorials, a leading Loyalist figure explains, 'it's better to have a memorial of somebody than to have the Grim Reaper or the hooded figures with guns. It wouldn't be seen to be an in-your-face thing, but it's just a change of emphasis. It's a different form of paramilitary presence, but equally paramilitary.'

Memorials encode into the territory the traditional intergroup division between Republicanism and Loyalism, inscribing onto the geography of the city the two opposing ethnic identities, political allegiances and ideologies. As of August 2009, Republican memorials are more than twice as numerous as Loyalist memorials in Belfast: of the 157 memorials analysed, 89 memorials (57 per cent) can be attributed to Republican paramilitary groups (IRA; Provisional IRA; Official IRA; INLA) or the political parties associated with them (Sinn Féin; Workers Party; IRSP) and 39 memorials (25 per cent) can be attributed to Loyalist paramilitary groups (UVF; UDA/UFF; Red Hand Commando).[9] However, a closer look at the group affiliation of memorials in Belfast reveals further intragroup dynamics (see Table 3.2).

Provisional IRA/Sinn Féin memorials account for the vast majority of Republican memorials in Belfast (74.1 per cent of total number), followed by the INLA/IRSP, which account for another 11.2 per cent of memorials surveyed. This is probably due to the fact that no smaller Republican paramilitary group has ever reached enough public support or political significance to challenge the Provisional IRA/Sinn Féin symbolic dominance in the streets of Belfast. In addition, it is a common occurrence for Republican memorials of different paramilitary groups to coexist within a few yards of each other.[10] Therefore, rather than serve as a function of territorial demarcation between zones of influence of different Republican paramilitary groups, it is more plausible to see memorials as differentiating Republican from Nationalist areas. As a Republican ex-prisoner explained in relation to the Clonard memorial garden,

I never thought [of Republican memorials] as marking out territory other than this is a Republican area rather than just a Nationalist area ... Certainly there would have been a sense that Clonard is [a Republican area] and has a very long tradition of resistance and struggle against British occupation. And certainly we wanted to demonstrate that. (Interview with the author)

Table 3.2 Memorials' distribution by group and type

Group	Memorials	Murals	Plaques	Total (per group)
Civilian (Protestant)	3	1	7	11
Civilian (Roman Catholic)	6	2	6	14
INLA/IRSP	2	0	8	10
IRA (pre-1969)	1	0	4	5
Loyalist history (pre-1969)	2	0	0	2
OIRA/Workers Party	2	0	1	3
Orange Order	1	0	0	1
Other	1	0	1	2
PIRA	28	16	18	62
Republican history (pre-1969)	3	1	1	5
RHC	0	1	0	1
Security forces	0	0	1	1
SF	0	0	4	4
UDA/UFF	12*	3	3	18*
UVF	6*	12	1	19*
Total (per type of memorial)	**67***	**36**	**55**	**158***

Note: *The joint memorial for the UVF and the UDA B Companies, Woodvale has been counted twice as it belongs to both organizations.*
Source: *Viggiani 2013*

In comparison, Loyalist memorials are almost evenly split in number between the two main organizations, with the UVF (together with the UVF-aligned Red Hand Commando) accounting for 51.2 per cent of the total number and the UDA/UFF 46.1 per cent. With the exception of a joint memorial in the Woodvale area, UVF and UDA memorials appear only within the respective areas of influence, even if these are only a couple of streets away from one another. With the outbreak of hostility between the UVF and UDA during the summer of 2000, visual displays of 'allegiance' have increasingly been used to mark out Loyalist territory along the lines of internal 'tribalism', rather than differentiating Loyalist areas from Republican ones. UDA brigadier Jackie McDonald, for instance, recalls how the Loyalist feud was fought in the Shankill area as well on the symbolic level, with both organizations 'out-flagging' each other in an attempt to gain the highest spot on a flagpole, with the result that 'it was dark by one o'clock in the Shankill Road because the sun couldn't get through all the flags and bunting' (Viggiani 2007). Loyalist murals and memorials make these internal divisions more tangible and permanent, to the extent that it was not uncommon to see gable walls 'claimed' by the different Loyalist organizations and 'reserved' for future murals (Loyalist representative in interview with the author; see also Vannais 1999: 25). Particularly in recent years, Loyalist memorials can be interpreted as largely directed inward towards the very same Loyalist community rather than outward towards its traditional Republican enemy, as a symbolic means of demarcating the spatial boundaries between rival Loyalist paramilitary groups (see also Graham and Whelan 2007: 486).

Memorials as Aide-mémoires

Memorials can be interpreted as memory's imprints on the topography of a place (Halbwachs 1992: 235). In the modern world where memory has become archival and 'relies entirely on the materiality of the trace, the immediacy of the recording, the visibility of the image' (Nora 1989: 13), memorials, among other artefacts, perform the function of *aide-mémoires* (memory aids), 'recalling the sights, sounds, and smells of former times and providing "frameworks through which people perceive and engage with the present and the future"' (Donnan 2005: 75). As Dawson (2005: 164) points out,

> the preservation in situ of material remains of . . . [the] past is widely considered to be an important resource supporting commemoration of what has taken place at that particular site; while conversely, the loss or destruction of such traces degrades the historical record and the potential for collective remembrance.

Thus, the 1915 Hiroshima Prefectural Commercial Exhibition, now known as the 'A-Bomb Dome' – the closest structure to the Hiroshima atomic bomb's epicentre to partially withstand the blast – has been preserved in its damaged state after much controversy (Gough 2000: 218; Williams 2007: 9) 'as a historical witness that conveys the disaster of the first atomic bombing in history' ('A-Bomb Dome' 2000). Similarly in Northern Ireland, Republican and Loyalist memorials provide a material trace, tangible reminder and visible testimony of the two communities' competing pasts, and help to reconstruct the violent history of the province in the last thirty years.

Memorials assume an even greater significance when the geography of places where atrocities or similarly iconic historical events occurred is altered beyond recognition. In Derry/Londonderry, for instance, road building and redevelopment programmes in the 1970s and 1980s have rendered unrecognizable the physical appearance of the Bogside area, the backdrop for Bloody Sunday (Dawson 2005: 163–65). Significant landmarks and points of orientation such as the Rossville Flats have been demolished over the years to the extent that some have suggested that it was done as if to 'wipe out the memories' and render 'the killing ground . . . now hard to imagine' (Pringle and Jacobson 2000: 1). It is now left to the numerous memorials and murals that dot the area between Glenfada Park and Westland Street, the stretch of ground where the majority of the fatal shootings occurred on 30 November 1972, to conjure up not only the memory of the individuals who lost their lives, but also the old geography of the place, acting as 'markers of the lost environment' against the obliteration of history (Dawson 2005: 165). Moreover, as Donnan (2005: 98) has shown in relation to Northern Ireland's border Protestants, 'the concreteness of place and the materiality of the signs within it' grant veracity to people's memories and accounts of their traumatic past. Memorials, together with other tangible signs of violence, become an externalized 'proof' of the past and project 'people's memories onto the landscape in a way that can then be read back as "history": as neutral, self-evident, and true' (ibid.). In situations of ethnic conflict where competing narratives about the past are often inextricably linked to rival groups' claims of legitimacy and victimhood, the translation of one's own 'story' into 'history' through permanent 'texts' such as memorials assumes clear political and ideological connotations, which will be the focus of the remaining chapters of this book. One last area remains to be investigated with regard to the relation between memorials and their physical environment – the sensitization of space.

Memorials as Sacred Places

In our everyday lives, it is not uncommon to pass floral tributes, photographs and various personal memorabilia left along the roadside to mark the spot where a fatal road accident occurred. Arranged by families and friends of the deceased soon after sudden, untimely, violent deaths, these 'spontaneous shrines' are expressions of personal love, grief, loss and remembrance; they are 'temporary monuments [that] *consecrate* the place where the unthinkable happened' (Santino 2004: 76–77; author's emphasis). The 'shrine' singles out a defined, limited section of neutral space and transforms it into 'sacred' place – in the Durkheimian sense of that towards which man feels respect (Durkheim 1948: 37–38). As Jack Santino (2004: 79) points out, the shrine communicates that 'here, evil has erupted into the everyday world . . . this place, the shrine says, is no longer mundane space. The shrine jumps out of the ordinariness of the street. It forces us to confront the humanity of those who were killed and those whose lives were left behind in the wreckage'.

Although erected in many cases years after the deaths that they commemorate, memorials to war casualties and victims of atrocities equally sensitize space and often arouse a quasi-religious sense of respect and *dignitas* in the beholder. In Northern Ireland, memorials to the casualties of the Troubles can be interpreted as permanent shrines that reify 'the deep seated feelings of loss, injury and the will to remember, felt by a community of individuals' (Brown 2006: 10).[11] Similar to spontaneous roadside shrines, some memorials – especially Republican ones – mark the exact spot where violent deaths occurred, thus singling these sites out as no longer ordinary space, but as a succession of 'sacred places'. It is interesting to note how the sensitization of the space can reach unexpected highs when memorials come under attack, either materially through acts of vandalism or symbolically, for instance when parades and symbols from one community are displayed close to commemorative sites associated with the other community. Any threat against memorials is interpreted as a symbolic attack against the community itself and reactions are usually emotionally tumultuous, as in the case of the rioting that occurred in Dublin in February 2006 when a 'Love Ulster' Unionist/Loyalist parade passed the Dublin and Monaghan Bombing memorial – remembering the victims of two UVF bombing attacks – in Talbot Street ('Clashes in Dublin over Loyalist March' 2006).

Memorials can also act as surrogate graves for relatives and close friends of the individuals commemorated, especially if the deceased are buried in a cemetery mainly associated with the opposing community, as in the case of Ronnie Bunting and Noel Little, two Protestants who joined the Republican INLA but whose graves are in Protestant cemeteries. As a relative of Little remarked, 'the thing about Noel and Ronnie, they are buried outside the traditional Republican areas. Ronnie Bunting is buried in Ballynahinch and Noel is buried up in Roselawn. They are not particularly cemeteries that Republicans of any shade would feel comfortable going into' (interview with the author); in this case, the plaque in memory of the two men that the INLA/IRSP erected in Republican West Belfast might well constitute a safer location to pay one's respects. Finally, memorials can also contribute symbolically to reclaim and 'detoxify' the site of the atrocity – a contaminated psychic site of trauma – by and for the local community (Dawson 2005: 166), thus 'exorcizing' locations where violent deaths occurred.[12]

The remainder of this chapter looks at the relationship between memorials to the casualties of the Troubles and the temporal dimension, drawing some conclusions from the analysis of the chronology of memorialization in light of major historical occurrences in Northern Ireland, in particular the 1998 Good Friday/Belfast Agreement.

The Temporal Dimension of Memorialization

The signing of the Good Friday/Belfast Agreement in 1998 brought about a monument-building 'frenzy' in Northern Ireland, with the majority (79 per cent) of the memorials examined having been erected since 1998 (Table 3.3).[13]

Although processes of memorialization occurred before and throughout the conflict, both communities witnessed an unprecedented increase in permanent memorials, with 84.5 per cent and 65.4 per cent of Republican and Loyalist memorials, respectively, completed from 1998 to 2009. On a practical level, the proliferation of memorials since 1998 is most likely linked to the formation of ex-prisoners' groups after the release of politically motivated detainees as a result of the provisions of the Agreement. On a theoretical level, there are a few possibilities as to why this monument frenzy has occurred since 1998.

Memorials: End of the War or Continuation through Different Means?

According to Nora (1989: 7), *lieux de mémoire* emerge at times and in places where a perceived or constructed break with the past occurs. This temporal and spatial rupture, 'bound up with the sense that memory has been torn' (ibid.), is followed by the necessity – for individuals, social groups, nations and other collectivities alike – either to mark the end of an era or to invent a 'cult of new beginning' that places the new system at as great a distance as possible from the old. History provides us with many examples of both practices. If we 'forget' processes of 'social amnesia' that have been attested throughout the world,[14] it is common practice for modern nation states to produce some sort of physical memorial soon after the end of a war to mark the cessation of hostilities and remember the human cost. As Sider and Smith (1997: 7) point out, war commemorations 'are attempts at closure, at decisiveness and imposition'; the beginning and end dates of the hostilities are carved in stone; the final list of casualties is drawn. Commemoration can, furthermore, construct a symbolic break with the past: from the French and American revolutions with their invention of a 'cult of new beginnings' to mark the novel era after, respectively, the *Ancien Régime* and the British domination to the desovietization of post-communist Eastern Europe; from the bombing of statues embodying the British establishment in Dublin after the proclamation of the Free State independence in 1921 to the scenes of dancing and cheering Iraqis in central Baghdad's Firdos Square when a colossal statue of deposed President Saddam Hussein was toppled by U.S. Marine armoured vehicles in 2003.[15]

Table 3.3 Chronological distribution of memorials in Belfast

Year of construction	Catholic/Republican				Protestant/Loyalist				Total
	Memor.	Murals	Plaques	Subtotal	Memor.	Murals	Plaques	Subtotal	
pre-1969	2	0	1	3	0	0	0	0	3
1969–1993	2	1	1	4	2	1	0	3	7
1994–1997	2	0	2	4	1	3	2	6	10
1998–2009	25	7	28	60	11	4	2	17	77
				71				26	97

Source: Viggiani 2013

For Northern Ireland, the 1998 Agreement can be considered a similar turning point creating a break with the (violent) past, a historical watershed marking the official end of a permanent state of conflict between the two opposing ethnic groups in the province (see Ruane and Todd 1999), though there have been numerous setbacks to the peace process, and the bloodiest episode of the Troubles – the Omagh bombing – occurred four months after the signing of the agreement.[16] It is, therefore, not surprising that the majority of Troubles-related memorials sprang up after 1998. Many interviewees – both Republican and Loyalist – agreed with the view that the appearance of permanent memorials marked the end of the conflict. Some of the responses collated during interviews mention memorial stones as 'a sort of closure', 'a recognition that the conflict is at an end', permitting 'those organizations [which] actively participated in it to draw a line under the conflict' (various interviews with Republican and Loyalist respondents). In the case of Northern Ireland, memorials do not so much symbolize a break between the past and the present; rather, as the following chapters will show, commemoration is actively employed by the four main paramilitary groups to anchor their opposing claims of historical legitimacy and ideological legitimation more deeply into the past, creating what Mosse (1990: 7) has termed a 'cult of the fallen soldier' which emphasizes the meaningfulness of the fighting and the human sacrifice.

Bar-Tal (2003: 88–89), however, warns us that 'memorials fulfil important functions to perpetuate the memory of the fallen and inspire the remaining society members with the will to continue the conflict and fight the enemy'; especially in situations of ethnic conflict such as Israel and, indeed, Northern Ireland, memorials 'represent concrete investment in the continuation of the conflict'. This view was shared by an almost equal number of interviewees, both Republican and Loyalist. Memorials are seen as 'regressive', in the sense that 'they don't heal the wounds, they in fact do nothing really to heal the divisions that exist in our community, but help to sustain those wounds and help to sustain division in the community'; they are 'insulating conflict, [maintaining] a little bit of the conflict, albeit not a physical conflict' and are seen as 'a continuation of the struggle' (various interviews with Republican and Loyalist respondents). Graham and Whelan (2007: 492) share this view, and comment that in Northern Ireland 'sites of commemoration symbolize the enduring importance of ethno nationalist and sectarian politics and the continuation of the conflict by other means'. This author believes that both explanations can be simultaneously applied to the case of Northern Ireland. Comments made throughout the interviews suggest that there is a genuine hope and belief that the conflict has finally come to an end among both ex-combatants and the local population. However, at a time when overtly paramilitary murals are disappearing as a consequence of numerous regeneration programmes, and 'shows of strength' are no longer on the agenda at commemorative parades, the use of more sombre forms of memorialization could be seen as an attempt by paramilitary groups to move their 'visibility' into a more acceptable civic space where the local authorities are reluctant to act, in order to continue their ontological claim.

A related issue is whether memorials act as a sort of 'danger signal' or 'recruitment poster', especially for the younger generation.

Memorials: Still Here or Never Again?

'Prepared for peace. Ready for war' read a famous UVF mural in the Loyalist area of Mount Vernon in North Belfast. Two gunmen with rifles in hand left no doubt as to the readiness of present (and future) UVF volunteers to take up arms should the need arise again. Although more recent memorials do not feature such proactive statements, their very existence appears to suggest that skeleton paramilitary organizational structures still exist, although now evolved into affiliated community or cultural groups promoting various commemorative projects.

From an opposite perspective, Winter (1995: 95) suggests that

> there is little in war memorials to suggest that they are there to instil in the young a belief in the virtues of *their* return to the battlefield. Citizenship is affirmed in war memorial art, but it is expressed in terms of a sacrifice which must never be allowed to happen again. The Abraham and Isaac myth, the Akedah, is the clear reference. As in Genesis, the message is the end of human sacrifice, not its eternal perpetuation. (Italics in the original)

For Sider and Smith (1997: 8), 'commemorative symbols invoke less a sense of *identity* with those remembered than a (very modernist) sense that we should remember them *precisely not to be like them* ... "Let us not forget, lest we do it again"; thereby follows progress' (italics in the original). In this perspective, memorials can be considered as 'warnings' against future conflicts, for society not to 'forget such inhumanity nor allow it to be repeated' (Mayo 1988: 67) and as 'benchmarks' for the measuring of progress and comparing a society's aspirations to change with its real achievements (Bort 2004: 2).

In Northern Ireland, many interviewees (both ex-combatants and members of local communities) believed that memorials do not carry any intrinsic message of triumphalism, romantic nostalgia or glorification of war, but they are simply 'a sad reminder of the price paid'; their function is to remember and to 'educate the people and say "Here, look what happened. Here's how it happened. Make sure it never happens again and that you don't recreate all the mistakes that we made in the past"'; in a post-conflict setting, they act as 'beacons of light toward peace; so, it's commemorating all the people who died, their lives and what they contributed, but also to light up [the way] so that we can actually see where we are going in the future and that we are not going back' (various interviews with Republicans and Loyalists). However, some respondents pointed out that paramilitary groups, though officially 'disbanded', are still quietly recruiting young members and that memorials to fallen comrades are evidence that 'paramilitaries have quieted down, but they'll never go away' and might contribute to the feeling in young people that they have 'missed out' on the action of the conflict. Commemorative activity is, therefore, seen as 'a sign that the conflict has never ended in [paramilitaries'] minds or never ended organizationally' (interviews with Republican and Loyalist respondents). While it is difficult to categorically exclude one or the other interpretation, in reality it is more likely that both rationales coexist: memorials act simultaneously as a warning for future generations of the pain and loss endured by previous generations during the conflict and as a signal that skeleton paramilitary organizations remain despite the disbandment and decommission of most active units.

Memorials as Identity 'Crutches'

The signing of the 1998 Agreement triggered a process of identity renegotiation within the two main communities in Northern Ireland, in particular within the Protestant community that felt victimized by the 'equality agenda' at the basis of the peace process and the Agreement, which they viewed as overtly benefiting Catholics (Hayward and Mitchell 2003; Mitchell 2003; Stevenson, Condor and Abell 2007). Donnan (2005) has shown how since 1998 the cultural war waged by Northern Ireland's border Protestants has escalated and how their social identity has hardened as a result of the increased fluidity of the border with the (Catholic) Republic of Ireland.

Recalling Nora's argument, *lieux de mémoire* emerge precisely at times when history threatens a group's social memory and identity; as he points out, 'we buttress our identities upon such bastions, but if what they defended were not threatened, there would be no need to build them . . . if history did not besiege memory, deforming and transforming it, penetrating and petrifying it, there would be no *lieux de mémoire*' (Nora 1989: 12). The emergence of permanent memorials in Northern Ireland since

1998 can, therefore, be explained also as a response to a perceived threat against one's own heritage and identity posed by shifting historical circumstances. Memorials embody not only the memory of past members of the community, but also a set of traditional values and 'identity traits' that the deceased shared with the surviving members of the same community. They can, therefore, act as 'identity anchors' at a historical time when these values and traits are irremediably changing and communities struggle to reconcile their shared meaning and interpretation of themselves and their past with the new political or social context they are moving to. Like murals before them, they provide 'a touchstone for cultural identity and a sense of belonging within communities struggling for meaningful identity' (Vannais 2000: 21). As Sinn Féin councillor Tom Hartley, author of *Written in Stone* (2006), explained in interview with the author,

> I think we're in a period of transition, and the memory of the dead becomes very crucial in a very uncertain world. Because politically I would have argued that the war is a very easy space to occupy, with 'baddies' and 'goodies', whereas negotiation requires a very different space to occupy psychologically . . . So I think there's something deeper happening around memorials in a period of transition, the memorials and the memory of those fallen dead, and the memory of community becomes a psychological anchor for community. So as we move out of a very intense period of conflict into a negotiating process and into a new political dispensation, the memorial becomes a consistent anchor to the past, the values for the future; anchors for getting us through this period.

Finally, it must be noted that the construction of memorials in specific places and times depends as much on practical as well as symbolic reasons. As Switzer (2007: 83) notes in relation to Unionist memorials to the Great War, the location of memorial sites was often determined by the availability of donated ground. Similarly, in post-conflict Northern Ireland the availability of waste ground or the location of land donated by private individuals has influenced the shape and form of the 'landscape of memorialization'. In terms of chronology, many interviewees pointed out that political activists and ex-combatants 'had other things in their minds during the conflict', whereas now 'have more time on their hands to think about memorials' (interviews with Republican and Loyalist ex-combatants). Or as Henry McDonald (2004) rather cynically phrases it, 'for the ex-paramilitary sitting twiddling his roll-up, commemorations and memorials rather than religion are the ultimate opiates. In short, it keeps them busy and their minds off the utter futility of the last 35 years of struggle'.

In summary, Belfast's memorials have contributed to its centuries-long process of ethnicization of space, encoding intra and intergroup divisions into the territory. They attempt to distil in a solid form the culture and identity of the community inhabiting that place and the veracity of the two communities' opposing versions of the past. They sensitize space and can support emotional and psychological attachment to sites where violent episodes occurred. They can concurrently be interpreted as signs that a permanent state of conflict is finally over and as a continuation of it through symbolic means; as warnings for future generations while reminding them of a reduced yet enduring paramilitary presence and as identity anchors at times of dramatic historical and social transformations. The next chapter investigates how and to what purpose paramilitary groups project discrete narratives about the conflict through memorialization, and reflects upon the relationship between the individual and collective memory of the Troubles.

Notes

1. On the political nature of landscape, see Cosgrove and Daniels (1988); Duncan and Duncan (1988); Harvey (1989); Monk (1992); Daniels (1993); Jackson and Penrose (1993); Charlesworth (1994); Johnson (1995); Atkinson and Cosgrove (1998).
2. The term 'cultural landscape' refers to the '"creative and imaginative" meanings and associations that are attached to a place through storytelling or practices of remembrance . . . enabling a community of people to orient themselves within and inhabit that place' (Stewart and Strathern 2003: 3–6, in Dawson 2005: 155).
3. On spatial segregation in Belfast, see Boal (1982); Doherty and Poole (1997); Shirlow and Murtagh (2006); Mesev, Shirlow and Downs (2009). For a recent interactive mapping of religion and identity affiliation in Northern Ireland, see 'Northern Ireland Census 2011: Religion and Identity Mapped' (2011).
4. On the ethnicization of urban space in Northern Ireland, see Boal (1982); Feldman (1991, 2000); Jarman (1993); Shirlow (2003).
5. On the relationship between violence and social class and deprivation, see Fay, Morrissey and Smyth (1999); Shirlow and Murtagh (2006); Mesev, Shirlow and Downs (2009).
6. It is interesting to note that fewer than ten memorial sites out of the entire corpus examined have been built along arterial routes.
7. On the territorial function of flags and painted kerbstones, see Bryan and Gillespie (2005); Bryan and Stevenson (2006); Bryan, Stevenson and Gillespie (2007, 2008); Bryan et al. (2010).
8. Interestingly, a leading paramilitary figure commented in relation to the space left on the Roll of Honour plaque on a memorial in South Belfast: 'somebody said you'd better leave a couple of spaces on it, which is a terrible thing to say, but it's a practical thing to say, because we have never been able to say, well it won't happen anymore; there won't be more [names] going on it' (interview with the author).

9. From this count, the following memorials have been excluded: fourteen memorials to Roman Catholic civilians, eleven memorials to Protestant civilians, one memorial to the Orange Order, one plaque to the security forces, and two 'other' memorials. The latter two memorials – a Celtic cross and a plaque in support of the Irish language – were counted as 'other', although they can be broadly associated with the Republican tradition.

10. An example of this can be observed in South Belfast where the Provisional IRA memorial garden in Stanfield Place commemorating the organization's fallen volunteers from the Market area stands only a few yards away from the INLA plaque in memory of volunteers Power, Power, O'Reilly and Gargan at the junction of Friendly Street and Stewart Street. (PIRA, South Belfast Fallen Volunteers and Power, Power, O'Reilly and Gargan, INLA – Viggiani 2013).

11. It should be noted that memorial sites can be considered as 'sacred spaces' in that they firstly recall the Christian graveyard/memorial garden tradition and that they assume a paramilitary significance at a later stage.

12. According to 'post-traumatic stress disorder' (PTSD) theories, 'psychic "sites of trauma" are formed within the internal landscape, that are derived from – and complexly related to – the material sites of violence within social environments, together with the meanings and memorial markers that constitute cultural landscapes of violence, horror, and mourning' (Dawson 2005: 156).

13. The following iconic dates were taken as temporal parameters of delimitation: 1969 (conventionally taken as the starting date of the Northern Irish 'Troubles'); 1994 (the first paramilitary ceasefires); and 1998 (the signing of the Good Friday/Belfast Agreement). It was possible to ascertain the exact date of completion for 97 of the 157 memorials investigated (around 62 per cent of total).

14. On the process of social amnesia, see Forty and Küchler (1999). Specifically on social amnesia in Ireland, see Leonard (1997a); Jarman (1999); Dolan (2003: 121–46).

15. On the French Revolution, see Ozouf (1988), Clarke (2007); on the American Revolution, see Lowenthal (1985: 105–13); on the desovietization of post-communist Eastern Europe, see Argenbright (1999), Verdery (1999), Foote, Tóth and Árvay (2000); on iconoclasm in Ireland, see Whelan (2003); on Iraq, see 'Saddam Statue Toppled in Central Baghdad' (2003).

16. It might be worth noting that the attack in Omagh which claimed twenty-nine lives on 15 August 1998 was conducted by dissident Republicans who were opposed to the Agreement. A permanent state of hostilities between (mainstream) Republican and Loyalist paramilitary groups was not reached again after 1998 and, since then, the four main paramilitary groups in Northern Ireland have officially declared that 'the war is over': the Provisional IRA was the first to announce an end to its armed struggle in July 2005, followed by the UVF in May 2007; the UDA announced the disbandment of its military arm, the UFF, in November 2007, and in October 2009 the INLA officially renounced violence.

Chapter 4

THE 'MEMORY MAKERS' AND THE PROJECTION OF NARRATIVES OF THE TROUBLES

$\Longrightarrow \bullet \Longleftarrow$

What happened, what we recall,
what we recover, what we relate,
are often sadly different.
The temptation is often overwhelmingly strong
to tell it, not as it really was,
but as we would wish it to have been.

– Bernard Lewis, in Keykhah 2003: 1

Most people in Belfast pass memorial gardens, monuments, commemorative murals and plaques dedicated to the casualties of the Troubles on their well-trodden ways to school, to work, to the local shops. Some glance at them and spare a thought for a loved relative or friend now gone; some stop and say a prayer; most walk past, too preoccupied with their everyday worries to notice. Although local residents have expressed a variety of individual opinions and reactions towards memorials, which are further investigated in Chapter 9, this chapter examines on a general level the interdependence between individual and collective memory and the asymmetry of power between 'memory makers' and 'memory receivers' in the production of public memory. The result is that individual memories of the Troubles are subsumed within shared mnemonic frameworks and used to construct dominant/sectional narratives of historical legitimacy and ideological legitimation by means of a selective use of the past.

Individual 'Stories' versus the Collective 'History' of the Troubles: The Power of the Narrative

On a day-to-day basis, individuals engage with the varied 'memory markers' that dot their environment to differing extents, based on their unique experience of the events or the individuals commemorated. As such, memorials and other permanent forms of memorialization act as 'vehicles for a conception' (Geertz 1973: 91) of that event or individual, representing different things to different people. The level of engagement can also vary upon the contingent frame of mind or occasion in which the encounter takes place: thus, the same memorial can mean different things to the same individual at different moments in time. If a symbol is defined as 'any object, act, event, quality or relation which serves as a vehicle for a conception – the conception [being] the symbol's "meaning"' (ibid.), memorials must, therefore, be considered symbols starting from the base level of private interaction.[1]

Anthropologist Dan Sperber (1975: 8–16) has argued that symbols per se do not possess a logical content or intrinsic meaning that must be elucidated or 'revealed' through interpretation; rather, it is the interpretative process that confers meaning to them: set in motion by a single image or idea that the symbol calls to mind, a series of cognitive associations take place, thus inevitably linking the symbol and its 'sense' to the agent that performs the interpretation and to the situation in which this action occurs. From this perspective, war memorials, like other symbols, do not possess *one* meaning that must be identified. They derive their signification from the complex interrelation and idiosyncratic permutations of discrete factors, including the memorials' physical structure and aesthetic form; the ideas and feelings that creators or promoting committees intend to communicate through them; the cognitive and emotional response of beholders; the social use to which they are assigned; and the historical and cultural contingencies in which the interpretative action takes place. Following the development of a vociferous debate on First World War memorials in Britain in the pages of newspapers, pamphlets and memorial committees' records of the time, King (1998: 3) has shown how, despite vigorous efforts to assign them a 'set-in-stone' meaning, war memorials were intrinsically 'elusive' and 'their capacity to convey a particular meaning was not entirely reliable'. Promoters and creators did originally ascribe to them deliberate meanings; however, such meanings were inevitably qualified and ultimately altered during the individual interpretative process. Applying Sperber's theory to the postwar culture of memorialization in Britain, King (ibid.: 12) has suggested that the symbols and rituals of commemoration, and the symbolic language commonly attached to them, did not themselves propose how people should make sense of the war, or of social relations in the postwar world. Rather, they were things which required sense to be made of them, offering opportunities for people to express the varied senses they were making of the war and its aftermath.

It is undoubtedly true that at an individual level 'readings' and interpretations of a war memorial are affected by the relative understanding and experience that the person engaging with the memorial has of the event that is being commemorated, thereby accounting for the expression or extrapolation of 'varied senses'. However, memorials neither stand as simple, objective reifications of a specific conflict nor are they open to *any interpretation* of that conflict. As previous chapters have shown, far from being merely historical markers, they function more importantly as ideology conveyors. Contrary to the view that symbols 'do not so much express meaning as give us the capacity to make meaning' (Cohen 1985: 15), memorials *do* attempt to propose how to make sense of every war for which they are erected as they are used by different societal agencies to present selective 'versions' of those wars, especially in situations of ethnic conflict, which limit and 'guide' the interpretative possibilities open to each individual. This is readily evident in the case of Northern Ireland, often achieved through a process of historical selection and a careful choice of language in translating one's own 'story' into 'history'.

The crucial factor narrowing the spectrum of possible interpretations is the asymmetry of power between 'memory makers' and 'memory receivers' in the process of asserting control over the multiple versions that can be given of the same past and, consequently, over the production of war memorials.[2] Memorials are one of many 'modes of exercising, or seeking to exercise, power along the cognitive dimension' (Lukes 1977: 68). While a necessary independence of judgment and analysis must be attributed to individuals, the ability to curtail the number of idiosyncratic interpretations of processes of memorialization is symbiotic with the power to project a symbolic collective narrative about the past that can accommodate these diverse individual positions within its structure. Individuals, therefore, remember by means of an independent mental act, but the act is influenced and constrained by the shared mnemonic framework proposed by memorials and other forms of collective memory. As Halbwachs (1992: 182) points out, 'the individual calls recollections to mind by relying on the frameworks of social memory': thus, 'for instance, individual memories of one's family cannot be dissociated from the whole images that comprise the "family memory"' (Misztal 2003: 51).

In Northern Ireland, casualties of the Troubles are remembered first and foremost as individuals, as beloved fathers and mothers, sons and daughters, friends and neighbours, but their memory is then placed and framed within a wider collective interpretation of the conflict as a result of which they lost their lives. As this study of Northern Ireland will show, when the Republican and Loyalist 'mnemonic families' come together to remember collectively, it is the 'history' that is *commonly shared*, within which all the individual 'stories' are subsumed, that is *collectively commemorated*. Although no two answers were identical when respondents were asked what memorials signified to them on a personal level – for some, a way to remember dead relatives and friends from the area; for others, a sad reminder of the history of the area and young lives lost; for yet others, nothing personal at all – those surveyed participate in commemorative events that present a collectivized view (and interpretation) of that past. Though it is unlikely that each participant agrees with the entirety of elements and messages presented at these events or recognizes them as pertinent to his or her experience of the conflict, the very same act of willing participation suggests that participants accept that the shared collective frameworks projected at commemorations sufficiently express and include their individual act of remembrance.

Sperber (1975: 137) has argued that in order to understand how cultural symbolism – of which the construction of narratives about the past can be considered an expression – seems to create a shared orientation among members of a given group, the simultaneous existence of two evocational fields of belief – a shared evocational field and an individual evocational field – must be postulated. Thus,

> when the evocational fields of two beliefs overlap, the evocation . . . takes place preferably in the overlapping area of the two fields and passes in review memorized information with the preferred aim of extracting from it a shared solution. The more numerous the beliefs, rituals, etc. which are taken into account, the more the evocational field is determined, the more restricted is the range of possible evocations, and the more the members of a single culture are led to similar evocations.

Successful narratives about the past are able to subsume different interpretations within a unifying, elastic structure, sharing this feature with the symbols that they utilize;[3] while an individual might agree with particular aspects of the narrative that fit with his idiosyncratic experience more than others, the result is that of a commonality of beliefs, if not a uniformity of opinion.[4] According to Cohen (1985: 108), a fitting image to understand the relationship between collective narrative and individual interpretations is that of an 'ideological hat stand – a single piece of furniture which, nevertheless, can accommodate a large number and wide variety of hats'.

This does not imply that official narratives cannot be subjected to radical criticism and fierce opposition nor openly challenged and denied – as will be illustrated in Chapter 6 in the case of the Irish Republican Socialist Movement's 'sectional narrative' against the mainstream Republican narrative.[5] In many instances, however, criticism and opposition are readily 'absorbed' through a variety of social mechanisms, ranging from social conventions to the use of repressive methods to silence dissenting voices. King (1998), for example, shows how on the occasion of First World War commemorative ceremonies in Britain, whatever the differences of opinion, motives and political outlooks among participants, 'all were united in their respect for the sanctity of the symbolic acts and objects on which [the commemoration of the dead] was centred' (ibid.: 228) and all complied with 'the conventions of behaviour expressing reverence for the dead' (ibid.: 234), such as the Great Silence or the recognition of memorial sites as sacred space. Failure to conform to the two-minute silence, for example, could result in being attacked by angry mobs of fellow participants (ibid.: 235–36). Similarly, in postwar Kosovo, voices in discord with the dominant narrative [the cult of KLA leader Adem Jashari as the 'Legendary Commander'] can be heard only in private conversations, 'since any public criticism of the legendary commander amounts to blasphemy' (Di Lellio and Schwandner-Sievers 2006a: 520). Asked about her opinion on the 'hero' Jashari, a young professional woman in Pristina replied: 'If you asked me, I would tell you that Adem Jashari was crazy ... But I would not give my opinion in front of anyone, and if you [the researchers] did it for me, I would deny I ever said it' (ibid.: 521–22). So, how are such powerful 'credible' narratives projected in practice in Northern Ireland?

Republican and Loyalist Memorials: The Projection of Opposing Narratives of the Troubles

The commission and financing of memorials to the casualties of Northern Ireland's Troubles are largely controlled by ex-prisoners' groups, associations and memorial committees who have overt links with paramilitary organizations and associated political parties. Aside from some privately erected memorials and the contemporary significance acquired by official

First and Second World War memorials, state-level practices of memorialization of the Troubles as witnessed in other Western countries are largely missing in Northern Ireland; as mentioned before, state-sponsored memorials related to the Troubles can only be found *outside* Northern Ireland, such as the Ulster Ash Grove in England. In their absence, paramilitary-related memorials are the most prominent reminder of thirty years of conflict in most working-class areas of Belfast.

Two Imagined Communities: Creating a Symbolic National Identification

Papadakis (1994: 409–10) offers an interesting perspective on any attempt to represent the past as a narrative. Recalling H. White's work (1990a, 1990b) on the use of the narrative form in representing reality, he stresses how such an exercise requires, among other characteristics, 'a social centre by which to locate events with respect to one another and charge these with moral significance'. In the modern era, after the fall of the religious community and the dynastic realm as cultural frames of reference, it is the 'imagined political community' of the nation – to quote Benedict Anderson (1983: 15)[6] – that constitutes the social and moral centre of most collective narratives about the past, in relation to which 'events may be judged as, say, tragedies or victories' (Papadakis 1994: 410). Fulfilling the narrative form's requirement of an actor who must appear as continuous or the same from the beginning to the end of the story, 'the idea of the nation comes to assume this role and as a consequence it is represented as coterminous with history and in this sense "eternal"'.[7] By linking the past generation's sacrifice to the present generation's readiness to die for the 'motherland' or 'fatherland', processes of war memorialization – particularly the construction of cenotaphs and 'Tombs of the Unknown Soldier' (Anderson 1983: 17–18) – are crucial to bolster a nation's imagined continuity and transcendence beyond time and mortality, and to foster a sense of national identification and ideals of citizenship and allegiance that have vital political significance for the present and future survival, both imagined and factual, of the nation state.

The unofficial nature of paramilitary-related forms of memorialization of the Troubles ascribes them to what Bodnar (1994: 14) defines as the sphere of 'vernacular memory', in that they aim at 'protecting values and restating views of reality derived from first hand experience in small-scale communities rather than the "imagined" communities of a large nation'. This has been readily evident in the previous chapter when considering their localized nature, both in regard to their geographical location and the 'spatial belonging' of the individuals commemorated. However, while they pertain to a microlevel of memorialization, they mimic state-led official forms of memory, which grants them the power to open up a macrolevel of interpretation and to project opposing narratives of a *national* nature given the state's abdication of its customary role in the production of official memory. The ontological existence of Northern Ireland as a nation state has been the subject of contestation between the Catholic and Protestant communities who have lived within its official boundaries since its very inception. Despite the increase in the number of people who identify themselves as 'Northern Irish', the majority of Northern Irish Catholics and Protestants still identify themselves as 'Irish' and 'British' respectively (NILT 2003: IDBRIT-IDNONE). As Northern Ireland cannot be considered de facto a nation state and its existence is always postulated in relation to the nation states of Ireland or the United Kingdom, paramilitary-related memorials, therefore, project opposing national narratives of a *symbolic* nature that supersede the geographic boundaries of the province and suggest two national imagined communities with which the Catholic and Protestant populations of Northern Ireland can respectively identify – and for which many of them have died. Most importantly, while these memorials recognize the individual sacrifice of single members of the (local) community, their deaths are invariably subsumed within a collective narrative of 'bloody sacrifice' in the name of a shared national 'imagined community'.

Looking at the landscape of memorialization in Belfast, thirty-five of the eighty-nine Republican memorials surveyed state that the commemorated individuals gave their lives for or devoted their lives to 'the cause of Irish freedom' (or the Gaelic equivalent '*ar son saoirse na h-Éireann*') or mention the word 'Ireland/*Éire*'. In addition, a symbolic link with Ireland is established through the iconography used, with the majority of memorials presenting one or more symbols drawn from different stages of the history of Irish Republicanism (see further). Loyalist memorials, on the other hand, do not directly mention the nation state of the United Kingdom in their inscriptions, continuing the tradition of Unionist Great War memorials in that 'they do not assert that those named gave their lives for any political entity' (Switzer 2007: 89): thus, the individuals commemorated 'made the ultimate sacrifice for (or in defence of) their country', but without specification of which country that might be. However, the association with Great Britain and the British Empire is made evident in fourteen of the thirty-nine Loyalist memorials surveyed through the widespread use of the Union Jack and the red poppy (symbol of the British Commonwealth war dead).

Cherry-Picking from History: Opposing Versions of a Shared Past

In situations of ethnic conflict, memorials are often used to translate one's own story into history against the opposing faction's version of the past. Despite some relatively successful official attempts – by both the Office of the First Minister and Deputy First Minister (OFMDFM) and non-governmental organizations – to promote a cross-sectional narrative of the Northern Irish conflict, particularly after the 1998 Belfast/Good Friday Agreement,[8] the 'history' of the Troubles is still primarily narrated by Republican and Loyalist partisan forms and practices of commemoration in the streets of Belfast. In order to understand the complex nature of memorialization in Northern Ireland, one must note that a fundamentally unresolved 'question' regarding the very nature and meaning of the conflict lies at the core of the sustained contestation occurring between the Republican and Loyalist factions (Shirlow and McEvoy 2008: 3). Republicans interpret and narrate *their* conflict primarily as an anti-imperialistic war against the British state and its agents – military corps like the Ulster Defence Regiment, the police force and, by extension, pro-state Loyalist paramilitary groups – with the ultimate goal of achieving an independent united Ireland. For Republicans, 'the British state has been engaged as an active and aggressive party at all stages in the conflict, [a conflict] which contains elements of territorial self-determination, assertion of civil rights and reactionary violence against torture, imprisonment and the violation of human rights'. On the opposite side of the 'narrative fence', Loyalists relate their conflict as a civil war primarily dictated by the need to defend themselves from both Republican violence against the Protestant population and any attempt to weaken or, even worse, sever the constitutional union of Northern Ireland with Great Britain – as attempted traditionally by military Republicanism and the Irish government, but in more recent years also by 'middle unionism' and the British government.

Paramilitary-related memorials act as a vehicle to assert control over the past by promoting these opposing 'readings' of the same conflict that cultivate intragroup cohesion and tend to discredit the 'other side's' version of it; at the same time, they project partisan narratives of historical and ideological legitimacy that establish continuity and ultimately foster the notion of a shared vision between the past sacrifices of a community's martyrs and the actions of modern-day volunteers. This is firstly achieved through a careful process of historical selection and accretion: as Jarman (1999: 193) rightly affirms, both Protestants' and Catholics' collective memories 'do not draw on some unquestioned mass of empirical facts, rather [they] are the product of a sifting through the confusion of the past for evidence that serves to substantiate existing beliefs'. A series of iconic events from the history of Great Britain and Ireland are 'chosen' to be remembered and commemorated in order to reinforce the social and political identity of both communities and to convert one's own version of the story into the 'unquestionable history' – in other words, to project and promote one's own narrative against the other. A similar process is attested in Cyprus, where Greek Cypriots and Turkish Cypriots follow distinctive calendars of commemorations that substantiate their opposing claims to the island (Papadakis 2003). Also interestingly, it has been observed how Greek Cypriot and Turkish Cypriot school textbooks and museums present, respectively, the 'history of Greeks in Cyprus' and the 'history of Turks in Cyprus' as the 'History of Cyprus' (Papadakis 1994).

In Northern Ireland, the most striking example is the use of the year 1916 by both the Provisional Irish Republican movement and the Loyalist Ulster Volunteer Force.[9] Both groups remember and commemorate this year, but whereas the latter celebrates the sacrifice of the 36th (Ulster) Division in the Battle of the Somme during the First World War as the ultimate testimony of their Britishness, the former honours the 'martyrs' of the Easter Rising that offered their blood in the name of a united free Ireland. At the same time, however, a process of 'social amnesia' takes place, whereby the divisive factors that foster the opposing social and political identities of the two groups are emphasized and 'grey areas' pointing towards the common ground ignored. For example, it is often 'forgotten' that over two hundred thousand Catholic Irishmen enlisted in the British forces during the First World War or that Ulster Protestants had been on the verge of an insurrection against the British government to oppose the third Home Rule Bill before the war broke out (Jarman 1999: 191–93). Among other interpretations, both events can be seen as focusing on the parallel (but opposite) supreme sacrifice that past members of one imagined community made in the name of their (symbolic) nation.

Ancestries of Resistance: Manufacturing Genealogies

Present day remembrance of events such as the Battle of the Somme or the Easter Rising fosters intragroup cohesion and a collective identification that stretches over centuries in an ideal and ideological unbroken line of resistance and struggle. Moreover, talismanic events like these provide, by setting a powerful example of sacrifice for the common good, moral justification and historical legitimation for further waves of violence. Following Papadakis's analysis of the use of a historical narrative in representing the past, commemorations – both through memorials and rituals –

> reveal their full meaning only if treated as components ('events') building a narrative that articulates a certain story ('a history'). Each commemoration focuses on an event and the events are linked into a story whose meaning lies in the whole, rather than in any commemoration (or the historical event commemorated) by itself. (Papadakis 2003: 253–54)

In Northern Ireland, events such as the siege of Derry/Londonderry in 1688–89, the 1690 Battle of the Boyne, and the Battle of the Somme for the Protestant community, and the 1798 United Irishmen rebellion, the Easter Rising, and the 1981 Republican hunger strike for the Catholic community possess what Zerubavel (1997: 8) has defined in relation to Israel's social memory as 'commemorative density': they are, therefore, better understood as 'episodes/chapters' of a long 'history/narrative' of, respectively, defence to maintain the union with Great Britain and struggle for a free independent Ireland.[10] Research conducted in Belfast shows that half of the memorials for the casualties of the Troubles present iconographic references to significant pre-Troubles episodes as interwoven threads of a unique discursive framework. Of the 132 memorials surveyed (excluding memorials to civilian casualties), 48 Republican memorials and 26 Loyalist memorials directly mention or allude to pre-1969 historical figures or events (Viggiani 2013).[11] A temporal continuum between past and current phases of struggle – and a direct lineage between past and present volunteers – is established through the often concurrent use of two devices: firstly, the remembrance of deceased volunteers from different eras through a single monument; and secondly, the collation of symbols linked to different seminal events at the same memorial site, carved adjacent to one another on plaques or displayed on flags.

Provisional IRA memorials often remember deceased Republicans who lost their lives from 1969 onwards (including the 1981 hunger strikers) together with the 1798 and 1916 rebels and the fallen volunteers who participated in the IRA's pre-1970s campaigns (Fig. 4.1; see Chapter 5 for further analysis of this memorial); IRSP/INLA memorials, for example their communal plot in Milltown Cemetery, emphasize more the link with the socialist James Connolly and his Irish Citizen Army. Modern-day UVF fallen members are often commemorated along with members of the homonymous organization founded in January 1913 and the 36th Ulster Division (Fig. 4.2; see Chapter 7 for further analysis of this memorial). The UDA, however, has been unable to claim direct 'historical forefathers' and has only recently tried to appropriate the memory – and myth

Figure 4.1 PIRA Clonard Martyrs Memorial Garden (central plaque)
Source: Viggiani 2006

– of the Somme, as the new memorial gardens in Sandy Row and Roden Street attest (see Chapter 8 for further analysis of these memorials).

In terms of the iconography used, Republican memorials usually present the following symbols drawn from different stages of Irish Republicanism's history, often adjacent to one another: the golden harp, emblem of the 1798 United Irishmen rebellion; the phoenix rising from the flames, originally used by the Irish Republican Brotherhood (the Fenians) in the 1860s; the Starry Plough, symbol of the Irish Citizen Army; the Easter Lily, worn to these days in remembrance of the 1916 Easter Rising; the orange sunburst, repeatedly used from the 1870s and now official emblem of the Fianna Éireann (the IRA's youth wing); the four shields of the historical provinces of Ireland; the lark in barbed wire, symbolizing Bobby Sands and the hunger strikers; and the Celtic cross, evoking a mythical Gaelic 'Golden Age'.

UVF memorials often feature quotes from the poem 'For the Fallen', written by Laurence Binyon during the First World War,[12] and mention significant battles such as the Somme, Thiepval, Messines, to name a few.

Figure 4.2 UVF 2nd Battalion Willowfield Memorial Garden
Source: Viggiani 2006

The UDA has, instead, attempted to position itself within the Loyalist tradition by means of more obscure historical references in the emblem and motto used at memorial sites and on flags and banners.[13] As mentioned earlier, both UVF and UDA memorials make widespread use of the Union Jack and the red poppy.

Forgetting to Remember: Social Amnesia and Euphemization

As noted before, processes of social amnesia have been observed in many historical and geographical settings. Similarly, in Northern Ireland what is 'forgotten' and 'written out' of Republican and Loyalist narratives of the Troubles is as important as what is remembered. For example, both Republican and Loyalist groups commemorate their fallen, but there is no mention on memorial stones of the pain and death they inflicted on 'the other side'; intragroup assassinations or civilian deaths accidentally caused within one's own community go unacknowledged. The only instance in which the accidental death of a civilian caused by a paramilitary group pertaining to the same 'side of the divide' has been publicly acknowledged is the plaque in memory of Angela Gallagher, a seventeen-month-old Catholic toddler caught in Provisional IRA cross-fire in 1971 (Gallagher Angela, Viggiani 2013). Given the particularly tragic circumstances of this death, the Provisional IRA leadership offered 'its sincere apologies to the family of Angela Gallagher for the pain and heartache that they have suffered as a result of our action', and Sinn Féin president Gerry Adams attended the unveiling ceremony of the plaque in 2007 (McCrory 2007). With respect to the individuals killed as a result of internal feuds within the same paramilitary group, a process of 'euphemization' takes place or no specifications regarding the circum-stances of their death are given. As Scott (1990: 53) points out, 'when-ever one encounters euphemism in language it is a nearly infallible sign that one has stumbled on a delicate subject. It is used to obscure some-thing that is negatively valued or would prove to be an embarrassment if declared more forthrightly'. Thus, for instance, INLA chief of staff Gino Gallagher, killed by his comrades in January 1986, is simply remembered as having been 'assassinated' (Loughran, Campbell, McLarnon, McCann, Tumelty, Gallagher and Dornan – INLA, Viggiani 2013).

It is important to note that, in a memorial context, group membership is deemed more important than religious or political affiliation. Thus, individuals who fought and died 'for the same cause' but belonged to a different organization are either remembered as civilians or omitted altogether, as in the case of the Provisional IRA memorial garden in Ballymurphy where local INLA volunteers are remembered simply as civilians (Ballymurphy Gairdin Cuimhneachain, Viggiani 2013). In addi-tion, killings perpetrated by paramilitary groups from the same side of the divide are remembered in inscriptions in the same way as killings committed by the traditional 'enemies'. YCV volunteer Samuel Rockett, for instance, was killed by the UDA during the 2000 Loyalist feud and is commemorated in Disraeli Street, Woodvale, as having been 'mur-dered by cowards' – an appellation traditionally referred to Republicans (Rockett Samuel – YCV, Viggiani 2013).

A most controversial issue is that of the informers, familiarly referred to in Northern Ireland as 'touts'. While acknowledging the hurt to their families, the majority of Republican and Loyalist interviewees recognized that no place exists on memorials for informers because they worked against their organization and community, they were 'talking about their own':

an informer is the worst of the worst. That is the bit that sticks in every-body's craw; that is the bit that if ever blood gets boiled, it's because of that

... So, although you might be an IRA, INLA or OIRA, you may be part of that movement, but if you are working for the other side you are really not and that goes across the board, you are really not socially acceptable ... The tout, informer, it's taboo. (Interview with an INLA ex-prisoner)

UVF volunteer Colin 'Crazy' Craig, for instance, had been suspected of supplying the security forces with intelligence for some years when he was shot dead in 1994 by the INLA together with two other men (a fourth survived the attack). In 1995, a commemorative plaque was erected in Spier's Place, off the Shankill Road, near the spot where the attack occurred. It read: 'This plaque is dedicated to the memory of Lt. Col. Trevor King Died 9th July 1994, Major Wm. (Frenchie) Marchant Died 28th April 1987 [another UVF volunteer who was killed on the Shankill Road in a different attack], Davy Hamilton Died 17th June 1994. These brave men were killed near this spot by the enemies of Ulster'. Colin Craig's name had been 'forgotten' (King, Marchant and Hamilton – UVF, Viggiani 2013).

Considered in a wider context, a ubiquitous process of appropriation and repudiation takes place in murals and memorials, where paramilitary groups claim individuals as their own or disown them in death. While during the conflict this was achieved at funerals, where individuals could receive a burial with full paramilitary trappings, in post-conflict Northern Ireland forms of memorialization act as permanent statements of affiliation or repudiation. For example, the IRSP/INLA memorial committee was created because IRSP/INLA volunteers 'were [getting] left behind ... were left basically out in the cold in memorial projects about the country'; instead, 'they should be recognized for what they are' and what group they belonged to, because in some [Provisional IRA] memorial gardens, 'they are named as civilians and that's derogatory. They are not civilians; they are INLA volunteers' (interview with one of the founding members of the Belfast Teach Na Fáilte [IRSP/INLA] Memorial Committee). Conversely, UVF volunteer Lennie Murphy, leader of the infamous 'Shankill Butchers' gang, has been excluded in UVF memorials in the Shankill area of West Belfast, somehow confirming the rumours that he was killed by a joint operation in which 'the IRA and Loyalists crossed the sectarian divide to eliminate a mutual problem' (The Irish News, in McKittrick et al. 2007: 924).

Delegitimizing the Enemy: Demonization and Stigmatization

If the promotion of partisan narratives of legitimacy and victimhood is necessary in order to gain symbolic and political capital, the deconstruction of similar claims made by the competing group is equally crucial. Bar-Tal (2003: 83–84) suggests that in situations of intergroup conflict the need for rationalization and justification of physical violence often results in the delegitimization of the adversary, who is depicted as 'evil, malevolent, immoral and inhuman . . . [a classification that] is the most economic and comprehensive way to explain why human lives are taken and why they should continue to be taken'. Similarly Scott (1990: 53) identifies a process of 'stigmatization', opposite to the process of 'euphemization', whereby 'rebels or revolutionaries are labelled bandits, criminals, hooligans in a way that attempts to divert attention from their political claims'. Although in Northern Ireland the enemy is not usually directly represented in any memorial, mural or banner (Jarman 1992: 153–54), this process of demonization is achieved through the language employed in plaques and inscriptions. The research carried out here indicates that Catholics are not simply killed but 'murdered' by 'pro-British/ pro-Unionist Loyalist death squads' or 'murder gangs'. On the other hand, Protestants are 'murdered' by 'cowards' or 'enemies of Ulster'; in one case, they are 'slaughtered by a Republican murder gang'. The brutality and inhumanity of 'the other side' is particularly stressed when civilians, who are always 'innocent', have been killed 'in unprovoked attacks' or 'atrocities' and, in the case of Catholics, 'for their faith'.[14]

Having identified some iconographic and semantic techniques used in both Republican and Loyalist memorials to present a selective version of the Troubles, one must consider how these 'official' narratives unconsciously – on the part of the viewer – limit the scope of interpretations to be garnered from a single memorial. As acknowledged at the start of this chapter, individuals can engage cognitively and emotionally with memorials of the Troubles and interpret them according to their own experiences – whether it is the loss of a family member, friend or comrade, or a sense of threat, discrimination or fear. A person's interpretation, however, is limited within a set of 'accepted' possibilities, since no public recognition is made of events that discredit or oppose the narrative, thus preventing unrestrained processes of signification and critical analysis.[15]

Talkative Dead Bodies: The Politics of Commemorations

By establishing a direct lineage with a 'noble' past, paramilitary memorials to the conflict provide a historical and ideological justification for the use of political violence during the conflict. Espousing Halbwachs' approach to collective memory as essentially determined by present contexts and readapted or reconstructed according to contemporary attitudes and historical occurrences, processes of memorialization are, however, seldom exclusively about the past (Halbwachs 1941); rather, they are reflections of present sociocultural values and needs and, above all, can be used to serve present purposes of political legitimation and ideological struggle. In times of political transformation or ideological takeover, in particular, the orchestrated stirring of 'selected' dead bodies presents another great advantage, in that

> dead bodies . . . don't talk much on their own (thought they did once). Words can be put into their mouth – quite often ambiguous words – or their own actual words can be ambiguated by quoting them out of context. It is thus easier to rewrite history with dead people than with other kinds of symbols that are speechless. (Verdery 1999: 29)

Memorial sites and commemorative events that take place around them are able to provide an ideologically reassuring setting and a legitimizing 'emotive filter' through which leaders and other public figures can, in times of change, mediate new political messages without incurring internal accusations of 'selling out'. Processes of signification and interpretation of war memorials, therefore, vary not only from individual to individual within a set spectrum of interpretative possibilities, but also in relation to the specific moment in time and history when this interpretation takes place. Since no permanent meaning or symbolic function can be eternally assigned to a war memorial, control over its signification is asserted through the projection of a narrative that is concurrently able to accommodate within its structure diverse individual positions and to adjust itself to shifting historical circumstances, relationships of power and cultural values in a society. It is precisely during these times of change that the projected narrative does not merely accommodate within itself a spectrum of different views, but actively seeks to shift such spectrum of views.

In Northern Ireland, this process is particularly evident in the case of the Provisional Irish Republican movement, whose most sensitive task since the mid-1990s has been the underlining of a continuity of beliefs, values and objectives despite a major shift in tactics, as they abandoned the use of violence for political negotiations and, eventually, participation in government. David Kertzer (1988: 45) has noted how a difficult political challenge presents itself when radical transformations in policies or strategies of action take place without a change of leadership. While architects of new political constructions may find legitimacy exactly in tearing down the old symbolic scaffolding of their predecessors, surviving

Figure 4.3 PIRA communal plot, Milltown Cemetery, Belfast
Source: Viggiani 2006

leaders must attempt to 'expropriate . . . [old] symbols for their new political purposes' because 'to challenge those symbols is to question the basis
of their authority'. As in many other geographical and historical contexts,
Republican dead bodies have proved to be very talkative when called to
address the gathered audience at commemorative events to endorse the
political choices and decisions made by the current leadership, thus reassuring base support and providing insulation from the attacks of rivals,
sceptics and doubters.

The author observed one of many examples of this process at the
commemoration for the 90th anniversary of the Easter Rising at the
Provisional Irish Republican movement communal plot in Milltown
Cemetery.

The plot clearly projects traditional tenets of Republican ideology through its physical configuration and iconography: the central
monument features a plaque inscribed with the 1916 Proclamation of
Independence and an Irish tricolour flies at its highest vertex; it is preceded by a long corridor on either side of which are entombed deceased

members of the Provisional Irish Republican Army and Sinn Féin, most notably the 1981 hunger strikers (see Fig. 4.3). Here, on Easter Sunday 2006, the president of Sinn Féin, Gerry Adams, delivered his commemorative speech for this poignant anniversary. The ghostly national imaginings of Pearse, Connolly, Sands and other heroes of the Republican 'Olympus of martyrs' were evoked to stress historical continuity and to give their opinion on – and ultimately their approval to – the contemporary Republican leadership's political attitudes and agendas. In the words of Gerry Adams (2006a):

> all of us are proud to be part of that struggle. It is a struggle which continues . . . Are there any real doubts about where Tom Clarke, Sean Mac Diarmada, Thomas MacDonagh, Padraig Pearse, Ceannt, Connolly or Joseph Plunkett, would stand on the great issues of our time? . . . Does anyone believe that they would block northern representatives being accorded speaking rights in the Dáil?

In an ideologically reassuring setting, protected by the emotive shields of legitimacy emanated by the spirits of the past at his side, Adams went on to present a series of images from the new post-1998 repertoire of Republican rhetoric. Whereas prior to the signing of the Agreement, Adams would affirm that 'Unionists should be given no more concessions' because of their 'intransigence', 'ultimatums, deadlines or threats' and 'their political efforts to minimise the potential for change [and] the impact of a peace process with which they were never happy and to which they never willingly contributed' (Adams 1994a, 1994b), in this new political dispensation it is 'fine' if

> Unionists have a different opinion [about an independent and united Ireland] . . . Let's talk about these matters. And let us begin by reassuring unionists that we are not in the business of coercing them into a united Ireland . . . We seek to build a shared space in which we can move forward . . . a meaningful, working partnership between nationalists and Republicans, unionists and Loyalists. (Adams 2006a)

As memorials 'open up' a national dimension by linking individual deaths to a wider narrative of collective sacrifice in the name of one's imagined nation, commemorative ceremonies can also become an arena where both macro (national or state) politics and micro (community) politics are played out: as will be illustrated further, orations given at memorial sites open up a communication channel with the greater 'Politics' of the state, while concurrently setting out the parameters for community 'politics', creating a sort of political 'mesolevel' that the leadership – whether of a political party or a paramilitary group – can utilize to convey a difficult political message in times of transition.

In conclusion, memorials for the Troubles do not convey a univocal or objective interpretation of the history of the province. Individuals may get from 'a poem in marble and granite, as in the case of a book, precisely what one takes to it' (King 1998: 3), influenced by the unique experience that each person has of the thirty years of conflict. However, memorials do not stand as neutral representations of the past with which one can freely and critically engage. Through a process of selection within the confusion of the past, they guide our reading and help us to make sense of what they remind us of, directing our understanding towards the narratives promoted by their commissioners and ultimate benefactors. In post-conflict Northern Ireland, memorials often reflect diametrically opposed readings of the same history, concurrently perpetuating each section's claim to historical legitimacy and victimhood. Control over the signification of memorials results in the projection of politically useful collective narratives that help to foster intragroup cohesion and identification, accommodating within their structures the idiosyncratic experiences of the past. In times of change, processes of memorialization can become a crucial weapon to mediate new messages, since 'memory, like history, is concerned not just with the past but with the legitimisation of the politically desired future' (Papadakis 2003: 254).

The four following chapters present one case study for each main paramilitary group in Northern Ireland. Chapters 5 and 6 consider memorialization from a Republican perspective. Chapter 5 is centred on the Clonard Martyrs Memorial Garden, associated with the Provisional Irish Republican Army. It illustrates how a dominant narrative of the Troubles has been successfully projected and maintained by the Provisional IRA and its political manifestation, Sinn Féin, and how memorialization subsumes individual experiences and acts of sacrifice within the wider dimension of the Republican imagined national community. It also documents the reasons behind the formation of ex-prisoners' groups and memorial committees since the mid-1990s, and the completion of local history and memorial projects in many Republican areas of Belfast. Chapter 6 follows the commemorative programme of the IRSP/INLA Teach Na Fáilte Memorial Committee Belfast to explore how a sectional narrative of the conflict is constructed and how a place in history for INLA volunteers is reclaimed in contrast to the Provisional IRA/Sinn Féin's dominant narrative. Both chapters also document the practical issues of memorialization in terms of funding, planning permission and the material process of building a memorial.

Chapters 7 and 8 look at memorialization from a Loyalist perspective and focus more on how memorial sites are used during commemorative events. Chapter 7 examines how the UVF has succeeded in projecting a dominant narrative of the Troubles, in opposition to Republicanism and mainstream Unionism, and follows the annual commemorations at three UVF murals in Disraeli Street from the early 1990s to the present day, highlighting how the political message conveyed at these events has changed in relation to shifting historical and political contexts. Chapter 8 examines how the UDA has so far struggled to project a credible narrative of the Troubles, and explores the different attempts to 'gain power' over what Brown (2009) has termed an 'ancestry of resistance'. It also illustrates how micro and macropolitics are played out during commemorative ceremonies, specifically the 2007 Remembrance Sunday service held at the UDA memorial garden in Sandy Row.

When considered collectively, the four case studies follow the 'lifespan' of memorials in Northern Ireland, from the formation of the memorial committee that oversees the building of the memorial to the diachronic use of memorial sites during annual commemorations.

Notes

1. For the ability of symbols to 'change' meaning in time, see Cannadine (1983: 101–64) and Schwartz (1991).
2. This author accepts Bertrand Russell's definition of 'power' (1960: 25) as 'the production of intended effects'. See also the definition of power as 'the capacity to produce, or contribute to, outcomes by significantly affecting another or others' (Outhwaite and Bottomore 1993: 504).
3. On the multivocal and ambiguous character of symbols, see Kertzer (1988: 11).
4. See Lukes (1977: 62–67) for an overview of the concept of 'value consensus' in cultural symbolism and ritual activity.
5. On 'sectional narratives', see Ashplant, Dawson and Roper (2000: 20–22).
6. For an explanation of the fall of the religious community and the dynastic realm as regulating cultural systems, and how this might have affected the appearance of nationalism towards the end of the eighteenth century, see Anderson (1983: Chapter 2).
7. The predominance of narratives of a *national* type is attested by many examples from different historical and geographical contexts. Among others, see Kapferer (1988) and Thomson (1994) for Australia; Mosse (1990) for Germany; Y. Zerubavel (1995) for Israel.
8. The first official attempt to deal with the legacy of the conflict was the appointment, in October 1997 by the then secretary of state Marjorie Mowlam, of Sir Kenneth Bloomfield, former head of the Northern Ireland Civil Service, to act as a one-man

victims' commission. His report 'We Will Remember Them', published in May 1998, recommended a series of practical measures aimed at 'providing greater recognition for those who have become victims in the last thirty years as a consequence of events in Northern Ireland' (Bloomfield 1998: 8), including a memorial scheme. Following the publication in March 2005 of the strategic framework for Good Relations in Northern Ireland, 'A Shared Future', the OFMDFM has funded a series of projects aimed at monitoring visual displays of identity such as flags and emblems in Northern Ireland – see, for example, Bryan and Stevenson (2006); Institute of Irish Studies (2006); Bryan, Stevenson and Gillespie (2007, 2008); Bryan et al. (2010). Among other non-governmental organizations, the most significant contribution on ways to deal with the legacy of the conflict has been made by the Healing Through Remembering initiative and the now defunct Democratic Dialogue.

9. The year 1916 also represents an important milestone in the narrative of the Irish Republican Socialist Movement, but while the Provisional IRA, in relation to the Easter Rising, tends to position Padraic Pearse at the top of their ideological hierarchy, the INLA/IRSP narrative places James Connolly as its primary ideological forefather. As for the Loyalist UDA, recent attempts at appropriating the myth of the Somme have been made, but the strongest ideological association remains with the homonymous organization UVF. It is significant, for example, that in the UVF-associated Mount Vernon area of North Belfast a historical garden dedicated to the memory of the Somme has been constructed in front of a (modern) UVF memorial garden, almost as if constituting a single memorial complex (16th Irish Division and 36th Ulster Division, Viggiani 2013).

10. On the siege of Derry/Londonderry and the Battle of the Boyne, see McBride (1997) and Walker (1992, 2000); on the Battle of the Somme, see Longley (1994), Jarman (1999), Officer (2001), Graham and Shirlow (2002), Graham (2004) and Brown (2007). On the United Irishmen rebellion, see O'Keefe (1992), Johnson (1994), Beiner (2000), Walker (2000) and Collins (2004); on the Easter Rising, see Longley (1994), Jarman (1999), Daly and O'Callaghan (2007), Doherty and Keogh (2007) and Higgins (2012); on the Republican hunger strike, see O'Malley (1990).

11. Republican memorials that displayed the Irish tricolor, the shields of the four provinces of Ireland, the Celtic hero Cuchulainn or a Celtic cross have not been included in this data, as these symbols cannot be related to a specific pre-1969 historical event or phase of the Republican struggle.

12. Specifically the fourth verse: 'They shall grow not old, as we that are left grow old:/ Age shall not weary them, nor the years condemn./At the going down of the sun and in the morning,/We will remember them.'

13. See Chapter 8. For a brief history of Republican and Loyalist traditional symbols, see Jarman (1997: 216–18, 236–39).

14. A similar process is observed by Picard (1991: 96–97) in his study of An Phoblacht's content. For another example of delegitimation of the enemy through language, see Papadakis on Cyprus (1994: 406–7).

15. On the control over critical analysis in war exhibitions, see Lisle (2006: 185–206).

Chapter 5

THE CLONARD MARTYRS
MEMORIAL GARDEN

Constructing a Dominant Republican Narrative

⋙•⋘

According to Halbwachs ([1926] 1950), 'the prominence, and there-fore also the duration, of a collective memory depends on the social power of the group that holds it'; in other words, the group's 'social standing ... provides an important indicator of its memory's durabil-ity, visibility and power' (paraphrased in Misztal 2003: 51). Since the early 1980s, the Provisional Irish Republican movement has increasingly consolidated its political power in Northern Ireland, to the extent that Martin McGuinness, ex-Provisional IRA member and leading figure of Sinn Féin, has been Deputy First Minister of Northern Ireland since May 2007. Among Republican paramilitary groups, the Provisional IRA has historically won, if not the outright support, the sympathies and respect of the majority of the Nationalist/Republican community, secur-ing a social and geographical dominance through the streets of Northern Ireland. Consequently, it is unsurprising that the narrative of the Troubles promoted by the Provisional Irish Republican movement has come to be synonymous with the Republican version of the Northern Irish conflict, a version that has been widely 'exported' internationally by the media, music and film industry (Ivory 2007; Connelly 2012).

Using as a case study the memorial programme carried out by the Provisional IRA-aligned Greater Clonard Ex-Prisoners' Association, this chapter investigates how the Provisional Irish Republican movement has succeeded in establishing and maintaining through the years a dominant narrative of the Troubles within Irish Republicanism. It also examines how the individual level, both in terms of personal remembering and individual sacrifice of members of Catholic/Republican local communities, is subsumed within the 'mnemonic collectivity' of the Republican imagined community and an overarching narrative of collective sacrifice in the struggle for national self-determination. Finally, it sheds light onto the practical side of memorialization, following the day-to-day activities in the process of 'memory making'.

The 1998 Agreement and the Prisoners' 'Issue': The Formation of Ex-prisoners' Groups

Under the terms of the 1998 Good Friday/Belfast Agreement, prisoners belonging to paramilitary organizations that had declared a ceasefire were to be freed from jail by July 2000.[1] As of 2008, this resulted in the release of 449 prisoners (196 Loyalists, 241 Republicans, 12 non-aligned) who joined approximately fifteen thousand Republicans and between five and ten thousand Loyalists who had already served prison sentences related to the Troubles (McEvoy 2001; Shirlow and McEvoy 2008: 2). The return to 'normal life' after long periods of imprisonment proved problematic for many of them, the most acute difficulties being experienced in the areas of physical and psychological health, family relationships and employment (Shirlow and McEvoy 2008: 76–93). In order to assist the reintegration of politically motivated prisoners into society, an increasing number of ex-prisoners' self-help groups have been established since 1995, primarily supported by funding from the European Union.[2] Most groups have similar aims and objectives, which include the provision of a range of services such as employment and housing advice, skills training and counselling. In addition, many of these groups have sponsored local cultural, historical and memorial projects as well as promoting various social initiatives, in particular with regard to youth provision. This chapter follows the lifespan and activities of one of the most active Republican ex-prisoners' groups: the Greater Clonard Ex-Prisoners' Association, based in the Clonard district.[3]

The Greater Clonard Ex-Prisoners' Association

An electoral ward of West Belfast situated between the Catholic Falls and the Protestant Shankill areas (see Fig. 5.1), Clonard was established in 1973 and owes its name to the local Clonard Monastery, founded in 1896 and home to the Catholic Redemptorists. In the annals of Irish Republicanism, Clonard holds a special place because Tom Williams,

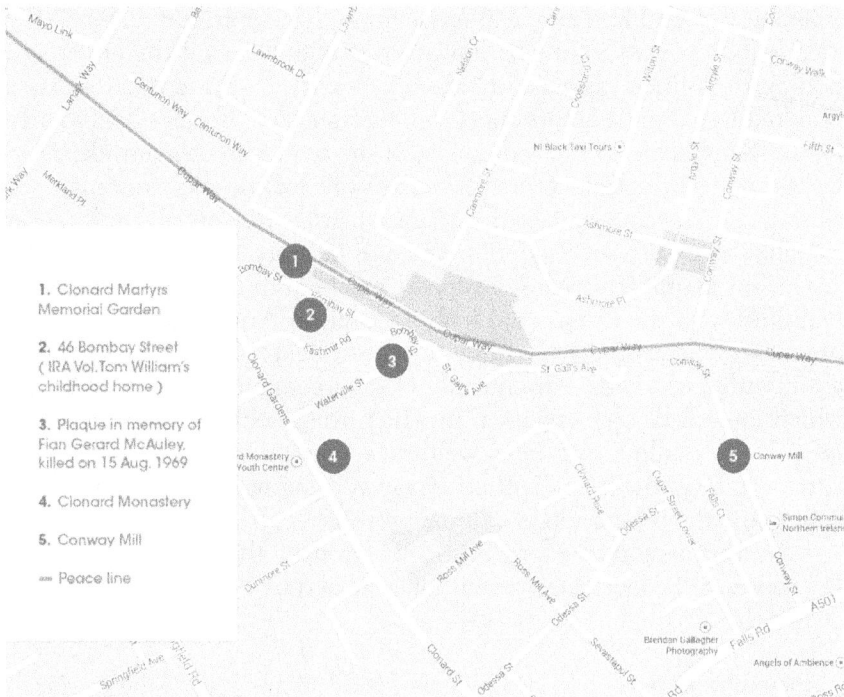

Figure 5.1 Map of Clonard
Source: Viggiani 2013

a celebrated IRA volunteer hanged in the Crumlin Road Gaol on 2 September 1942, grew up at 46 Bombay Street. During the civil disruption that broke out in Belfast in August 1969, Clonard acquired an even greater significance. On 15 August, fierce sectarian clashes erupted around the Clonard Monastery and the adjoining Bombay Street, which housed Catholics on the border between the Falls and the Shankill. Numerous buildings in the street were set alight by Protestant mobs and, during the fighting, fifteen-year-old Fian Gerald McAuley was shot dead by a Loyalist gunman in Waterville Street. He was the first Republican to die and the first IRA member to be killed during the Troubles (McKittrick et al. 2007: 38).

Here in Clonard, the Greater Clonard Ex-Prisoners' Association held its first official meeting in February 2000. According to what has been reported in the pamphlets and monthly bulletins that the group has regularly produced since its inception, the first few months of activities witnessed 'mature but very difficult' discussions around structural issues such as the organization, raison d'être, function and remits of the group

(Greater Clonard Ex-Prisoners' Association, henceforth GCEPA, 2001); a constitution was eventually drawn up that established the group as a non-party political association, open not only to the estimated three hundred Republican ex-prisoners coming from the Greater Clonard area but to Republicans in the wider sense of the term – an element identified by many local activists as one of the reasons for the success, prolonged existence and steady support for the association in comparison to other Republican ex-prisoners' groups. It must be noted, however, that the group was mainly created as a support mechanism for ex-prisoners who had links with the Provisional Irish Republican Army, and the majority of group members interviewed by this author expressed a political affiliation with Sinn Féin. An annually elected committee was established, which identified some key areas in which the association could become involved, including prisoners' welfare, education, youth provision, an extensive local memorial initiative, networking with other community groups and the promotion of cultural projects.

Like the majority of ex-prisoners' groups, the Greater Clonard Ex-Prisoners' Association was initially created as a support network to deal with

> the problems many of us [ex-prisoners] faced in adapting to the outside after in some cases twenty years in jail. The re-adjustment to family life, employment, technological development, work visas, etc. are just some of the problems; we also realised the psychological impact of so many years in jail. (GCEPA 2001)

Bonds of friendship developed among prisoners while incarcerated played an important part in the formation of the group: 'we all had a special friendship and bond which, we feel, should not be allowed to fall apart' (GCEPA 2001). As one of the Republican activists involved in the association aptly summarized,

> the ex-prisoners' group itself . . . was used as a sort of means to keep people together – especially ex-prisoners, [as] they have a sort of a bond that they were incarcerated together; it was a means of providing support for people coming out of prison, reintegrate prisoners back in the community; and it was a support mechanism for the prisoners' families as well. (Interview with the author)

A second fundamental reason for the establishment of the Greater Clonard Ex-Prisoners' Association was 'to ensure that Clonard and its people is never forgotten' (Greater Clonard Ex-Prisoners' Association Bulletin, henceforth GCEPAB, August 2001: 3) and to address 'a need for recognition of local people, [because] people were concerned about being forgotten about and written out of history' (interview with local Republican). As in many other Republican areas, this has resulted in the promotion of local history projects and an extensive memorial programme over the years to honour all people from the area who lost their lives as a direct result of the conflict. As will be investigated in this chapter, both personal and ideological motivations play a part in such ventures.

Enlisting the 'Unsung Heroes' in the Republican Narrative: Local History and Memorial Projects

To give testimony is to bear witness; it is to tell the unofficial story, to construct a history of people, of individual lives, a history not of those in power, but by those confronted by power, and becoming *empowered*. (This author's emphasis; Perks and Thomson 1998: 231)

Ashplant, Dawson and Roper (2000: 3) believe that the rekindled interest in war memory since the 1980s can be ascribed, among other reasons, to the fact that 'social groups suffering injustice, injury or trauma that originates in war have become increasingly prepared to demand public recognition of their experience, testimony and current status as "victims" or "survivors"'. Among such groups, a prominent position is held by civilians whose lives have been affected by war; hence, a proliferation of oral history projects and studies on the long-lasting effects of war on different sections of the local population in war zones.[4] In situations of ethnic conflict or civil war, in addition, the collective war memory of groups who find themselves in a position of social, economic or political inferiority seldom finds public expression, as attempts are made by the state and its agents, or by the more dominant group, to suppress it. Once the conflict is resolved or a more balanced social, economic or political position is achieved by previously repressed groups, their 'untold' collective war memory is likely to enter the public arena as a sectional narrative parallel to the dominant narrative or, in some cases, to replace the very same dominant narrative of the conflict.

In Northern Ireland, the 1994 paramilitary ceasefires and the signing of the Good Friday Agreement created 'the space for people to begin to reflect upon and discuss the past thirty years of political conflict', the space for 'a period of reflection and reassessment at the individual and community level' (Ardoyne Commemoration Project, henceforth ACP, 2002: 2), in particular among the Catholic population and the Republican community, whose public expression of memory, as mentioned in Chapter 2, had been restricted under the Stormont regime. As the past 'must be articulated to become memory' (Huyssen 1995: 3), many local history projects were carried out in Republican areas across the province: taking a variety of forms – booklets, photographic or artefacts exhibitions being the most popular – their common aim was to write a 'history from below' that gave communities the opportunity to 'set the record straight' and prevent *their* version of history from being 'lost, rewritten or misrepresented' (ACP 2002: 1). One of the most ambitious projects was undoubtedly the 543-page book *Ardoyne: The Untold Truth*, produced in 2002 by the Ardoyne Commemoration Project. Based on more than three hundred interviews with victims' relatives, friends, eyewitnesses and key individuals within the Ardoyne community, it records 'the story of 99 ordinary people, living ordinary lives, who became victims of political violence in a small, close-knit, working-class, nationalist community in North Belfast . . . between 1969 and 1998' (ibid.). Its main aims were to 'give control and ownership over what is written about victims to their relatives and friends' and 'to ensure that these unheard voices of ordinary people will enter the public discourse [so as to] reclaim an important part of their history for future generations' (ACP 2002: 1–2).

Charting the transition from personal to collective memory, Ashplant, Dawson and Roper (2000: 18) assert that war memory is 'first of all the possession of those individuals, military or civilian, who have experienced war'. Individual war memories are, therefore, 'formed from the specific, immediate personal experiences [of the war]'; however, they are also 'in part shaped through pre-existing cultural narratives, both those specific to that individual and their immediate social environment (such as family myths), and those which circulate through wider social discourses (such as national or generic – for example, warrior-myths)'. In addition, it has been observed (Humphrey 2002: 116) how, in situations of political violence,

> victims tell their stories in terms of the stories that have already been told. Their testimony more often reinforces established narrative themes than creates fresh ones. Through their testimonies they forge their own culture and identity around group discourses of memory.

If we analyse the agencies that have facilitated the work behind many oral history and memorial projects in Northern Ireland, victims' groups, ex-prisoners' organizations and memorial committees that are aligned with various political movements feature prominently, in particular those linked to the Provisional Irish Republican movement. Through these projects, then, previously 'silenced' individuals and local communities have been able to voice and find public recognition for their idiosyncratic memories of the Troubles; however, their recollections of the past do not live in isolation, but are influenced and restricted by common social (and ideological) representations, promoted by the various agencies that have 'facilitated' these recollections.

In Clonard, for example, individual testimony, engagement and participation has been paramount to all local history projects championed by the Greater Clonard Ex-Prisoners' Association, such as the 2000 photographic exhibition 'Clonard in Conflict' that charted the Republican history of Clonard (GCEPAB January 2001: 2–3; GCEPAB April 2001: 4) or the commemorative event 'Remembering '69' that included the showing of a video in which local people retold their stories of the events of August 1969 in Bombay Street (GCEPAB January 2001: 2–3). The underlying principle, however, is that the history of Clonard, like that of other Republican areas, is seen as a 'microcosm of the overall struggle for national independence' (GCEPA 2001), thus subsuming the localized experiences within the general Republican narrative of sacrifice and resistance while still granting public recognition for the courage shown and the suffering borne by each community. Similarly, individuals from a specific area who lost their lives as a result of the conflict are recognized and publicly remembered, but their sacrifice is subsumed within this collective narrative of national sacrifice: hence, the high number of casualties compared to the overall population of Clonard is 'indicative of both the intensity of the [national] struggle and of the direct contribution to that struggle by the Greater Clonard community' (ibid.). We will see how this is achieved in the most ambitious of the memorial projects carried out by the Greater Clonard Ex-Prisoners' Association – the Clonard Martyrs Memorial Garden; here it suffices to note how the series of seven commemorative plaques commissioned by the same association since 2001 to mark the spots where fallen local volunteers lived or died on active service has been erected 'to demonstrate to those people's families that [the volunteers] aren't forgotten, that their sacrifice wasn't in vain' but at the same time 'to demonstrate [that] this is where we came from as a community and . . . what we contributed to the cause of Irish freedom' (interview with one of the association's promoters).

In summary, both the Greater Clonard Ex-Prisoners' Association's local history projects and memorial programme allow people to tell their stories or remember the dead based on their individual experience of the past. On the one hand, there is recognition for the individual sacrifice and reassurance to families and friends that each person will not be forgotten; on the other hand, these personal engagements, individual stories and memories are subsumed under the hat stand of the wider Republican collective narrative of 'powerlessness, marginalization and resistance' (ACP 2002: 1). In telling the stories and remembering the people, the past members of the Republican 'imagined community' are conjured up to foster the present members' shared identity and collective memory:

> the stories of the people who died . . . are, in the first place, . . . the personal memories of those who knew and loved them. In another way they are also, however, a key component of a collective memory through which a shared identity takes shape. They are part of the fabric of what makes this community see itself as a community. (ACP 2002: 7)

This dual dimension of memory – individual and communal – is also at the heart of the formation of many ex-prisoners' groups. On the one hand, ex-prisoners felt a genuine *individual* desire and need to pay homage to fallen friends and comrades – people who they may have known because they were neighbours or comrades in arms or fellow prisoners; on the other, however, there was a conscious effort on their part to keep alive and foster a sense of community and shared identification. As a member of the Clonard ex-prisoners' group stated in conversation with the author,

> why have people decided to do [these things]? Of course it's individual, it's me wanting to pay tribute and respect to people, to friends that I have lost. . . . I'm sure for everybody there's a personal motivation or personal connection maybe to one individual or a number of individuals. But then, again, people come along because of the community side of it . . . people consciously got involved in this also because they had a sense of Clonard as a community and they wanted to maintain that sense of community and they wanted to maintain a respect of those bonds.

This attention to a shared 'sense of community' and to collective memory by ex-prisoners' groups is, in turn, concurrently genuine and politically strategic. It is undeniable that there is a sincere and altruistic desire to 'put something back into the communities' from which ex-prisoners came. It has been noted how the relationship between ex-combatants and communities is often misrepresented in the international literature on conflict transformation (Shirlow and McEvoy 2008). In many geographical contexts former prisoners and ex-combatants 'are viewed as a managerial headache, portrayed as largely passive recipients to whom measures such as Disarmament, Demobilization and Reintegration should be applied to remove them from the transitional equation as quickly as possible lest they prove a destabilising influence' (ibid.: viii). Contrary to this postulation, what has happened in Northern Ireland 'provides a useful corrective to those assumptions prevalent in the international literature on how to "deal" with former prisoners and ex-combatants in a transition from conflict', in that here former prisoners and ex-combatants have assumed a 'much more dynamic role' and have become key agents of conflict transformation, providing leadership and guidance at grassroots level for the communities to which they belonged (ibid.). As a religious representative involved in community politics for many years has pointed out in the case of Northern Ireland,

> paramilitaries in this community are the sons, the boyfriends, the partners, the grandsons, the fathers of the community. They are not something outside it, they are not something parachuted in; they are an integral part of that community as much as any other whether it'd be the church or the other infrastructures that are there. (Interview with the author)

At the height of the conflict, paramilitaries 'needed a community behind to sink into after engaging in conflict, because that was your cover, that was what protected you, that was your wall around you . . . So, the communities were behind them' (Loyalist ex-paramilitary in interview with the author). With the transition to a post-conflict setting, many ex-combatants have chosen to get involved in community work as a genuine way of 'putting something back' into the communities, as a 'payback' and 'empowerment' mechanism:

> the communities are coming to the front and the new analysis is paramilitaries behind the communities but in a different sense . . . Ex-combatants and a lot of people are going into community work and trying to build positively within the communities, trying to move them forward positively, because the community has missed out; they haven't got the capacity within them to know how to do things, which is why ex-combatants like myself are guiding them in that direction. (Interview with Loyalist ex-paramilitary)

Since its inception in 2000, the Greater Clonard Ex-Prisoners' Association has, for example, promoted a successful series of social and cultural initiatives in the area 'to contribute constructively to our local community' and 'improve our/their quality of life' (GCEPA 2001). These have ranged from the re-establishment of the Clonard Amateur Boxing Club and the erection of bilingual (English/Gaelic) street signs in the area to the setting up of the Lower Clonard Residents' Association that lobbies on behalf of the Clonard community with respect to housing, youth provision, and employment, and has promoted initiatives aimed at tackling antisocial behaviour in the area.

However, this involvement in community politics and the promotion of collective memory by Republican ex-prisoners and activists undoubtedly also have a more premeditated and strategic dimension. As one local Republican recognizes, 'this was part of a very conscious, deliberate strategy on the part of Republicans to become deeply embedded within the community'. While the genuine reasons cited above are acknowledged,

> the other part was as well that of course we wanted to extend the influence of Republicans, we wanted to be relevant; we wanted to bring as many people as we could into the struggle . . . of course, we soon realized that the struggle is about community politics; it's about projects like [these]; it's about getting the respect of the local community. (Interview with the author)

In Clonard, the Greater Clonard Ex-Prisoners' Association's most ambitious project of building a memorial garden for all the people from the area who lost their lives as a direct result of the conflict assumed, therefore, a multi-layered meaning. Like other memorial initiatives in the area, its most obvious aim was to remember the local dead and reassure their families that their sacrifice had not been forgotten. However, its promoters also saw the project as 'a great means of mobilizing the community' around something which could provide 'a sort of common aim' (interview with one of the promoters). Notwithstanding the differences of opinion among local residents, the building of the memorial garden was 'a project that basically everybody could buy into, regardless of what they thought of the political direction, the things they were taking out of the political developments' (local Republican activist in interview with the author). While the extent to which the local community has 'bought into' this project will be investigated in Chapter 9, it is clear that a conscious attempt was made to project a unifying framework within which the idiosyncratic experiences and interpretations of the conflict could be subsumed. In addition, the building of the memorial garden, together with other initiatives, would have been very much regarded as a 'continuation of the [Republican] struggle'. As an ex-member of the Clonard ex-prisoners' group acknowledged,

> here was a large group of people [Republican ex-prisoners] who had been involved in struggle at some point, but had left for whatever reason, personal reasons or political reasons, and it was a huge constituency . . . If we could get two thousand ex-prisoners to become involved in this garden, even just on the basis of the garden, that was strengthening the struggle; that meant we had twice as many activists.

Such an involvement – both of the local community and the ex-prisoners – was seen, therefore, as a way of strengthening the Provisional movement's political presence, influence and relevance at a grassroots level and at an electoral level.

The remainder of this chapter focuses on the Clonard Martyrs Memorial Garden. It illustrates some of the practicalities behind the erection of paramilitary-related memorial gardens, in particular in relation to government legislation and local state agencies, and demonstrates how a dominant narrative of the conflict is successfully projected by the Provisional Republican movement through a process of historical selection and a careful choice of language and iconography.

The Clonard Martyrs Memorial Garden

Soon after the establishment of the Greater Clonard Ex-Prisoners' Association, a committee was formed to oversee the 'most daunting' task that the group had set for itself – the building of the Clonard Martyrs Memorial Garden (GCEPA 2001). An overgrown neglected area was identified in the quiet back street of Bombay Street and, after a series of public meetings held in Clonard Hall, construction work began in the spring of 2000.

Planning Permission and Relationship with Local Authorities

Like all memorials on public soil, paramilitary-related memorials are theoretically subject to planning regulations. According to official records, however, no planning permission request for the Clonard memorial garden was submitted to the Planning Service, the executive agency within the Northern Ireland Department of the Environment that is responsible for developing and implementing government planning policies and development plans in Northern Ireland. This is by no means an uncommon practice for 'unofficial' Troubles-related memorials, at least in the city of Belfast. As of May 2008, the Divisional Planning Office had received planning permission applications for only two of the 157 memorials surveyed.[5] While this was not considered an issue by either Republican or Loyalist ex-prisoners before 1998, many interviewees have suggested that in recent years applications have been submitted for present (and future) memorial projects and that retrospective planning permission requests were being presented for older memorials; however, no official record was found to sustain this claim.

It is interesting to note that, while there is a formal protocol with respect to sectarian symbols such as flags and emblems displayed on arterial routes and in sensitive public spaces in Northern Ireland (such as city or town centres, churches, hospitals and schools), no governmental body has so far agreed an official policy specifically related to permanent forms of memorialization. Given the high sensitivity of the topic and the 'sacredness' of these sites, a policy of tolerance and common sense has hitherto prevailed whereby the local authorities seem to have 'signed a non-written agreement' with the promoters of 'sectional' memorials and 'turned a blind eye' (interview with Clonard Republican activist). As a representative of the Northern Ireland Roads Services admitted, 'we don't have a policy as such; because of the political and human sensitivities associated with [these memorials], we tend to operate a toleration policy'. As in the case of the Clonard Martyrs Memorial Garden, the location chosen for most memorial gardens in Belfast depends, therefore, upon practical constraints rather than official legislation: since no land is granted for this purpose by the authorities, local circumstances – the availability of waste ground in the area or the location of land donated by private individuals – influence how the 'landscape of memorialization' takes shape probably to the same or a greater degree than the ideological and symbolic considerations analysed in Chapter 3.

Funding, Building Materials and Manpower

The exact cost of permanent memorial projects is impossible to estimate since materials for construction or decorative elements are often donated or provided at a lower market price by sympathizers of the group promoting the project, but average prices for memorials as elaborate as the Clonard memorial garden can be as much as £30,000–£40,000. Funds to support the building and upkeep of memorial gardens are raised entirely at a local level by voluntary donations through door-to-door envelope collections, sponsored walks, lotteries, fundraising social events and financial donations from local businesses; in the case of the Clonard example, there was no use of public money as far as this author is aware.

The donation of building materials such as bricks, sand, stones and cement by private individuals or local building suppliers as well as sponsorship of different parts of a memorial – plaques, gates, commemorative benches – by residents and local businesses is common practice for the majority of memorial gardens in Belfast, particularly Republican ones. In some cases, materials are 'put aside' to build a memorial site during redevelopment projects undertaken by the Housing Executive or other public bodies, as in the case of the Provisional IRA 'A' Company, 2nd Battalion Memorial Garden in Beechmount Avenue, Falls (interview with a local Republican).[6] Although the service of external professional architects, surveyors and sculptors may be sought for the most complex elements, the memorial garden is, in most part, built through the effort of a community: from local bricklayers, labourers, painters and electricians 'donating' their time to street collections and cleaning tasks carried out by local youth and even the provision of tea and refreshments for the workers by local residents. Such participation of (some) local residents in memorial projects has been quoted by many promoters of memorial initiatives as unquestionable proof that local communities welcome the erection of memorial gardens in their areas, which, therefore, should be considered as 'people's gardens' rather than being associated with a particular group. As one Clonard ex-prisoner asserted, 'people are delighted to see it there, given what it's for: not so much the IRA, it's about really the local people who died'. While the extent to which local residents do genuinely support such projects will be discussed in Chapter 9, it is interesting to note how these memorial gardens are usually portrayed as being the result of a 'community effort'. Thus, a uniformity of opinion is often advocated in the name of an 'imagined community' who share the same views and beliefs.

Construction of a Successful Dominant Narrative: Iconography, Language and Historical Selection

The Clonard Martyrs Memorial Garden was unveiled on 20 August 2000. Its structure makes it one of the most elaborate and among the largest Republican gardens in Belfast.[7] The twenty-five fallen volunteers on the Roll of Honour of the 'C' Company, 2nd Battalion, Belfast Brigade, Oglaigh na h-Eireann (IRA) and fifty-eight civilians from the area who lost their lives as a result of the conflict are commemorated on the same plaque situated at the centre of the garden (Fig 4.1). Along the walls of the right yard, 182 names of deceased Republican prisoners from the Greater Clonard area who died from 1916 to the 1970s are listed on a series of plaques.[8] In the left yard, two more recent plaques pay tribute to the members and friends of the Greater Clonard Memorial Garden Committee and to 'the people of the Greater Clonard who have resisted and still resist the *occupation of our country*' (this author's emphasis). As the latter plaque exemplifies, the Clonard memorial garden clearly reflects the mainstream (Provisional) Republican interpretation of the conflict as an anti-imperialistic war – a struggle of self-determination against the British state.

As the previous chapter outlined, the language and iconography used in this memorial project a symbolic national narrative that supersedes the geographical limitations of Northern Ireland and establishes a clear connection to the nation state of Ireland: the plaque in the left yard asserts, for instance, that the reward for the people 'who have resisted and still resist the occupation of our country by Britain ... will only be a united Ireland' and an Irish tricolour permanently flies against the iron peace line running along the back wall of the Clonard memorial garden, which separates the Catholic Falls from the Protestant Shankill. Symbolic 'national' connections can also stretch back millennia to the mythical Gaelic Ireland. The central plaque, for instance, prays that the Clonard dead 'be in the midst of Gaelic warriors/heroes' (*i measc laoċra na ngae deal go rad siad*); the four provinces of Ireland adorn two plaques in the garden; Celtic crosses are engraved on the pavement of both lateral yards; and a seven-foot granite Celtic cross is prominently positioned at the centre of the main yard.

As explained earlier, memorials in Northern Ireland tend to portray significant pre-Troubles episodes as interwoven threads of a unique narrative framework; this can be achieved either by means of collating symbols linked to different seminal events at the same memorial site or by remembering the deceased from different eras through a single memorial component. Unlike the majority of Republican memorials which assemble many symbols from different iconic events of the history of Irish Republicanism,[9] the Clonard memorial garden presents only the image of the phoenix engraved on its iron gates (see Figure 5.2), possibly a symbolic representation of Bombay Street which rose from the ashes of August 1969 with strengthened resolve, commitment and dedication to the cause of Irish freedom. On the 'C Company' 2nd Battalion's Roll of Honour plaque, however, fallen volunteers from the area who died between 1920 and 1944 are listed together with volunteers who died between 1969 and 1992, with no differentiation between the IRA who fought in the early decades of partition and in the Border Campaign of 1956–62 and the post-1969-split Provisional IRA.

Similarly, deceased Republican ex-prisoners who died between 1916 and 1962 are listed in a stream of names together with those who died from 1970, without any distinction. As outlined earlier in this chapter, the struggle of Clonard during the Troubles is seen just as a phase in the century-long struggle for Irish independence and the individual sacrifice subsumed within a collective narrative of wider resistance and martyrdom. Thus, past martyrs of the Republican 'imagined community' are conjured up all together in order to foster the present generation's social cohesion and collective identification. On some Republican memorials, the forefathers of (mainstream) Irish Republicanism such as Wolfe Tone and Padraig Pearse are remembered alongside Troubles-related casualties

Figure 5.2 PIRA Clonard Martyrs Memorial Garden
Source: Viggiani 2006

from a specific area of Belfast.[10] Although the Clonard garden makes no mention of ideological forefathers, the garden itself is built opposite the native home of Tom Williams, another legendary figure of Irish Republicanism.

In a careful exercise of historical selection, what is 'forgotten' in the Clonard garden is as important as what is remembered. It is interesting to note how memorial features that were once central tenets of the Provisional Republican dominant narrative have changed to accommodate the movement's political, ideological and strategic shifts. For many years until 2007, a mural in memory of Fian Gerald McAuley stood on a gable wall a few yards away from the Clonard garden; it depicted a dramatic scene of the burning out of Bombay Street with the caption 'Bombay Street Never Again! Decommission No Mission' (Fig. 5.3).

The mural has since been renovated and moved to a more prominent position next to the garden itself. The central image depicting families fleeing burning homes – in other words, the section of the narrative that has been retained – has been reproduced, while the caption beneath has

Figure 5.3 Mural in memory of Fian Gerard McAuley
Source: Viggiani 2006

been substituted with three historical photographs from the time, since its statement no longer complied with the direction taken by the Provisional Republican leadership in terms of arms decommissioning (Fig. 5.4).

As a local black-taxi driver commented,

> because they [the Republican leadership] have gone into politics . . . It suited them to have that removed, because they had decommissioned and they had moved on . . . But I would say the people of Bombay Street would still be saying 'No decommissioning'. (Interview with the author)

A more complex issue is posited by who is and who is not commemorated in the memorial garden. According to the Republican activist who compiled the list of names for the plaques in the garden, strict criteria of inclusion/exclusion were outlined at the very outset of the project to avoid any potential controversies. Officially, an individual acquires the right to be on the Provisional IRA's Roll of Honour if he/she has been killed on active service or is a lifelong Republican. Of the twenty-five

Figure 5.4 Mural in memory of Fian Gerard McAuley
Source: Viggiani 2008

individuals listed on the 'C Company' 2nd Battalion Roll of Honour, for instance, two (Liam Hannaway and Proinsias Mac Airt) died of natural causes but their high profile in the Republican movement earned them mention on the memorial; all civilians remembered on the central plaque died as a direct consequence of the conflict and every effort was made to comprehensively represent ex-prisoners from the area, the list compiled over years of research through prison files held at the Public Record Office, books, newspaper cuttings and oral testimonies from veteran Republicans. In addition, private individuals who donated the decorative benches for the garden were allowed to dedicate them to deceased family members and friends, even if they were not Republicans in the strictest sense of the word.

As mentioned in earlier chapters, remembering IRA volunteers together with civilian casualties from a particular area is a common feature of Republican memorial gardens throughout Belfast. It is less common, however, to list deceased Republican ex-prisoners one by one, or to have commemorative plaques adorning each bench, as is the case in the Clonard garden.[11] This has led all ex-prisoners and activists from the area that were interviewed to remark upon the 'inclusiveness' of the Clonard garden and to stress how the sacrifice of each member of the Clonard community had been recognized. The addition of these plaques was seen by many as a practical way to overcome the strict limitations for inclusion in the IRA Roll of Honour and to recognize the contributions of volunteers who, for example, died of illness or as a result of tragic accidents while not on active service.

> There was a lot of recognition. The fact that the ex-prisoners' names were put up, it was good for some people as well that their loved ones may not have necessarily been recognized otherwise, they weren't killed in active service or anything like that there, but they [had] done probably a lot of time within jails. . . . That was an attempt to be as inclusive as we could to those families who felt, rightly so, that the contribution that their own particular loved one had made during the course of the Republican struggle was as good as Seán Savage. (Interview with local Republican)

Undoubtedly, the Clonard memorial garden is one of the most inclusive gardens in Belfast in the sense that it represents and recognizes the contribution made by different constituencies of the mainstream Republican family – Provisional IRA volunteers, ex-prisoners and 'unsung heroes'.

While these individuals contribute positively to the construction of a dominant mainstream Republican narrative of oppression and heroic resistance, individuals whose actions while alive or whose circumstances of death are seen as undermining this narrative are, instead, 'forgotten'.[12] No mention is made, for instance, of Catholic civilians from the area who had been killed by the IRA. Informers are also excluded and, interestingly, deceased volunteers who were members of other Republican paramilitary groups share the same fate. Although 'there was never any question of informers being included, [because] they are enemies of the struggle', a more controversial issue was posited by the situation of INLA volunteers, because 'these were people who were for the most part good Republicans' (interview with local Republican); they fought for a very similar, if not the same cause, but under different banners. Though recognizing the hurt that their families must have felt, few interviewees seemed to be expecting any mention of INLA volunteers (or of other smaller Republican organizations) on memorials promoted and sponsored by Provisional IRA-affiliated ex-prisoners' groups and vice versa.

As mentioned in the previous chapter, the promotion of partisan narratives of legitimacy and victimhood to gain symbolic and political capital runs in parallel with the deconstruction of similar claims made by the competing group. The enemy is often dehumanized and demonized through the language employed in memorial inscriptions. In Clonard, volunteers Sean Gaynor, the Duffin brothers and Sean O'Riordan were 'murdered' and not 'killed' by the Royal Irish Constabulary (the Irish pre-partition police force)[13] and the British Army (in the case of O'Riordan), while civilian casualties remembered in the Clonard memorial garden 'were killed by Crown forces and Loyalist *murder gangs*' (author's emphasis). Thus, a selective version of the conflict is portrayed and a partisan narrative projected to stress historical legitimacy, foster intragroup cohesion and discredit the other side's 'story'. As Chapter 9 will investigate, disagreement and discontent with the dominant narrative are often kept behind closed doors, or if expressed, are promptly absorbed through social mechanisms of 'acceptance' and 'respectability' in the name of a 'united community'.

Perpetuating Collective Memory: Periodic Commemorations in Clonard

This unity of opinion, if not a uniformity of belief, was readily evident at the unveiling ceremony of the Clonard memorial in August 2000, when two thousand Republicans and local residents paraded through the streets of Clonard. Since then, the garden has served as a focal point for the local Republican community who gather here three times a year 'to pay their respect to the local patriot dead'. On the Sunday closest to 9 March – a date rich with significance for Republicans in Clonard[14] – a wreath-laying ceremony takes place at the old Republican plot in Milltown Cemetery, followed by a commemorative parade through the Greater Clonard area, starting at Conway Street and proceeding to the memorial garden in Bombay Street for the main commemorative event. This is preceded by an evening function on the Friday night in the Felons Club, where a gift presentation is usually made to local Republicans and their families, and the crowd is entertained by guest speakers, live music and a discotheque. This annual event in the Republican calendar of commemorations was observed until 2004, when the organizers decided that, due to habitually adverse weather conditions, only the Friday function and the Sunday wreath-laying ceremony in Milltown were to be held in the month of March. Since 2005, the main Clonard Martyrs Memorial Parade has been moved to the Sunday closest to 15 August in memory of the burning of Bombay Street. Finally, on Easter Sunday local Republicans gather for a wreath-laying ceremony at the memorial garden before joining the mainstream Republican Easter parade marching from Beechmount Avenue to the new Republican plot in Milltown Cemetery.

Echoing Connerton's (1989) analysis of commemorative activity, this periodic reunion of the Clonard community has been consciously encouraged to ensure that 'the community spirit that was fostered in the old district remains' (GCEPA n.d.), and its collective memory and identity are transmitted to younger generations. Due to redevelopment and demographic change, many Republican communities have 'broken up' and

> this [having periodical commemorations] is another way of trying to draw a line in the sand and say 'No', Clonard is an old community, it's a proud community and let's keep it as a community and let's keep some community pride and sense of our place and our history. (Interview with local Republican)

Thus, these occasions are seen as 'a very unifying force' and provide the opportunity for residents who once lived in the district but have now moved away, as well as current residents and older and younger Republicans, to gather together and 'see that that sense of community is still there, that sense of pride is still there'. Despite the fact that these commemorations still take place to the present day, the Greater Clonard Ex-Prisoners' Association no longer exists in its original form. A smaller committee – the Clonard Martyrs Memorial Garden Committee – is still in place to oversee the maintenance and upkeep of the memorial garden, while the majority of ex-prisoners have 'moved on' or have concentrated their efforts on the Clonard Residents' Associations. As many interviewees recognized, ex-prisoners' groups had their heyday between 2001 and 2003; they provided a particular function at a particular time and, once the issues they were there to address had been dealt with, they ceased to have a raison d'être. Many of them no longer exist and former prisoners are now active in the areas of trade unionism, community politics, political tourism (the so-called 'black tourism') or in some cases have been reabsorbed into normal patterns of employment.

Following the lifespan and daily activities of one of the many ex-prisoners' groups associated with the Provisional IRA, in particular the construction of the Clonard Martyrs Memorial Garden, this chapter has examined how a dominant Republican narrative of the Troubles has been projected by the Provisional Irish Republican movement and how the individual experience – both in terms of personal memory and individual sacrifice – is subsumed within an overarching narrative of collective national sacrifice. The following chapter turns its attention to a different ex-prisoner's group, the Teach Na Fáilte Memorial Committee, affiliated with the smaller Republican paramilitary organization the Irish National Liberation Army. Focusing on the group's memorial activities in Belfast, the chapter attempts to establish how a sectional narrative is carved out and negotiated within the mainstream Republican narrative by the Irish Republican Socialist Movement, and how a place in history for INLA volunteers is reclaimed in spite of the Provisional IRA/Sinn Féin's dominant 'version' of the conflict.

Notes

1. See Section 10 'Prisoners'. For the Agreement's text, see Elliot (2002: 223–34).
2. As a response to the positive developments in the peace process (most notably the IRA and Combined Loyalist Military Command's 1994 ceasefires), in July 1995 the European Union established a funding programme called the Special Support Programme for Peace and Reconciliation in Northern Ireland and the Border Region, most commonly known as the PEACE programme. Its aim was to provide financial support to a series of local community initiatives that promoted social inclusion, economic development, employment, conflict transformation and reconciliation. From 1995 to 1999, PEACE I accounted for approximately €500 million, while the second phase of the programme, PEACE II (2000–06), provided a further €467 million, supporting more than 5,300 projects. Finally, €225 million was allocated for the PEACE III Programme for the period 2007–13. For more information, see Special EU Programmes Body.
3. The Greater Clonard Ex-Prisoners' Association was also part of the umbrella organization for Republican ex-prisoners' groups, Coiste na n-Iarchimí (Committee of Ex-Prisoners). Established in 1998 in order to 'secure the full integration of the Republican former prisoner community by securing recognition of the contribution they have made to the community in the past and can make in the future' and 'facilitate Republican former prisoners in deepening and developing their contribution to justice and peace in Ireland' (Coiste na n-Iarchimí 1999a: 3–4), Coiste included at its peak twenty-four ex-prisoners' groups and employed ninety-five staff throughout Ireland (Gormally 2001).
4. See, for instance, the Recovery of Historical Memory (REMHI) project in Guatemala or the UCLA Armenian Genocide Oral History Project. On the impact of sectarianism and the conflict on young people in Northern Ireland, see Smyth (1998) and Roche (2008).
5. These are the St Matthew's Chapel memorial in Bryson Street, Short Strand (Divisional Planning Office record, application ID Z/2000/1169/F) and the Provisional IRA Gairdin Cuimhneachain in Donore Court, off New Lodge Road, New Lodge (Divisional Planning Office record, application ID Z/2003/0193/F).
6. See PIRA, "A" Company, 2nd Battalion, Belfast Brigade, Viggiani 2013.
7. For a description of the Clonard Martyrs Memorial Garden layout, see Clonard Martyrs Memorial Garden, Viggiani 2013.
8. This includes nine deceased Republican prisoners from 1916; fifty-one from the 1920s; thirteen from 1921 to 1922; eighty-two from the 1930s and 1940s; five from 1956 to 1962; and twenty-two from 1970.
9. See, for example, the Provisional IRA memorial in memory of the fallen volunteers from the Greater Lenadoon Area in the Roddy McCorley's Club, Glen Road,

Andersonstown (PIRA, Fallen Volunteers from the Greater Lenadoon Area, Viggiani 2013) and the Provisional IRA garden in memory of the fallen volunteers from the Greater Turf Lodge Area at the junction of Norglen Road and Monagh Crescent, Turf Lodge (PIRA, Fallen Volunteers of the Greater Turf Lodge Area, Viggiani 2013).

10. For example, a quotation from Wolfe Tone is engraved on a plaque set in the pavement outside the Provisional IRA memorial for the Twinbrook and Poleglass Fallen Volunteers in Twinbrook Road, Twinbrook (PIRA, Twinbrook and Poleglass Fallen Volunteers, Viggiani 2013). At least five Republican memorials among those surveyed refer to the famous oration of Padraig Pearse at the grave of O'Donovan Rossa ('The fools, the fools, the fools . . .').

11. See also the Provisional IRA Falls Garden of Remembrance, Lower Falls Road, Falls (Falls Garden of Remembrance, Viggiani 2013).

12. An interesting admission of the selective nature of Republican memorialization can be found in the commemorative booklet *Green River: In Honour of Our Dead*. Here, the Beechmount Commemoration Committee (aligned to the Provisional Irish Republican movement) recognizes that the booklet pays tribute to the sacrifices made by Republican patriots 'with a certain sensitivity and circumspection because the IRA has also hurt and killed civilians . . . has also bereaved the families of these people and those of informers or members of British forces'. However, 'inevitably, in a work of this nature there are bound to be omissions – and for any unwitting oversights we apologize' (Beechmount Commemoration Committee 1998: 4).

13. After the partition of the island, the Royal Irish Constabulary (RIC) was disbanded and replaced with the Royal Ulster Constabulary (RUC) in Northern Ireland and the Garda Síochána in the then Irish Free State.

14. This date was chosen in memory of Provisional IRA volunteers Gerard Crossan, Sean Johnston, Tony Lewis and Tom McCann, who died in a premature bomb explosion in Clonard Street on 9 March 1972. It assumed further significance after 1988 when volunteers Seán Savage and Dan McCann (both on the Clonard 'C' Company 2nd Battalion Roll of Honour) were shot dead by the SAS in Gibraltar on 6 March 1988 together with their comrade Mairéad Farrell.

Chapter 6

The IRSP/INLA Teach Na Fáilte Memorial Committee

Constructing a Sectional Republican Narrative

⋙•⋘

> It is important that we keep their memories alive and prevent the historical revisionism that we currently see coming into play time and time again by those who would rather see the IRSM [Irish Republican Socialist Movement] airbrushed from history.[1]

Following what Ashplant, Dawson and Roper postulate in relation to the process of war memories articulation, 'shared' or 'common' memories emerge 'when individuals can express and compare their memories with the experience of contemporaries, can begin to formulate a shared language and identify common themes'. They are usually formulated and transmitted through 'face-to-face groupings, ranging from . . . gatherings of old comrades to local communities and interest groups' (Ashplant, Dawson and Roper 2000: 18). However, it is only when these shared memories are articulated in 'some cultural or artistic form' such as memorials that they enter the public arena and become *political* narratives, whether dominant or sectional (ibid.: 20). A publicly articulated sectional narrative can then be 'subordinate [to the dominant narrative], if accorded only limited or partial recognition; marginalized, if simply neglected or not deemed worthy of recognition; or suppressed, if treated . . . as incompatible with the parameters of the dominant narrative', potentially becoming 'oppositional' if sufficient sociopolitical mobilization around it can be achieved (ibid.). This chapter examines how a sectional – and at times oppositional – narrative of the Northern Irish Troubles is constructed by the Irish Republican Socialist Movement, in contrast to the Provisional IRA/Sinn Féin's dominant 'version' of the conflict illustrated in the previous chapter. Following the commemorative activity of the Teach Na Fáilte Memorial Committee Belfast, it illustrates how the IRSM has attempted to reclaim a place in history for the INLA, highlighting similarities and differences between Provisional Republican and Republican Socialist commemorative practices. This chapter also investigates how memory is shaped by the present and how a narrative about the past is able to adjust itself to shifting historical and political circumstances, relationships of power and cultural values in a society.

The IRSP/INLA Teach Na Fáilte Memorial Committee

One morning in June 2002, a man walking along the Falls Road in West Belfast noticed a small plaque hung on a wall in a side street away from the busy main road. The plaque had been erected the previous summer by the Sinn Féin-aligned Lower Falls/Clonard 1980/81 Commemoration Committee in memory of Nora McCabe and Peter Doherty, two Catholic civilians killed by plastic bullets in 1981, and Emmanuel 'Matt' McLarnon, an INLA volunteer shot dead by the British Army in the same year (McLarnon, McCabe and Doherty, Viggiani 2013).[2] The man rushed to his office close by, sat down at his desk and wrote a letter to the editors of the *Andersonstown News* and *The Starry Plough* calling all Republican Socialist ex-prisoners to meet the following week at Costello House, the Irish Republican Socialist Party's Belfast head office, in order to institute a memorial committee. On 6 June 2002, eleven Republican Socialist ex-prisoners 'from as far back as 1975 and right up to 2001' (Teach Na Fáilte Memorial Committee Belfast, henceforward TNFMCB 2004) gathered for the first official meeting of the newly formed IRSP/INLA Teach Na Fáilte (House of Welcome) Memorial Committee Belfast. The group immediately agreed to erect a series of plaques in the Belfast area in memory of the sixteen volunteers and four comrades on the IRSP/INLA County Antrim Roll of Honour ('Irish Republican Socialist Movement Roll of Honour' 2000).[3] Other immediate resolutions were to organize fundraising events, canvas local businesses for donations, and intensify publicity efforts both locally and internationally. While the Belfast branch was the first to be established (in 2002), since its inception other local branches have been established in Derry/Londonderry, Strabane, Dungiven and Dublin, which all work independently, but maintain regular contact and attend each other's commemorative functions and unveiling ceremonies.

As in the case of the Greater Clonard Ex-Prisoners' Association, the need to remember the fallen members of the Irish Republican Socialist Movement who lost their lives as a direct result of the Troubles has primarily been dictated by a genuine *individual* desire among ex-prisoners to pay homage to fallen friends and comrades: as ex-prisoner Gerard Murray pointed out in his opening remarks during an unveiling ceremony in the Markets area in 2003, '[O]ur committee is composed of comrades, ex-prisoners and ex-combatants who survived the struggle. We felt it appropriate that we should honour those of our comrades who did not' (Murray 2003b). On a more public, politically strategic level, however, the memorial committee embarked upon a task of 'reclaiming' a place in history for the Irish Republican Socialist Party and the Irish National Liberation Army in spite of the Provisional IRA/Sinn Féin's dominant Republican narrative. Historically much smaller, both in terms of members and political support, and 'much more vulnerable than the broad church itself [the Provisional movement]', the IRSM has always faced the daunting challenge of demonstrating that 'its history is as old, as honourable and as brave as that of any other sections of the Republican movement' (McAliskey 2002). Therefore, one of the key reasons why the man rushed to his office in June 2002 to 'summon' the small Republican Socialist family to leave an official mark of their existence on the landscape of memorialization in Belfast was that he felt that

> we should remind the future generations that there was another organization fighting a war. It wasn't the case that it was just the Provisional IRA or Provisional Sinn Féin . . . there was the INLA, there was the IRSP . . . But if you put monuments, plaques, murals up to one side of the protagonists, if that's the right word, future generations will only believe it was one side doing everything, and it was not. And unfortunately that's the way it happened, so that is why we took that decision of putting up plaques to INLA volunteers. (Belfast Teach Na Fáilte's founding member in interview with the author)

Reclaiming a Place in History for the INLA: The 1981 Hunger Strike

Sectional memories or 'counter-memories' often present an alternative view of the past to the 'version' promoted by the hegemonic or dominant narrative, claiming a more accurate or wider representation of history. As Zerubavel (1995: 10–11) points out in relation to Israeli counter-memories,

> this challenge not only addresses the symbolic realm, but obviously has direct political implications ... The commemoration of the past thus becomes a contested territory in which groups engaging in a political conflict promote competing views of the past in order to gain control over the political center or to legitimize a separatist orientation.

An exemplary case to examine the relationship between the Provisional movement's dominant narrative and the Republican Socialist sectional narrative is provided by the 1980–81 hunger strike. In 1981, ten Republican prisoners died in the Maze prison: seven Provisional IRA volunteers and three INLA volunteers.[4] Historically, however, the ideological differences between the two organizations have been underemphasized and the memory of the ten hunger strikers has been incorporated into the Provisional Republican narrative of resistance and struggle for independence as 'a watershed in modern Irish history credited with accelerating the growth of Sinn Fein' (National 1981 Hunger Strike Commemoration Committee 2006).[5]

A look at the landscape of memorialization in Belfast shows how the ten men are habitually remembered together, often in conjunction with Provisional IRA volunteers Michael Gaughan and Frank Stagg who died on hunger strike in 1974 and 1976 respectively. Of the six memorials in honour of the hunger strikers commissioned by groups that can be linked to the Provisional IRA and Sinn Féin, none officially recognize that three listed volunteers did not belong to the Provisional movement. In addition, the three INLA hunger strikers are also remembered on a plaque at the IRA County Antrim communal plot in Milltown Cemetery. Though this may seem if not normal at least justified, since all ten men died within 107 days of each other in similar circumstances and for the same political reason – the concession of political status to Republican prisoners – it is worth recalling that in post-conflict Northern Ireland a memorial is a statement of belonging and appropriation. Chapter 4 demonstrated that different organizations claim their volunteers 'in stone', whereas volunteers who died for a similar 'cause' but belonged to a different paramilitary group are excluded and 'forgotten'. The affiliation of the dead with the group that commissioned the memorial becomes, therefore, implicit unless otherwise stated, as in the case of the plaque mentioned at the beginning of this chapter. In an exercise of iconographic accretion, the symbolic capital provided by the unified and communal sacrifice of the hunger strikers overcomes ideological differences, and the fact that three volunteers belonged to a different organization is, if not forgotten, not emphasized in Provisional IRA/Sinn Féin memorials.

As a consequence, the Teach Na Fáilte Memorial Committee Belfast set out to 'reclaim' the memory of the three INLA volunteers who died on hunger strike. As an IRSP member stated in interview with the author,

> for us it was very, very important for ensuring that Patsy O'Hara and the other men were not lost in the great misconceiving of the hunger strike. It's not to say that there was any human difference between the ten men that died, there wasn't; but there were political differences there and it's important that the struggle that those volunteers raised, that was a revolutionary struggle, is not caught up in the great nationalist narrative.

The first public statement was made in 2000 with the joint unveiling of a hunger strike memorial and the North West Republican Socialist Plot in the grounds of Derry/Londonderry City Cemetery (Fig. 6.1).[6] Since 2001, a series of murals in memory of the three INLA hunger strikers have also been completed, both in Belfast and Derry/Londonderry, characterized

Figure 6.1 INLA communal plot, Derry/Londonderry City Cemetery
Source: Viggiani 2006

Figure 6.2 INLA mural in memory of the 1980–81 hunger strikers
Source: Viggiani 2006

by a red stars design on a bright yellow background (Fig. 6.2 illustrates an example of this in Shaws Road): this recurrent artistic device creates a stark stylistic contrast to Provisional IRA/Sinn Féin murals and establishes a distinctive and easily recognizable 'template' that leaves no doubt as to the group commissioning the artworks. In addition, a highly public space has been appropriated in Dungiven, with the unveiling of a memorial to hunger striker Kevin Lynch strategically positioned along the busy thoroughfare connecting the cities of Belfast and Derry/Londonderry (Fig. 6.3).

Conscious of its secondary position in the history of Irish Republicanism, the IRSM set out to achieve recognition through this memorial activity not of a primary, but of an equally important place in history for the INLA hunger strikers, thus accepting its role of 'sectional narrator' of this shared chapter of the wider Republican narrative of resistance and struggle against the British state. The ten men are remembered as a homogenous group by the INLA/IRSP because 'it is fitting [to] spare a thought for them all' (Murray 2006), but their differences in personal political

ideology and organizational affiliation are stressed at every commemorative occasion to avoid that 'the political story gets lost and you bulk
everybody in together' (Republican Socialist activist in interview with
the author) and that 'by default, people who never knew them assume
them to have been simply members of the broad Republican movement
and represented by the Irish Republican Army' (McAliskey 2002).

Unlike the dominant narrative that tends to absorb sectional threads
allowing them limited or partial acknowledgement, the counter-memory
cannot but recognize that there were 'many other Republicans in other
organizations who were good, decent, honest men and women who lost
their lives fighting against injustice . . . [and that] from whichever organizations volunteers came, their sacrifice should be honoured by us all'
(Ruddy 2003a). Occasionally, the IRSM sectional narrative assumes
oppositional tones when the legacy of the hunger strikers is invoked
against the current political direction of Sinn Féin's leadership. At the
unveiling ceremony of a mural in memory of Patsy O'Hara in Derry/
Londonderry, for example, the main speaker affirmed that

Figure 6.3 INLA Kevin Lynch memorial, Dungiven
Source: Viggiani 2008

recently it has been said that Patsy and his comrades would in all likelihood have supported the Good Friday Agreement. We cannot speak for all the hunger strikers, but we can speak for Patsy O'Hara, Kevin Lynch and Mickey Devine. They joined our movement to end British rule and establish a socialist republic. That is what they believed then . . . Others can change their views; that is their prerogative. We have not. And we do not believe Patsy, Kevin or Mickey would have either. (Murray 2006)

This contingency to become an openly defying oppositional narrative is, however, never wholly fulfilled, due to the heterogeneous nature of the IRSM and the limited political support and social mobilization it generates in Northern Ireland. For this reason, the sectional narrative portrayed by the Republican Socialist movement is generally tolerated by the dominant Provisional narrative and, to the best of this author's knowledge, there have been no public attempts to suppress it. The relationship is one of coexistence, facilitated by the shared nature of the hunger strikers' sacrifice, with the sectional narrative not deemed incompatible with the parameters of the dominant narrative, but almost acting as a specification of it. It is also possible that while the Republican Socialist is adamant to stress its political and ideological difference from the Provisional Irish Republican movement, the ideological 'halo' projected by the myth of the hunger strike must be safeguarded and, therefore, the projection of a too strong oppositional narrative that would tarnish such a halo is seen as counterproductive for the greater Republican good.

Advancing a Sectional Narrative of the Troubles: The Belfast Teach Na Fáilte's Memorial Programme

Unlike the hunger strikers, less prominent INLA volunteers were left unacknowledged before the formation of the Teach Na Fáilte Memorial Committee Belfast, or simply remembered as civilians, as in the case of volunteers Ronnie Bunting and Noel Little in the Provisional IRA Garden of Remembrance in Ballymurphy (Ballymurphy Gairdin Cuimhneachain, Viggiani 2013). As mentioned earlier, the main aims of the memorial committee were to 'give true recognition to our comrades . . . for what they were' (Murray 2003a) and to leave a permanent testimony and public acknowledgement of the contribution made by members of the IRSM to the cause of national liberation and the socialist struggle. A secondary aim, perhaps less structured but mirroring the motivation behind the promotion of local history projects by the Provisional movement, was to start an intragroup 'historical' inquiry into the circumstances surrounding the death of some of the volunteers and to reach a symbolic closure, for the families in particular. Thus, a relative of Noel Little, who was killed together with Ronnie Bunting on 15 October 1980 in an operation supposedly masterminded by the British SAS, points out that

> when you're engaged in struggle, you don't often get the liberty to enquire what's going on, what's happening, but it's all very fresh in a lot of the minds. And I suppose this [memorial programme] is an attempt to try and get that aspect of things together . . . that they didn't die for nothing . . . People start looking into cases and backgrounds . . . Republican Socialist people were killed in very dodgy circumstances, including my uncle Noel and Ronnie Bunting, and nobody has taken those cases on board . . . I don't know if we'll ever get there, but I think that the public acknowledgment of the people who were lost and the circumstances are very important.

According to Leerssen (2001: 220–21), both Catholics and Protestants in Northern Ireland have suffered from a form of 'traumatic remembrancing' – that is 'a wound-licking impulse which returns to, and revives, the painful memory in an ongoing recurrence' – resulting from the fact that 'injury or loss was initially unacknowledged, lacked proper "official" recognition and catharsis'. To deal successfully with trauma and achieve a symbolic closure with the past, the traumatic experience must be 'verbalized', put into discourse in 'a form of self-historicization' (ibid.: 221) and victims/survivors, including collective groups, must be able to see their 'uttered grief' addressed, acknowledged and respected. Memorials – together with other so-called 'symbolic acts of reparation', such as truth commissions, reburials, public apologies and compensation payments or other material acts of reparation – can therefore play a 'therapeutic' role both on a personal and communal level, for they verbalize and objectify formerly silenced memories (Hamber and Wilson 2003). Though they 'do not tell who pulled the trigger or who gave the order' – in the words of Little's relative – as a public enquiry might do, memorials can catalyse a symbolic closure both for individuals and social groups (i.e. the Republican Socialist movement); they act as a public acknowledgment that a person did not die in vain and as an 'official' recognition of the circumstances and reasons behind their death: they 'stabilize the ghosts, they domesticate them and tame them by representing the compensation for their death' (ibid.: 157). In addition, as seen in Chapter 5, memorials allow subsuming each individual death within a shared and standardized collective narrative of national struggle, which infers 'meaning' to the interpretation – and representation – of why they died, making their sacrifice worthwhile, a significant pebble in the long path for the advancement of the ideological greater 'Cause' of whichever movement they belonged to.

Finally, on a more politically strategic dimension for the Republican Socialist movement, the formation of the Teach Na Fáilte Memorial Committee Belfast was consciously seen as a way of maintaining control over the members of the Irish National Liberation Army and regulating their actions, especially in the latest phase of the peace process. Less structured and disciplined than the Provisional Republican movement, the IRSM has historically been prone to intragroup feuding and organizational splits; the lack of a clear strategic direction after 1998 – the INLA did not support the Good Friday Agreement, but agreed to call a halt to its military struggle after the referenda in May 1998 – was seen by many in the movement as cultivating a risk of defection in favour of smaller dissident Republican groups such as the Real IRA and Continuity IRA.[7] As a member of the memorial committee explained in interview with the author,

> that is a problem in its own; you have people there who went out and used the guns, but they are controlled because they are in a movement and they are told what way to go and have a vision, but if they are left to fester, the only thing they know is guns, so it wouldn't take too much for them to adjust their discipline . . . There is nothing worse than people who have been trained in a certain way of life and have nothing to do. If they are trained in a certain way, they go and look to do that way, but without being controlled.

The formation of the memorial committee was, therefore, intended as a reference point for INLA ex-combatants and as a mechanism to help them to channel their energies in a post-conflict setting towards a symbolic, rather than physical, continuation of the struggle: '[W]ith no war on, [the committee] gave people a focus to keep the whole bandwagon going . . . You keep going and you keep your wee groupings together rather than splinters . . . rather than let the thing fester' (Interview with a member of the memorial committee).

To these purposes, the committee has, since its inception in 2002, unveiled seven plaques in Belfast in memory of the twenty volunteers and comrades on the County Antrim IRSP/INLA Roll of Honour.[8] Funds were raised through voluntary donations from sympathetic individuals and businesses, evening social functions, raffles, internet auctions of handicrafts made by the Republican Socialist prisoners in Portlaoise and Castlereagh prisons, and the sale of an ex-prisoner's badge. A template design for the plaque was agreed and their locations determined by the committee, following the rule that volunteers' names would

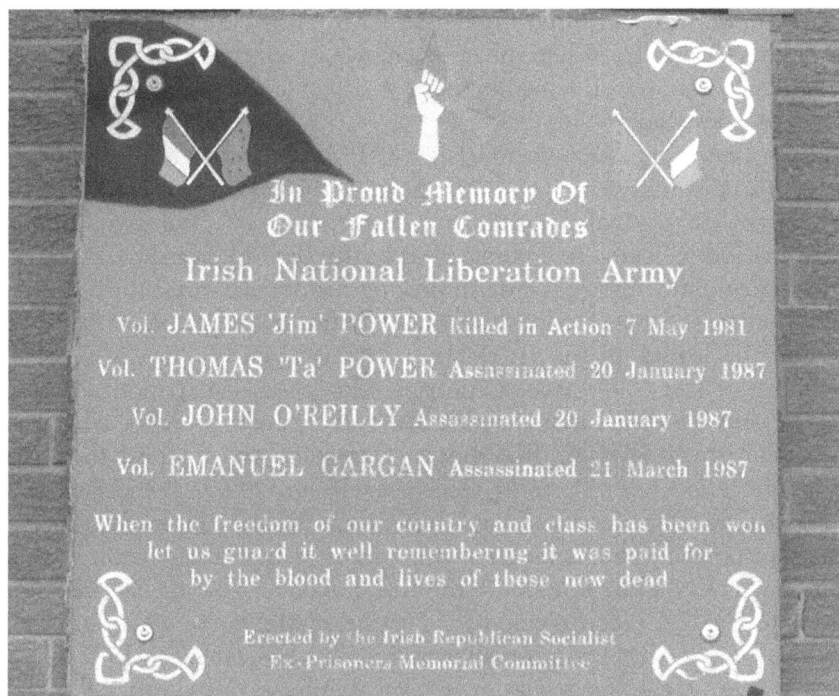

Figure 6.4 INLA plaque in memory of Power, Power, O'Reilly and Gargan
Source: Viggiani 2006

appear on the plaque for the area where they were born, raised or killed (Fig. 6.4).

INLA memorials also suggest a traditional Republican interpretation of the conflict as a struggle of self-determination against the British state, and they establish a clear symbolic connection with the nation state of Ireland through the language and iconography used. Volunteers Brendan McNamee and Miriam Daly, for example, 'remain an inspiration to everyone who believes in Irish freedom' (plaque no. 7); the Irish tricolour can be found on all seven plaques; five plaques present a Celtic motif (plaque nos. 1 and 3–6); and one plaque depicts the shields of the four provinces of Ireland (plaque no. 7). However, iconographic references to the national question are always accompanied by symbols linked to the socialist class struggle, thereby setting the IRSP/INLA ideology into stone. It is significant that the Irish tricolour appears on every plaque juxtaposed with a Starry Plough, the symbol of James Connolly's Irish Citizen Army. In addition, plaque nos. 5 and 6 depict the IRSM emblem – a rifle in a clenched left-handed fist with the five-pointed red star of socialism in the background – and plaque no. 6 bears the following quotation from Connolly: 'When the freedom of our country and class has been won let us guard it well remembering it was paid for by the blood and lives of those now dead'.

Like Provisional IRA memorials, IRSP/INLA memorials establish a symbolic continuity with pre-1969 phases of the Republican struggle, but where the Provisional Republican movement has its ideological forefathers in Wolfe Tone and Padraig Pearse, the IRSM places at the top of its iconographic totem pole the following historical figures: the socialist trade unionist James Connolly, founder of the Irish Citizens Army and one of the leaders of the 1916 Easter Rising; Liam Mellows, a founder member of the 1913 Irish Volunteers who participated in the Easter Rising and the War of Independence; and Seamus Costello, who was involved in the 1956–62 IRA Border Campaign and founded the Irish Republican Socialist Party in December 1974, having abandoned the ranks of the Official Republican movement.[9] Other important figures that are often 'evoked' alongside the fathers of Irish Republican socialism are James Larkin, founder of the Irish Labour Party, and Thomas 'Ta' Power, an INLA volunteer and IRSP member who wrote a famous essay on the history of the Irish Republican Socialist Movement in 1987 while imprisoned. However, some 'genealogical intersections' can be found between the Provisional and Republican Socialist movements: James Connolly and the Irish Citizens Army are often symbolically referred to on Provisional IRA/Sinn Féin memorials, while a quotation from Pearse can be found on an INLA commemorative plaque.[10]

Similarly to the Clonard Martyrs Memorial Garden, the language used in the inscriptions of INLA memorials also tends to demonize the 'enemy': thus, Joseph Craven is 'murdered' rather than 'killed' by Loyalists (plaque no. 2). As noted earlier, elements that undermine a social group's narrative about the past are often 'forgotten'. In the case of the INLA, the five volunteers who were killed as a result of the internal feud with the Irish People's Liberation Organization (IPLO), a small group of INLA veterans who splintered from the main organization in 1986, are simply remembered as having been 'assassinated' or 'killed in action';[11] also, Patrick Campbell is said to have been 'killed in action' during what was, instead, a supposedly drug-related dispute with a West Dublin criminal gang.

Unveiling Ceremonies

Typically held on Sundays on dates chosen to coincide as closely as possible with the anniversary of one of the commemorated individuals, the unveiling ceremonies of the first two plaques of the series were low-key

events. A short informal parade, opened by a three-man colour party carrying a Starry Plough flag, an Irish tricolour and a red flag of socialism,
led participants to the place of the unveiling. Galvanized by the high
level of attendance and support received for these early initiatives, the
group decided to make a more prominent statement and formalize their
presence. Starting with the unveiling ceremony of the third plaque of the
series in memory of volunteers Kearney and Campbell in January 2003,
the ceremony took the form that has become the traditional format of
INLA/IRSP commemorations to date: members of the movement parade
around the district in the 'civilianized' uniform of white shirt, black tie
and black trousers, and the colour party has been expanded to include
four additional people carrying the flags of the four provinces of Ireland
and a colour party sergeant who ensures the carriers march in step. Once
at the place of the unveiling, the ceremony unfolds according to the following running order: the chair's opening remarks are usually followed
by a family member of the deceased giving a short statement and then
unveiling the plaque, while the colour party's flags are lowered and a
piper's lament is played. After the laying of the wreaths, a prominent
speaker addresses the gathered crowd. The ceremony closes with the
chair's final remarks and the playing of the Irish national anthem. While
the extent to which Loyalist commemorations differ from Republican
ones will be investigated in the following chapters, it is important to
note here that, despite some variations, the format and style of IRSP/
INLA commemorations are similar to those organized by the Provisional
Republican movement.

Provisional Republican and Republican Socialist Commemorations

The historic continuity and ideological genealogy of the Republican
struggle is asserted by the Provisional movement through a series of ever
more elaborate and evocative iconographic elements, whereas the INLA/
IRSP continues to this day to establish its ideological connections with
the past through the use of a less sophisticated symbolism on memorials and flags. In recent years especially, an increased use of 'spectacle,
costume and theatricality' has been observed in Provisional Republican
commemorations (Brown and Viggiani 2009). For instance, in August
2006 columns of Republican ex-prisoners dressed as blanketmen and
women and as eighteenth-century United Irishmen marched along the
Falls Road on the occasion of a large commemorative parade and rally
organized in Belfast to mark the twenty-fifth anniversary of the 1981

hunger strike; along the route they passed a 'series of street theatre enact-
ments and tableaux . . . each depicting events from the Hunger Strike
period familiar to members of the Republican community', such as police
raids, interrogations, prison protests and a satirically rendered trial of
the infamous Diplock courts (Brown and Viggiani 2009; *An Phoblacht* 17
August 2006).

Differences between the two strands of Republicanism are also evident
in the content and tone of the main speech that, in the tradition of Easter
Sunday commemorations, represents the climax of local commemorative
ceremonies. As noted in Chapter 4, commemorative events in conjunction with permanent forms of memorialization have assumed an ever-
increasing importance in post-conflict Northern Ireland as a means of
projecting 'fluid' ideological narratives, able to advance evolving political
projects while reassuring base support and providing insulation from the
attacks of rivals, sceptics and doubters. As Brown (2009: 10–11) aptly
summarizes,

> rather than simply drawing a line under conflict, memorialization has
> been used as a means of negotiating the Republican and Loyalist proj-
> ects through this difficult [peace] process . . . It can be used to reassure
> grassroots members and doubters or to anchor new political directions by
> embedding them in the past. It has also served to maintain the cohesion of
> Loyalist and Republican political projects and to maintain links with their
> communities and beyond.
>
> Commemoration has also helped to repel challenges to legitimacy
> and authority, and it has been used to rededicate, reinvigorate and recast
> traditional tenets of Loyalist and Republican ideology.

While the Provisional Republican movement has faced the daunting task
of averting accusations of 'selling out' by carefully stressing a continuity of
beliefs, values and objectives despite a major shift in their tactics, as they
permanently put aside the Armalite to fight only with the ballot box, the
Republican Socialist movement has progressively taken upon itself the
role of oppositional narrator with its critical analysis of the political situation in contemporary Northern Ireland. The latter part of this chapter
turns to investigate how a parallel, although opposing, narrative to the
Provisional Republican dominant narrative is constructed at Republican
Socialist commemorations, with particular attention to the main speech
that represents the openly political element of these events.

During both Provisional Republican and Republican Socialist commemorations, a party member or veteran of the movement takes the centre
of the stage to address the congregation after the laying of wreaths, which
are usually donated by various party branches, paramilitary organizations'

brigades, local or national sympathizing groups and families. After a brief eulogy for each individual commemorated on the memorial, often recalling both their personal life and their public/political life as a volunteer, and the customary thanks to the families and the organizers, the key speaker invariably reaffirms the doctrine or philosophy of the movement – whether Provisional Republican or Republican Socialist – and recalls its history and diachronic development. The ideological forefathers are evoked to look benignly upon the gathered 'sons and daughters', and a sense of connection and identification with those now gone who belonged to the same 'imagined community' is established by stressing the unaltered persistence of beliefs and commitment to the cause throughout successive generations despite changes in tactics, thus ensuring a symbolic continuity through time. In the case of the IRSM, the courage and faith in the socialist cause that prompted James Connolly to 'lead the linen workers in Belfast in the 1907 strike . . . to form the Citizen Army to protect the Dublin workers from the scabs, employers, and police in 1913; . . . and to march into the GPO on Easter Monday 1916 to begin the Irish Revolution' is, for instance, the same that inspired Miriam Daly and Brendan McNamee 'to do what they did'; that same faith will encourage the comrades and friends of today 'to be Republicans . . . to be socialists . . . to oppose imperialism wherever we find it . . . and to organize to oppose [injustice]' (Ruddy 2003b). Group cohesion and a shared collective identification that conceptually stretch over centuries are thus achieved.

Moreover, as explained in Chapter 4, the remembrance of past members of one's imagined 'national' community who fulfilled the patriotic 'oath' of loyalty by sacrificing their lives for the common good binds the living to a moral obligation to follow their example, compelled by a sense of indebtedness and gratitude towards them. Thus, at the unveiling of the plaque in memory of Ferguson and O'Neill, Eddie McGarrigle felt that, although like many at the event he personally did not know them, he was 'indebted to them because they died so that I, and each of us gathered here, had the basic right to be a Republican Socialist' (McGarrigle 2003). While both permanent and performative forms of memorialization serve an educational function in that they materialize history, remembering and contextualizing the sacrifice of volunteers so their deaths were not in vain, the value most sought by organizers lies in the inspirational appeal they have for present and future generations: the Republican heroes' names are carved in stone for posterity, to set an example for others to live up to, if not their deeds, their integrity, dignity and devotion. IRSP Ard Chomairle (National Executive) member Terry Harkin at the unveiling of the plaque in memory of volunteers Kearney and Campbell opened his speech as follows:

in today's hectic world with everything happening so fast it is little wonder that the youth of today, spoon fed on a continuous diet of wall-to-wall trash TV and designer music to deaden the soul have swallowed whole the manufactured cardboard heroes, held up by a partisan mass media for them to admire ... As our children walk past this plaque many of them will be more concerned with 'Rave' culture than the plight of the community in North Belfast, where kids of the same age or younger are blackmailed into spying on their defenders. They'll stand under it and talk about 'Big Brother' as their every move is observed by the Ascendancy's cameras. They would be wise to emulate both Patrick and Mickey, look beyond the hype and have something more to believe in. (Harkin 2003)

However, it is the ability to provide an ideologically reassuring setting for the projection of evolving political narratives that renders commemorative events in post-conflict Northern Ireland the preferred arena to negotiate new political programmes without incurring accusations of 'selling out' the true spirit of Irish Republicanism.

Opposing the Dominant Republican Narrative: Post-1998 Republican Socialist Rhetoric

Similarly to the Provisional Republican movement's leadership that has employed the emotive 'shields' of legitimacy emanating from the spirits of the past to advance its post-conflict strategy, the IRSM has also made use of commemoration to anchor its new post-1998 political direction. Not represented during the multi-party talks that brought about the 1998 Agreement, and excluded from the various power exercises that succeeded until the current power-sharing government co-led by Sinn Féin and the DUP, the Republican Socialist movement's position was one of rejection of the Agreement while supporting a military ceasefire. Since the INLA ceasefire in August 1998, the efforts of the IRSM's leadership have been aimed both internally at maintaining organizational cohesion and externally at providing an oppositional critique to mainstream Republicanism. On the one hand, INLA units must be reassured that, despite no change in beliefs and aims, armed struggle has to be replaced by a more prominent political position for the IRSP, utilizing a rhetoric that resembles that of early Sinn Féin political orations. As McGarrigle (2003) cries from the platform, 'whilst our methods may change and alter, our commitment to the freedom of our country and of our class will never diminish. The INLA and the IRSP have not, and will not, go away until the objective of a socialist republic is achieved'. Echoing one of the reasons at the heart of the formation of the Teach Na Fáilte memorial committee, organizational cohesion becomes a particularly sensitive issue in a post-conflict setting for a movement historically prone to internal schism and vicious intra and intergroup killings. The importance of forgetting 'the quarrels of the past, especially when those quarrels were between former comrades and fellow Republicans' is periodically remarked upon and, while recognition is granted to the pain inflicted by Republicanism 'on its own people' and to the fact that 'no one Republican organization holds the high moral ground in this regard, [but] we are all guilty', the recurring message is one of unity, respect and a constructive confrontation of opinions, rather than arms in the 'interests of the Irish People' (ibid.).

> Whatever disagreements we all have, whatever quarrels that may arise within the various Republican traditions, be warned friends and comrades, that those who would turn such disagreements into armed confrontations, are in effect doing the work of our enemy, British Imperialism. Let us as Republican Socialists heal, where possible, the divisions of the past; let us draw a line in the sand and embrace each other as comrades; let us build the Republican Socialist Movement that our fallen comrades died in defense of. (ibid.)

The unanimous voice of the leadership encourages supporters to convey all their energies and enthusiasm in the exercise of socialist and community politics, since 'it has been clear for some time that the vast majority of the Irish people favour Republicans using peaceful methods of struggle [and] that has to be respected for we all realize that different situations require different methods of struggle' (Ruddy 2003a).

However, on the other hand, the Republican Socialist movement looks outwards to express a sectional, at times oppositional, voice that counters Sinn Féin's confident tone that 'we are closer today to our goal of Irish unity than at any other time in our history' (Kelly 2007). Although the organizers of the memorial committee are adamant about reminding the main speakers that, in the words of one of them in interview with the author, 'they are there to commemorate and not to castigate', the narrative projected at commemorations portrays the Republican Socialist movement as the true defender of the ideal of a united socialist Irish republic in the light of Sinn Féin's 'betrayal'. While the need to maintain a peaceful setting is reaffirmed, Republican Socialists reflect upon the 'set back' of the Republican and class struggles, since Sinn Féin are seen as having 'forgotten everything James Connolly wrote about' when they 'signed up to the new, liberal economic agenda that . . . will take [Ulster] back to capitalism' (McMonagle 2007). As Bernadette McAliskey (2002) reminisces following a police raid on Stormont, there was a day when [Sinn Féin MLA] Gerry Kelly would have walked out on his heel and told them where to stick their Assembly. There was a day when [Sinn Féin MLA] Bairbre de Brun would have walked down the steps of Stormont pulling the door behind her and saying, 'When you are serious about democracy, call me back'.

IRSP member Terry Harkin (2003) echoes that statement, further affirming that

> Stormont is a farce, a charade, a joke! A place for place-seekers, for the gin and tonic set – for the great and the good, for the wannabes and for the has-beens, a place for the small minded, for the YES men and women to swan about in. It is an obscenity for any self-respecting Republican to give credence to that administration in the White House on the hill.

Following the examples of Connolly, Costello and all the dead Republican Socialist martyrs conjured up, it is the Republican Socialist movement that 'constitute[s] the people who can't be bought, who can't be fooled, who can't be intimidated . . . we constitute the soul of socialism in this country: we constitute the spirit of Republicanism in this country' (McAliskey 2002).

Applying Ashplant, Dawson and Roper's theoretical framework to Northern Ireland, this chapter has illustrated how the IRSM has attempted to project a sectional narrative of the conflict in contrast to the Provisional movement's dominant narrative and to reclaim a parallel, if not equal, place in history for INLA volunteers. In an exemplification of how narratives about the past can adapt themselves to contemporary historical and political circumstances, the Republican Socialist narrative, while normally acting as a non-threatening specification of the mainstream Republican narrative, becomes at times oppositional, assuming critical tones towards the present political direction of the Provisional movement. In particular during commemorative events, the forefathers of Irish (Socialist) Republicanism are invoked to foster intragroup cohesion and give legitimacy to the IRSM as the true heir of the ideal of a 32-county socialist republic. The following two chapters turn their attention to Loyalist forms of memorialization and focus on the interaction between memorials and rituals held around them in the process of anchoring new political directions through the spirits of the past. Chapter 7 follows the diachronic development of memorial activity around three UVF murals in Disraeli Street from the early 1990s to the present, investigating how the UVF has succeeded in constructing a dominant version of the conflict, in particular through the use of the 'myth of the

Somme', and how such narrative has changed and adapted itself to shifting historical and political circumstances.

Notes

1. Republican Socialist muralist Gerard Foster, speaking after the completion in 2008 of the mural in memory of INLA Volunteers Brendan McNamee and Miriam Daly in the Andersonstown area of West Belfast (*Spotlight* 2008: 1).
2. It is interesting to note that, as far this author is aware, this plaque represents the only example where a member of a paramilitary organization has been officially commemorated – i.e. his military role has been recognized – on a memorial commissioned by a different paramilitary group or an association of a different political orientation. For the unveiling ceremony, see 'Belfast 1981 Victims Remembered' (2001).
3. The distinction between 'volunteer' and 'comrade' on the IRSP/INLA Roll of Honour depends upon the number of years of commitment in the IRSM.
4. The three INLA volunteers were: Patsy O'Hara (died 21 May 1981), Kevin Lynch (died 1 August 1981) and Mickey Devine (died 20 August 1981).
5. Ideologically, the main difference between the two organizations is that whilst the Provisional IRA interpreted the Northern Irish question mainly as a war of national liberation against the imperialistic British state, the IRSP/INLA considered the national question in the six counties to be inextricably linked with the socialist class struggle throughout the island of Ireland.
6. This ten-foot-high sculpture of a paramilitary in combat clothing, scarf, beret and dark glasses sparked heated controversy and calls for its removal by DUP members ('Call Made to Remove INLA Monument' 2007).
7. The two groups received renewed media coverage in March 2009, after the Real IRA killed two British soldiers at Massereene Barracks in Antrim on 7 March and the Continuity IRA shot dead Constable Stephen Carroll, the first member of the PSNI to be killed in Northern Ireland, in Craigavon, Co. Armagh, on 9 March. See 'Real IRA Was behind Army Attack' (2009) and 'Continuity IRA Shot Dead Officer' (2009).
8. For an individual description of the seven INLA plaques' layout, see Viggiani 2013: Bunting Ronnie and Little Noel – INLA (plaque no. 1); Craven Joseph – INLA (plaque no. 2); Kearney Michael and Campbell Patrick – INLA (plaque no. 3); Ferguson Hugh and O'Neill Hugh – INLA (plaque no. 4); Loughran, Campbell, McLarnon, McCann, Tumelty, Gallagher and Dornan – INLA (plaque no. 5); Power, Power, O'Reilly and Gargan – INLA (plaque no. 6); and McNamee Brendan and Daly Miriam – INLA (plaque no. 7).
9. A bronze relief portrait of Seamus Costello can be found at the entrance of the IRSM headquarters on the Falls Road.
10. 'If you strike us down now, we shall rise again and renew the fight. You cannot conquer Ireland. You cannot extinguish the Irish passion for freedom. If our deed has not been sufficient to win freedom, then our children will win it by a better deed', on plaque no. 5.
11. The five INLA volunteers killed in the feud with the IPLO are: Gino Gallagher, Thomas Power, John O'Reilly, Michael Kearney and Emmanuel Gargan.

Chapter 7

THE 1913 UVF AND THE MYTH OF THE SOMME

Constructing a Loyalist 'Golden Age'

≥•≤

In Flanders fields the poppies blow
Between the crosses, row on row,
That mark our place; and in the sky
The larks, still bravely singing, fly
Scarce heard amid the guns below.

We are the Dead. Short days ago
We lived, felt dawn, saw sunset glow,
Loved and were loved, and now we lie
In Flanders fields.

Take up our quarrel with the foe:
To you from failing hands we throw
The torch; be yours to hold it high.
If ye break faith with us who die
We shall not sleep, though poppies grow
In Flanders fields.
                    – John McCrea, *In Flanders Fields*, 1915

We have examined so far how the two main Republican paramilitary groups make use of memory to project a narrative – either dominant or sectional – that legitimizes their historical presence and their military and political actions in Northern Ireland. The following chapters turn to

Loyalist forms of memorialization, investigating, in particular, the relationship between memorials and the commemorative rituals that periodically take place around them. Drawing from Smith's definition of 'Golden Age' and its significance in shaping a group's collective memory (Smith 1997), this chapter investigates how the Ulster Volunteer Force (UVF), one of the two main Loyalist paramilitary organizations in Northern Ireland, has succeeded in projecting a credible dominant narrative of the conflict in opposition to the Republican 'version': tracing their lineage directly to the 1913 UVF and appropriating the 'commemorative density' attached to the Battle of the Somme, they have established a powerfully legitimizing Loyalist 'Golden Age' that vouches for their historical presence and ideological legitimacy in Northern Ireland. This chapter also follows the memorial activity carried out by the UVF throughout the years, in particular the annual commemorations held at three murals in Disraeli Street from the early 1990s to the present day, and highlights how the political and ideological message conveyed at these events has changed in relation to shifting historico-political contexts, corroborating the theoretical stance that sees memory as fundamentally shaped by the present rather than the past.

'Lest We Forget': Loyalist Landscape of Memorialization

As seen in Chapter 4, a primary difference between Republican and Loyalist 'modes of memory' lies in the interpretation of the nature and meaning of the Northern Irish conflict, duly reflected in their respective memorial activity: for Republicans, it is a struggle of national self-determination, an anti-imperialistic war against the British state and its military presence in Ireland, maintained with the co-participation of other pro-British agents; for Loyalists, a civil war, a prolonged reactionary defence against many attempts to weaken or sever the constitutional tie with Great Britain (Shirlow and McEvoy 2008). This 'under siege' mentality often observed with regard to the Protestant community in Northern Ireland, together with the perception that the 1998 Good Friday Agreement represented a defeat for Unionism (Hayward and Mitchell 2003), is somewhat reflected in the format and more militaristic tone that the Loyalist landscape of memorialization has assumed in post-conflict Northern Ireland.[1] Unlike Republican memorials that often take the shape of gardens of remembrance – in some cases with fountains and greenery – open to the public until sunset, Loyalist memorials are generally more enclosed, often surrounded by fences and locked gates, and resemble miniaturized strongholds that are seldom accessible to the public, though more recent Loyalist memorials are more spacious and offer some seating facilities.

Whereas Republicans have set in stone their century-long unwavering symbolic identification with the nation (state) of Ireland and cultural confidence in their Catholic and Gaelic roots, Loyalists partake of the confused 'national' identity theorized for Ulster Protestants: they are 'Irish and not Irish, defender of Ulster as ideal, British but not resident in Britain, not this and not that but always Protestant and at risk' (Bowyer Bell 1996: 115). Despite some attempts by radical thinkers to advocate for an independent Ulster and shape an Ulster identity,[2] Loyalist symbolic affirmations of identity remain, however, firmly British – if not the nation state of the United Kingdom, an imagined, ideal Britishness. The physical structure of Loyalist memorials and the format of their annual commemorations resemble the British Commonwealth's Great War forms and practices of memorialization. Many Loyalist memorials feature, for instance, a central memorial stone that 'invokes the Stone of Remembrance found in all Commonwealth and War Graves Commission cemeteries' (Graham and Shirlow 2002: 895). In addition, Loyalist 'memorial murals usually mimic cenotaph displays, not only in portraying the Loyalist with bowed head and upturned rifle, but also in the accompanying captions: "Lest we forget" or "At the going down of the sun, we will remember them"' (Rolston 2003b: 7); depicting volunteers with heads bowed and weapons at rest, in fact, emulates the pose adopted by the Guard of Honour at official British Commonwealth Armistice Day commemorations (Jarman 1997). Finally, both the UVF and UDA make widespread use of iconographic references to Great Britain and the Empire, such as the Union flag and the red poppy, on their memorials, flags and emblems.

Historically less organized than mainstream Republicanism, both on a military and political level, Loyalist organizations reflect this lack of a centralized structure in the attainment and coordination of local memorial programmes. Despite the formation of Loyalist ex-prisoners' groups from the mid-1990s – most notably the Ex-Prisoners' Interpretive Centre (EPIC) in Belfast for ex-prisoners from a UVF and Red Hand Commando background and their families[3] – there is no tradition of purposely formed memorial committees, as seen for Republican ex-prisoners, with weekly meetings, bulletins and bespoke commemorative publications.[4] EPIC, for example, oversees the UVF memorial programme, specifically in the Shankill and Woodvale areas, but, unlike Republican ex-prisoners' groups, does not directly commission the painting of murals or erection of memorials, nor does it materially carry out their execution, but simply acts as a reference point, for instance, to liaise with governmental agencies and other paramilitary groups, in particular the UDA, in the recent phase of re-imaging of Loyalist neighbourhoods.[5] Loyalist memorial projects are habitually organized and carried out on a local basis, directly overseen by ex-prisoners and/or community workers based in the area, and are less grandiose and publicized than their Republican counterparts. In many instances, they have been the result of individual initiatives rather than the orchestrated effort of structured collectivities. Despite high levels of interest and in some cases of ownership, local community involvement is less widespread in Protestant areas, both in terms of funding and active involvement in the memorial-building process (see Chapter 9). Possibly due to this lack of structural organization, the collective narratives projected by Loyalist paramilitary groups are somewhat more problematic and at times confused in their articulation than mainstream Republicanism, but they are nonetheless as impactful and important to investigate.

'From the Battlefields of the Somme to the Barricades of the Shankill': Borrowing Legitimacy

According to Smith (1997: 48–51), memories of a social group's 'Golden Age' fulfil its need for authenticity, help to define its 'true spirit' and establish a sense of continuity between generations, reminding its members 'of their past greatness and hence their inner worth . . . [and] collective dignity' (ibid.: 50). The quest for and symbolic return to the 'Golden Age' of the community we belong to imply that 'despite the ravages of time and the vicissitudes of social change, we are descendants of the heroes and sages of that great age' (ibid.). From the Pharaonic past in modern Egypt to the 'Old Russia' in nineteenth-century Russia, from the Founding Fathers of white America to the splendour of the Aztec civilization in modern Mexico (ibid.), emerging nation states, ethnic and social groups alike have founded their historical, political and ideological legitimacy on a specific historico-mythological epoch or event which condenses and incarnates the highest qualities and identity traits of the collectivity.[6]

In Ulster Unionist history, it is the years between 1912 and 1916 that provide 'a central organizing mythology' which in latter day Unionist/Loyalist oratory and iconography came to represent 'a "Golden Age" of solidarity, communal mustering . . . and an acceptable, adventurous sense of political militancy' (Brown 2007: 712). Threatened by the implementation in 1912 of the Third Home Rule Bill, which would establish a self-governing Nationalist parliament in Dublin, the Ulster Protestant community mobilized across class and religious denominations as never before in history. On 28 September 1912 – a day commemorated to the present as 'Ulster Day' – around half a million Unionists, led by leaders Sir Edward Carson and Sir James Craig, signed the Ulster's Solemn League and Covenant, pledging

> to stand by one another in defending, for ourselves and our children, our cherished position of equal citizenship in the United Kingdom, and in using all means which may be found necessary to defeat the present conspiracy to set up a Home Rule Parliament in Ireland. (PRONI D627/429/95)

In January 1913, a civic militia under the name of Ulster Volunteer Force was set up. This organization enjoyed a wide support and membership, supposedly numbering a hundred thousand men, and its leadership had close links – when it was not directly drawn from – the Ulster Unionist Party ruling establishment and the Orange Order. At the outbreak of the First World War, the original UVF reinforced the British Army ranks as a distinct bloc – the 36th (Ulster) Division – and proved its bravery and patriotic spirit on the first day of the Battle of the Somme, on 1 July 1916, when it advanced the furthest of any other British Army unit but was almost decimated. The Battle of the Somme instantly came to be interpreted by the wider Protestant/Unionist community as the epitome of Ulster loyalty to Britain, with *The Belfast Newsletter*, soon after the battle, carrying headlines such as 'Ulster's Sacrifice for Empire' (McIntosh 1999: 14); more importantly, it provided Unionist mythology with an iconic originary blood sacrifice during which the 'paradigmatic model of the ideal Ulsterman' was forged (Officer 2001: 182).

After the First World War, the original UVF was disbanded. In 1966, however, a newly formed armed group appropriated the name, symbols and crest of the 1913 organization.[7] The modern UVF was born 'for God and Ulster' and has profusely reiterated through its commemorative activity its *direct* lineage from the homonymous older organization – although the historical links between the two are in reality rather tenuous. An analysis of contemporary UVF murals in Belfast shows that murals commemorating the Battle of the Somme and the 36th Ulster Division have substituted depictions of King Billy and other traditional Loyalist imagery as the most substantial corpus of historical murals.[8] This group of murals usually depicts members of the old UVF and soldiers of the 36th Ulster Division counterpoised with modern paramilitary figures, immortalized on a shared timeless and aspatial battlefield, crouched in trenches or marching to their death over the top of a hill, similar to the original depictions of the Battle of the Somme.[9]

The mural in memory of the (modern) UVF No. 4 Platoon, A Company, 1st Battalion, Belfast, in Glenwood Street, near the Shankill Road, for instance, pictures a battlefield strewn with headstones, half

Figure 7.1 UVF 4 Platoon, A Company, 1st Battalion, West Belfast mural
Source: Viggiani 2006

marked with the 36th Ulster Division emblem and half with the modern UVF emblem (Fig. 7.1). On the left-hand side, a First World War soldier and a black-clad hooded paramilitary figure pay their respects with bowed heads and upturned rifles, while on the right-hand side a modern UVF volunteer fires a volley of shots over the graves; in the background two volunteers lower their flags in sign of respect while a piper sounds his lament. A headstone portraying an emblem formed by the conjoining of the 36th Ulster Division and modern UVF emblems with the caption 'Lest We Forget' and the 1966 UVF logo surrounded by a wreath of red poppies form the centrepiece of the mural.[10] Modern UVF volunteers are thus presented as the embodiment of Ulster's early volunteers' 'true' self and spirit: 'from the battlefields of the Somme to the barricades of the Shankill . . . the same blood courses through our veins, as we [the modern UVF] breath [sic] the same air and are nurtured by the same families and communities' (*Combat* [November/December] 2005: 12). An illegal paramilitary organization, whose mass support and political voice is constantly declining, the modern UVF 'borrows' legality from the widely supported and respected 1913 UVF, thus claiming a 'legitimate' place in the wider Protestant/Unionist history by presenting itself as 'a natural organic growth budding out from the parent stem of mainstream Unionism' (Brown 2007: 714). A powerful symbolic connection with mainstream Unionism is, for instance, established through the memorial built in Cherryville Street, off Woodstock Road, in remembrance of the UVF 2nd Battalion Willowfield, East Belfast Regiment (Fig. 4.2). Two large memorial stones, mirroring each other, remember, respectively, the members of the Willowfield Battalion of the 1913 UVF who fought in France during the First World War as part of the 36th Ulster Division and the equally 'brave men of Ulster' of the 1966 UVF who 'without favour or reward . . . fought militant Republicanism on it's own terms'. It is, however, the location of this memorial that opens up further associations with the wider Protestant/Unionist history and invests this site with a higher symbolic significance. As one of the memorial stones informs passers-by, the memorial was erected where the old Willowfield Unionist Club, a drill hall for the old UVF that was officially opened in 1913 by Ulster Unionist leader Sir Edward Carson, once stood. An ulterior layer of meaning is added by the fact that (modern) UVF volunteer Robert Seymour was killed by the IRA in 1987 while working in one of the shops that replaced the old Unionist hall after it was demolished in the early 1980s. The site, therefore, 'wraps the old Ulster Volunteers, the dead of the First World War, mainstream Unionism's one time embrace of militancy and the martyrdom of a modern paramilitary member together in one ideologically packed space', creating a 'politically imagined kinship across decades' between the Unionist establishment and the 36th Ulster Division on the one hand, and modern illegal Loyalism on the other (Brown 2007: 715–16).

'Politicized' memory, however, 'establishes itself as not only a source of a sense of lineage and inheritance, but also as identities' sole justification and legitimization' (Misztal 2003: 47). Unlike the mainstream Unionist narrative that has 'forgotten' its early-twentieth-century militancy, the sacrifice of the old UVF at the Battle of the Somme has provided the modern UVF with a powerful 'beacon of resistance' that ultimately justifies the organization's military actions during the Troubles, giving them 'a mandate for the defence of Ulster and its people' (*Combat* [November/December] 2005: 12).

> Little did our forefathers realise that what they, as the Ulster Volunteer Force, began so many years ago, would be emulated and indeed finalised, decades later, in the highways and by-ways of modern day Ulster. They gave their lives for the Cause in 1916, as did Ulster's Volunteers in the

recent conflict from which we are emerging . . . With time, the uniform, the Battlefields and the enemies have changed . . . [but] Ulster's resistance throughout the century has been as one. (*The Purple Standard* [May/June] 2007: 1; *Combat* [November/December] 2005: 13)

Thus, the necessity of the old UVF to take up arms for the United Kingdom's wider sake and freedom, and their proneness to die for a higher ideal – loyalty to the Crown and the State – finds historical repetition in the necessity of the modern UVF to take up arms to defend Ulster, its freedom and right to remain British, against the more recent attacks of Irish Republicanism, and to pay the ultimate sacrifice 'for God and Ulster'. Uncovering and fostering this political and ideological genealogy through its commemorative activity, the modern UVF waves back through history an unbroken line of commitment to the 'Cause', 'ageless virtue' and 'timeless values of honour' (*Combat* [November/December] 2005: 13), in an attempt to show that 'our struggle has been a noble one' (ibid.). A significant example of this is the four-panel mural in Canmore Street, off the Shankill Road, painted in 2002 (Fig. 7.2), each

Figure 7.2 UVF The People's Army mural
Source: Viggiani 2006

panel of which depicts a military 'chapter' in the history of the UVF: the training of its first volunteers in 1912; the Battle of the Somme; the defence of the Protestant community in 1969 when the 'Troubles' erupted; finally, the present ideological position – the readiness to take arms again in case any concession towards a united Ireland is made. The thread linking these four images in time, legitimacy and aim is further underlined by the central caption 'The Peoples Army 1912–2002 – 90 Years of Resistance'.

Mainstream Unionism, Republicanism and the Modern UVF Narrative

The narrative projected by the UVF posits an ambiguous and dialectical relationship between modern Loyalism and mainstream Unionism: by positioning itself as the direct descendant of the old UVF, the modern UVF attempts to 'conquer' a legitimate place within the wider Protestant/Unionist narrative of the Northern Irish (nation) state, but simultaneously seeks moral justification for its militarism, long 'forgotten' and condemned by Unionism. In particular, the sacrifice of the 36th Ulster Division at the Battle of the Somme is concurrently interpreted as the epitome of Ulster's loyalty to Britain – in accordance with the wider Unionist/Protestant interpretation – and as an example of patriotic courage and resistance that justifies Loyalist paramilitary actions during the Troubles. Moreover, in recent years, the modern UVF's narrative has also assumed oppositional tones in relation to wider Unionism, expressing criticism of that same political tradition of which it wishes to partake. It is interesting to note how the myth of the Unionist/Loyalist 'Golden Age' is evoked to advocate that modern Loyalism remains the sole and true defender of British Ulster, in light of the recent political developments that saw the Unionist DUP agreeing to a power-sharing government with Republicans after decades of refusal at the cry of 'Ulster Says No'. Although the Protestant people of Ireland pledged, when signing the Ulster Covenant, that 'as long as they drew breath, there would never be Home Rule in this land', 'the principles and traditions of Ulster are slowly being eroded by those in Government' and some Loyalists may rightly say that 'as a result of Government in power at present we *have* effectively been sold down the river to Ireland, by those who would shout the loudest and promise the most' (The Purple Standard [September] 2007: 1). To the then Unionist First Minister Reverend Ian Paisley, who led the government with Sinn Féin Deputy First Minister Martin McGuinness, the editor of The Purple Standard compellingly reminds that it was armed Loyalist paramilitaries in the form of the Ulster Clubs who guarded the City Hall on the day of the signing of the Covenant. It was Loyalist paramilitaries who formed the 36th Ulster Division and sacrificed their all at the Somme and other WWI battles. It was Loyalist paramilitaries (and not your 'clever' negotiating, bellowing or threats), that unreservedly defeated the Republican Movement, and First Minister, it will be the Loyalist paramilitaries who will bravely step forward once again, should their people call! (ibid.)

The UVF's narrative, however, exists not only in relationship to mainstream Unionism, but also in opposition to the Republican 'version' of the Northern Irish conflict. Recalling Papadakis's theorization of the use of a historical narrative in the representation of the past (see Chapter 4), the Battle of the Somme and the struggle of the modern-day UVF reveal their full meaning only if treated as components ('events') of an overarching narrative that articulates a certain story ('a history'). Far from being an independent 'memory cluster', they become chapters of the century-long Protestant narrative of resistance against any attempts to weaken the union with Great Britain, of which the 'Troubles' are the most recent phase. As in 1688–89, 1690 and 1916, the conflict that broke out in 1969 is interpreted as the umpteenth attempt of the 'traditional enemy' – Catholic Irish Nationalism/Republicanism – to coerce the Protestant population into a united Ireland; the actions of the modern UVF are, therefore, justified as the umpteenth historical contingency when 'Ulster saw its duty to resist' (*Combat* [November/December] 2005: 8).

In by gone days of yore, the brave 13 closed the gates of Derry, 'gainst King James' rebel hordes ~ **the cry, No Surrender!** On 28th September 1912, Sir Edward Carson signed the Solemn League and Covenant, again the cry was **No Surrender!** We have withstood Two World Wars, four decades of IRA atrocities all across the UK . . . But we, the people of this land, are still united as one and our cry is still No Surrender! (ibid., bold in the original)

Therefore, references to the 'Golden Age' of the 1913 UVF and the Battle of the Somme are used by the modern UVF to project a narrative of historical legitimacy and ideological legitimation, both in relation to mainstream Unionism and Republicanism.

While the way in which the myth of the Somme is regularly evoked at UVF commemorations will be discussed later, this chapter now turns its attention to the periodical commemorative activity that takes place around three murals in memory of modern UVF volunteers in the Woodvale area of West Belfast: specifically, a diachronic analysis of memorial activity around these murals from the early 1990s to the present will highlight how the political and ideological message conveyed by the UVF leadership at these annual commemorative events has changed in relation to shifting historico-political contexts.

Disraeli Street: An Iconic Cluster of Memory

On the morning of 2 September 1989, UVF volunteer Brian Robinson was shot dead from close range by a female soldier; he was making his escape, together with another man, minutes after killing Catholic Patrick McKenna in the Ardoyne area when their motorcycle was rammed near Flax Street, off the Crumlin Road, by an unmarked car carrying an undercover British Army surveillance unit who had witnessed the incident.

On 16 June 1994, UVF 'Lieutenant Colonel' Trevor King was standing at the junction of Spiers Place and the Shankill Road, talking to fellow UVF volunteers Colin Craig, David Hamilton and a third man, when an unmasked INLA gunman got out of a car and fired several shots at them, killing Craig instantly. Hamilton died three days later, while Trevor King fought for his life in hospital for three weeks and was eventually taken off life support machines on 9 July 1994.

Six years later, on 23 August 2000, during the Loyalist feud between the UVF and the UDA, 22-year-old YCV volunteer Samuel Rockett was visiting his girlfriend and baby daughter in Summer Street in the Oldpark area when he was shot dead by UFF gunmen in retaliation for the killing of UDA Bobby Mahood and Jackie Coulter, despite having received reassurances that he was not considered a target.[11]

Three commemorative murals (with plaques) in their memory were painted alongside one another in Disraeli Street, Woodvale, each a few months after the volunteers' death occurred (Figs 7.3, 7.4 and 7.5).[12] Some local residents and activists who were interviewed considered this 'memory cluster' to be a key example illustrating the complexities of the Northern Irish conflict, as all of the different agencies that played an active role are 'represented' and their deathly capability demonstrated. Moreover, the Woodvale area represents a remarkable example in that both main Loyalist paramilitary groups and their displays of identity coexist here and, at times, coalesce. Unlike South Belfast, where territorial loyalties are clearly demarcated (see following chapter), the three UVF murals are painted only a few yards away from a mural commemorating the Woodvale Defence Association, precursor of the UDA (WDA, 'B' Company, Viggiani 2013); in addition, the only example among the memorials surveyed of a joint UDA/UVF memorial can be found in Disraeli Street: erected in the mid-1980s, a now almost illegible memorial

Figure 7.3 Mural in memory of UVF volunteer Brian Robinson
Source: Viggiani 2006

stone remembers the fallen members of the UDA 'B' Company Woodvale together with the deceased volunteers of the UVF 'B' Company (UVF, 'B' Company and UDA, 'B' Company, Woodvale, Viggiani 2013).[13] Despite this, results from the survey conducted in the Woodvale area for this study seem to suggest a community preference for the UVF. As one

Figure 7.4 Mural in memory of UVF volunteer Trevor King
Source: Viggiani 2006

local community representative suggested in interview with the author, 'one organization (the UVF) is reaching out to you and the other one (the UDA) is not, and the community can reach to it . . . so, it's only seen to be one organization working for the community, so that's who the community are favouring'.

If we analyse their iconography, the three UVF murals in Disraeli Street perpetuate and reinforce the traditional narrative elements of Loyalist memorialization, as outlined in Chapter 4. Although there is no direct mention of the nation state of the United Kingdom, a symbolic national association with Great Britain and the British Empire is projected through the use of the red poppy (murals in memory of Trevor King, henceforth TK; and in memory of Brian Robinson, henceforth BR) and the Union Jack (incorporated in the UVF logo on the three plaques). Legitimizing references to the UVF's pre-Troubles 'Golden Age' can be found in the use of the 1912–13 UVF flag (TK and BR) and the First World War Battle Honours on the YCV flag (TK and BR). The 36th Ulster Division and the Battle of the Somme are further evoked in the outline of a hill (BR)

Figure 7.5 Mural in memory of UVF volunteer Samuel Rockett
Source: Viggiani 2006

and by quoting famous First World War poems: Laurence Binyon's *For the Fallen* (TK's plaque; mural and plaque in memory of Samuel Rockett) and Siegfried Sassoon's *Suicide in the Trenches* (TK).

Annual events in memory of the three UVF volunteers take place at these murals: on the first Saturday in July a commemorative parade takes place in the area in memory of Trevor King; on 23 August the YCV usually gathers in the evening for a ceremony in memory of Samuel Rockett; and the first Saturday in September is dedicated to remembering Brian Robinson. In addition, the UVF Remembrance Sunday service is held in the proximity of the murals.[14] An analysis of *Combat* magazine reveals that the tradition of memorial parades to commemorate individual UVF fallen volunteers originated in Disraeli Street, as the first record of this practice is a band parade in memory of Brian Robinson in September 1992 (*Combat* October 1992: 12). Although initially held mainly as a display of skill, with prizes being awarded to bands for categories such as best melody, or best blood and thunder, these events evolved over the years into the now traditional format of contemporary Loyalist commemorations.

Loyalist Commemorations in Memory of Paramilitary Casualties

Both Loyalist and Republican paramilitary groups make a similar use of commemorative parades, though there are some differences in the format and tone of these events (Jarman 1997: 152–55). Whereas Republican marches recall funerary processions, and participants – including many women and children – follow the colour party and band that open the cortege in a relaxed and collective atmosphere, Loyalist events are much more militarized and 'macho' in nature, with a more rigid separation between mainly male bandsmen and spectators, and a clear division of participants into separate bands, each carrying their banners and flags and wearing a distinctive uniform.

UVF parades in memory of fallen volunteers, such as those that take place in Disraeli Street, are usually opened by the colour party's sergeant calling for representatives of the different UVF battalions and companies to come forward and lay their wreaths in front of the mural and militarily salute the dead volunteer (Fig. 7.6). Dozens of bands from different parts of Belfast, Northern Ireland and Britain gather for these occasions and at regular intervals begin to march from the mural through the district, performing their varied musical repertoires. Once the bands have returned to the starting point, the UVF 'officer of the day' or a PUP representative takes centre stage to deliver the main oration. After a minute's silence, the 'Last Post' is played, as the colour party lowers all flags except for the Union Jack, which is given honorary treatment as a reaffirmation of Ulster Loyalism's sense of Britishness and national identification with the United Kingdom.[15] The colour party, wearing a black combat-like uniform with white gloves, a white flag-holder around the waist, and a black woollen hat with the UVF logo, is then officially dismissed. The commemoration ends with the band members and gathered crowd heading off to the sound of Loyalist tunes towards the various private members clubs and pubs in the area for an evening of further celebrations. Until 2006, a balaclava-clad armed honour guard would appear midway through the proceedings and fire a volley of shots in the air to pay tribute to their fallen comrades.

Although the format and style of Loyalist commemorations has not changed dramatically through the years – apart from the absence of overt

Figure 7.6 Trevor King memorial parade, 8 July 2006
Source: Viggiani 2006

paramilitary 'shows of strength' since 2006 – the ideological and political message conveyed through the main oration has undergone significant 'adaptations' in light of shifting historico-political circumstances, reflecting the narrative's ability to accommodate itself to times of change, as outlined in Chapter 4.

The last section of this chapter focuses on the diachronic development of memorial activity around the three UVF murals in Disraeli Street from the early 1990s to present, highlighting how these commemorations have represented an arena for negotiating changes in the organization's military and political strategy throughout the peace process, while still projecting a consistent claim to historical legitimacy and national identification.

Changing with the History Tune: The Evolution of the UVF Narrative

Rituals have the ability to be 'at once unchanging and yet ever change-able', their paradox lying in the fact that while they maintain a continuity of form, their meaning inevitably varies with historical and social circumstances (Jarman 1997: 10); as Abner Cohen points out (1974: 39), in rituals 'old symbols are rearranged to serve new purposes under new political conditions'. Many examples from around the world attest to this semantic adaptability of rituals.[16] Narratives about a collective past are often projected and sustained through rituals, such as commemorations, and they partake of this flexibility: as seen in Chapter 4, they are not only able to subsume within themselves individual experiences and beliefs, reducing idiosyncrasies to a seemingly shared framework of remembrance, but they are also capable of 'changing with the history tune', adapting themselves to transformations in the political scenario while maintaining ideological coherency of a group or organization and a sense of continuity with the past.

In a Northern Irish context, in the orations given from the early 1990s to the present at the annual commemorations in memory of Brian Robinson, Trevor King and, since 2000, Samuel Rockett, the UVF has been adamant about reiterating the necessity and ideological justification for their existence: thus, the self-proclaimed 'People's Army' could not 'stand idly by to allow a defenceless people to face slaughter without reply' (*Combat* September 1994: 3) but needed to be there 'in constant readiness to defend you . . . our people' (*Combat* [October] 2003: 7). Its 'long and illustrious record' is seen as testament to the fact that the UVF 'will not let you down' (*Combat* [Christmas] 2001: 7) and, as long as there are agencies 'who might hurt, maim or intimidate our people', 'the Ulster Volunteer Force, want you the people to know that we are never going away, we trust the people and we are certain that the people trust us; our guard will not drop' (ibid.). Ultimately, the UVF has stood as 'a servant to our people and our Country' (*Combat* [September/October] 2005: 10) in the defence of Protestant Ulster's unremitting national allegiance with the United Kingdom: 'the brave Volunteers in the Ulster Volunteer Force . . . gave their lives so that we can stand here today as British citizens' (*Combat* [September] 1999: 11), during this 'ongoing campaign of cultural aggression against our British way of life' (*Combat* [August] 2005: 9).

Recalling what was examined earlier in relation to the UVF 'Golden Age', it is unsurprising that references to the 1913 UVF and the Battle of the Somme are consistent, even from the first documented orations at the three murals in Disraeli Street. As Brown (2007: 714) suggests, this ideological and political kinship with 'our father organization' is 'actualized and made flesh in memorial orations, as family histories are traced back through to the old UVF' and the individual volunteers' 'ancestry of resistance' is clearly delineated to attest to their valour, patriotic spirit and virtue. The individual deaths of modern UVF volunteers are thus subsumed within a wider narrative of 'sacrificial continuity' with the past, and a direct descendance between the old and modern UVF delineated as a warranty of the latter's historical legitimacy: 'from the fields of The Somme to the streets of Ulster . . . throughout the pages of our history, generation after generation [of UVF volunteers have been] sacrificing their lives for the defence of their people and the love of their country' (*Combat* [October] 2002: 9). In a temporal isotopy, modern UVF volunteers could have fought on the First World War battlefields: thus, 'if Trevor King had lived in July 1916, he would have been among those heroic Volunteers who, with rifle and pack, trudged down that long, lonely road to the Somme . . . to glory . . . to oblivion!' (*Combat* [October] 1997: 13). As commitment to the (same) cause and patriotic virtues are handed down through history, the myth of the Somme also provides a moral validation for the actions of the modern UVF: 'the annals of history aptly show that the actions implemented by our forebears of 1912/1913, and the generations that spawned our modern day Ulster Volunteers, was necessary and justified, if our people and culture were to survive' (*The Purple Standard* [July/August] 2007: 16). UVF memorial orations tend to suggest an interpretation of the modern Troubles as the most recent phase of a century-long struggle to maintain the union with Great Britain: 'as history dictates, orders were handed down *once again*, to the gallant Volunteers of the Ulster Volunteer Force, to take up arms and engage the enemy that would slaughter our people' (this author's emphasis; ibid.).

If these ideological, historical and moral claims of legitimacy together with the delineation of a powerful genealogy and a sense of continuity with the past can be seen as the UVF narrative's 'unchanging' features from the 1990s to the present, the political message that is conveyed through the commemorative speeches accounts for its 'ever changeable' dimension. Memorial orations of the early 1990s abound with praises for the military actions of 'soldiers' and 'heroes' of the Ulster Volunteer Force, who gave a 'fearless example in the pursuit of the enemy lives' (*Combat* [September] 1995: 7) and had 'an extensive, illustrious and greatly valued war record' (*Combat* [July] 1994: 7). The message is one of confidence and faith in the armed struggle; thus, the friends and comrades of the fallen volunteers

> will see the struggle through, capitulation does not exist for us, defeat is a negative expelled from all our thoughts. The Ulster Volunteer Force is not tired enough nor wounded enough. The *means of war* are at our disposal. The men of courage and fortitude are here and this country will one day be free. (This author's emphasis; *Combat* [December] 1996: 4)

However, with the onset of the multi-party talks that brought about the 1998 Agreement, which included the PUP, a clear shift occurred and the voice heard was that of an organization which had 'come of age politically'. Rather than eulogizing his military actions, Trevor King was remembered as 'a thinking man who was convinced that a political solution could be found to our many problems here in Ulster'. The armed struggle gave way to 'the primacy of politics', because 'this is what the people want at this point in time'; Loyalist political representatives were now at the forefront working for the people's sake, exhausting all their 'policy and patience in a genuine attempt to reach an honourable and equitable settlement, thus assuring a peaceful and viable future for everyone' (*Combat* [October] 1997: 13) and exploring 'the possibilities of finding a safe Government which can be trusted by all the people of Northern Ireland' (*Combat* [October] 2003: 8). In addition, throughout the peace process, memorial orations given during commemorations at these three murals have been the preferred vehicle to express the UVF leadership's stance on various contemporary political issues: from their position during the feud with the UDA in 2000 (*Combat* [October] 2000: 2) to their mistrust of the 2003 Joint Declaration by the British and Irish Governments (*Combat* [October] 2003: 8); from strong pronunciations in support of the 'right to march' during the annual summer parade issue (*Combat* [September] 1999: 11; [August] 2001: 7; [July/August] 2004: 8–9; [August 2005]: 9–10; and [September/October] 2005: 10–11) to their anger at the disbandment of the Royal Irish Regiment and disillusionment with the British Labour government and its 'never-ending concessions to Republicans' (*Combat* [September/October] 2005: 10–11, 16).

Finally, in more recent years, the message has become one of transformation and evolution of the very same organization from paramilitarism to 'community work', in order to bring about a positive contribution 'in the era of building a multi-cultural and diverse society' in Northern Ireland (*The Purple Standard* [September] 2007: 9).[17] It is time for the Ulster Volunteer Force to 'transform and remould once again', in order to 'remain a vital and indeed integral, mechanism in building a safe and prosperous future for our people' with different 'tactics and weaponry' (*The Purple Standard* [July/August] 2007: 16). Ex-combatants can play an important role among their communities in facilitating them to move forward and 'truly rise from the ashes of conflict', because 'where once the defence of our communities fell to those of military inclination, today a role exists for everyone' (*The Purple Standard* [July] 2008: 11). The reinvented UVF must, therefore, 'prepare our people well for the next stage . . . [and] equip our people with new skills, hence enabling them to competently meet the challenges that lie ahead' (*The Purple Standard* [July/

August] 2007: 16); the clear call from the leadership is to join 'community organizations, political parties, cultural groups and historical societies', because 'unless the Loyalist people stand united, we will fall divided, and so will the culture, heritage and identity that has been forged over centuries' (*The Purple Standard* [July] 2008: 11).

Applying Smith's definition of 'Golden Age', this chapter has explained how the UVF has appropriated through its memorial activity the legitimizing aura surrounding the 1913 UVF and the myth of the Somme in order to project a narrative of historical and ideological legitimacy and moral justification for its military actions during the Troubles, both in relation and opposition to Unionism and Republicanism. Orations given at annual commemorations in memory of the three UVF volunteers in Disraeli Street from the early 1990s highlight how claims of ideological legitimacy and a sense of continuity with the past have remained constant, while the political and ideological messages conveyed at these events have adapted themselves to shifting historico-political circumstances. The next chapter turns its attention to the second main Loyalist paramilitary organization in Northern Ireland, the Ulster Defence Association, and investigates how a more difficult task has presented itself to this 'fatherless' organization in constructing a coherent and lasting political and ideological narrative over the years.

Notes

1. As noted in Chapter 3, this is also a consequence of the intragroup territorial competition between the UVF and the UDA.
2. The earliest supporter of an independent Ulster from the United Kingdom (without reunification with the Republic of Ireland) was the South Tyrone UUP MP W.F. McCoy, who, in the mid-1940s, advocated for more fiscal independence for Northern Ireland (Walker 2004: 112–13). Following the disbandment of the Northern Irish parliament and the introduction of Direct Rule in 1972, the Vanguard movement, later the Vanguard Unionist Political Party, of William Craig became the champion of Ulster nationalism (ibid.: 216–18). After the Ulster Workers Council Strike in 1974, the UDA also began to strongly advocate for an independent position for Ulster, which culminated in the publication in March 1979 of the proposal *Beyond the Religious Divide* by the newly formed New Ulster Political Research Group (Wood 2006: 71–73).
3. Since the opening of a drop-in centre along the Woodvale Road in the Shankill area in 1995, EPIC has diversified its services to include youth intervention, initiatives of 'humanization' and 'de-stereotypization' through dialogue, the opening of a communication channel with Republicans to resolve interface violence, the provision of welfare rights advice to ex-prisoners and the wider Loyalist community, and the organization of political tours (Shirlow and McEvoy 2008: 68–70).

4. The bi-monthly/monthly UVF-aligned *Combat* magazine (renamed *The Purple Standard* in 2007) has documented the UVF memorial activity since the mid-1970s, but there is no equivalent for the UDA. The UDA published periodicals over the years (the *UDA Bulletin*, *Ulster* and *New Ulster Defender*) but these have all been discontinued.
5. A significant example of this is constituted by the mural 'Hidden Treasures' on Beverley Street, Shankill, painted in 2005. The completion of this mural was overseen by EPIC, in consultation with the UDA as it replaced a UFF mural. It depicts various cultural and historical images related to Northern Ireland, such as the Titanic, the cranes of Harland and Wolff, a DeLorean car and characters from *The Chronicles of Narnia* ('Mural Giving Shankill a New Image' 2005).
6. Other common theoretical conceptualizations are those of 'blood sacrifice' or 'myth of origin', whereby it is necessary for an ethnic group or nation state to possess a primeval blood sacrifice, a mythical or historical event that becomes idealized as the 'founding' moment of one's collective ethnic and national identity. Examples of these are the Battle of Kosovo for Serbia or Anzac Day for Australia.
7. Although the original UVF was officially instituted in 1913, the commemorative 'historical' flag flown by the modern UVF in the streets of Belfast carries the year 1912, as this was the year of the Ulster Covenant, as a consequence of which the original UVF was formed.
8. In 2007, for instance, only one King Billy mural could be found on Donegall Pass in South Belfast among the fifty-four Loyalist murals that were counted on the main roads in Belfast. In 2008, of fifty-four murals depicting Loyalist imagery, eleven related directly to the First World War, ten of which also displayed UVF symbols (Bryan 2010). There was, however, a resurgence of King Billy murals in mainly UDA areas in 2012, with new murals depicting King Billy appearing in Sandy Row and the Lower Shankill.
9. Most famously, the painting *Battle of the Somme, the Attack of the Ulster Division* by James Prinsep Beadle depicts Lt Francis Thornely leading soldiers over a hill towards the German line while bombs explode around them.
10. It is interesting to note how different UVF-aligned 'Somme Associations' have been formed in recent years; these organizations have appropriated the name of the official Somme Association, which is a cross-community charitable organization, but they have no link or direct contact with it.
11. For a more comprehensive account of the death of the three volunteers, see for Robinson: *Belfast Telegraph* 2 September 1989: 1–2; 5 September 1989: 1; *Irish News* 4 September 1989: 1; McKittrick et al. (2007: 1177–78). For King: *Belfast Telegraph* 9 July 1994: 1; *Irish News* 17 June 1994: 1; 11 July 1994: 1; McKittrick et al. (2007: 1368–67). For Rockett: *Belfast Telegraph* 24 August 2000: 1; 26 August 2000: 1; *Irish News* 24 August 2000: 1; 28 August 2000: 4; McKittrick et al. (2007: 1482).
12. See Viggiani 2013: Robinson Brian – UVF; King Trevor – UVF; Rockett Samuel – YCV.
13. A joint UVF/UDA Remembrance Sunday service was held at the memorial in November 1987 and 1988 (*Ulster* December 1988/January 1989: 17). In more recent times, three separate Remembrance Sunday ceremonies are held in the Woodvale area on the same day, but at different times: at 9 A.M. the first service is 'hosted' by the UDA; at 11 A.M. the UVF gathers in front of the three murals in Disraeli Street, and finally at 3 P.M. the local Orange Order lodge holds a ceremony at a memorial

plaque in Bray Street (Deceased Protestants and Members of the Security Forces in the Greater Shankill Area, Viggiani 2013).

14. See Chapter 8 for a more detailed analysis of Remembrance Sunday services.

15. It is interesting to note how similar proceedings and rituals are followed at Orange Order commemorations (Jarman 1997; Bryan 2000). It seems, therefore, that Loyalist paramilitary groups have adopted pre-existing structures from other Loyalist functions and adapted them to their commemorative needs.

16. See, for example, Sanson (1976) on Bastille Day in France; Kertzer (1988) on the rituals of the Italian Communist Party; and Cannadine (1983) on royal ceremonies in Britain.

17. For a more detailed analysis of the evolution of Loyalist paramilitary groups from paramilitarism to community work, see Chapter 9.

Chapter 8

THE UDA SANDY ROW MEMORIAL GARDEN

Attempting a Narrative of Symbolic Accretion

≫•≪

The previous chapter has illustrated how the UVF has managed to project a dominant Loyalist narrative of the conflict, both in opposition to
Republicanism and 'middle Unionism', and how the annual commemorations at three murals in the Woodvale area have been the chosen arena
for negotiating changes in the organization's military and political strategy throughout the peace process, while still maintaining a consistent
claim to historical legitimacy and national identification. This chapter
looks at how the second major Loyalist paramilitary group in Northern
Ireland, the Ulster Defence Association (UDA), has struggled to construct a coherent and lasting political and ideological narrative of legitimation over the years. Using the 2007 Remembrance Sunday service in
Sandy Row as a case study, this chapter also highlights how both community and national politics are played out at commemorative events,
and how paramilitary-related memorial activity can create what has previously been defined as a political 'mesolevel', a gateway to a symbolic,
ideological national identity and national politics while still pertaining to
a microlevel form of memorialization.

'You Are Now Entering Loyalist Sandy Row'

Whether a proud statement of identity, territorial demarcator or threatening warning against unwanted visitors, the once (in)famous mural

painted across an entire gable wall at the lower entrance of Sandy Row left no doubt for interpretation: you are now entering the 'Heartland of South Belfast Ulster Freedom Fighters'.[1] A predominantly Protestant working-class area, Sandy Row is contained within Sandy Row to the east, Donegall Road to the south, Linfield Industrial Estate to the west and the Boyne Bridge to the north (NIDSD 2004). Once a vibrant and growing neighbourhood that attracted even non-residents to its many shops, the area has been experiencing a serious economic decline in the past few decades despite its close proximity to the city centre and the university quarter, with an outflow of people and businesses, a reduction of disposable income and a lack of external investments. Although Sandy Row presents no interfaces with Nationalist/Republican estates and little contact habitually occurs with the Catholic population, the local community perceives itself as isolated and under threat. This threat – or fear of being under threat – is posed by the traditional enemy *outside* (the Nationalist/Republican community), but more insidiously by a new enemy *within*, in the shape of residents who are moving out without a new demographic wave to replace them and developers who are buying out old buildings and factories, repositories of local history and culture, and converting them into aseptic apartments void of identity (Viggiani 2007). In general, it has been observed that 'the community has feelings of apathy and sometimes resentment with the perception that [the] Government has forgotten Sandy Row' (NIDSD 2004).

A perceived lack of leadership and the absence of confidence in the political structures have given way to the grasp of paramilitarism, to the extent that 'many acknowledged that paramilitaries have a firm grip on Sandy Row and may have a veto over most things that happen in the area' (NIDSD 2004). Despite the fact that Sandy Row is situated between two areas mainly controlled by the UVF – the Village and Donegall Pass – and resonates with particular symbolic significance for this organization in that the original South Belfast Ulster Volunteer Force had its headquarters in the Brewery Buildings once located here,[2] it has been the UDA that has asserted almost full control over the area: since the early 1990s the UDA South Belfast Brigade has, in fact, established its unofficial 'headquarters' in the John McMichael (ex-prisoners') Centre along Sandy Row, a few doors away from the office of UUP MLA Michael McGimpsey.

As seen in Chapter 3, Loyalist visual displays of identity have assumed an additional 'meaning' in recent years. Rather than differentiating Loyalist areas from Republican ones, flags, murals and memorials appear to have been used more to mark out Loyalist territory along the lines of 'tribalism' within Orangeism/Loyalism, particularly in South Belfast. As

Jarman (1997: 220–21) has noted, 'the sense of antagonism and differ-ence between locales within the Loyalist community is here made vis-ible in the patterns of allegiance that are displayed on the walls' – and in more recent years through permanent memorials. While Sandy Row and the Roden Street area have traditionally displayed UDA emblems and hooded UFF gunmen, the nearby Donegall Pass and the Village have proclaimed support for the UVF and the smaller UVF-aligned Red Hand Commando. In contrast to the Woodvale area and, to a certain degree, the pre-feud Shankill, there is 'no common space for combined displays' of identity and allegiance in South Belfast (Jarman 1997: 222). As UDA brigadier Jackie McDonald stated in regard to paramilitary visual displays,

> it's not a Protestant/Catholic thing, or a Nationalist/Unionist or Republican/Loyalist thing . . . If you come here any time in this area [Sandy Row] you will not see a UVF flag. If you were down in Donegall Pass, you will not see a UDA flag. So it's not against the other community, it is mark-ing out territories . . . It's saying this is our patch, and that's their patch . . . The Orange would have developed the different Red Hand Commando, UVF, UFF, and UDA flags. They'd be more splintered if you like. So it's not just a cross-community thing. It's tribalism within. (Interview with the author)

Born out of the merger of a number of vigilante groups (Knox and Monaghan 2002: 38), the UDA never achieved the degree of structural centralization, membership discipline or political acuteness that histori-cally characterized the UVF. Much larger in number than the latter, the single brigades of the UDA have acted almost as independent units, loose and undisciplined – despite the existence of a ruling 'inner council' – maybe explaining the perceived behavioural difference between the two organizations (Wood 2006: 236–59). Whereas the UVF claims a moral superiority and relative freedom from common criminal activity (Bruce 1992, 1994), the UDA has often lent itself to be portrayed as a collection of individual 'kingdoms' based on racketeering and drug dealing, as in the case of the reign of Johnny 'Mad Dog' Adair in the Lower Shankill, or the Shoukri brothers in North Belfast. This reality found less ground in Sandy Row, where the progressive leadership of John McMichael and, in more recent years, of the present South Belfast brigadier Jackie McDonald has brought about a relationship of 'mutual protection' with the local com-munity. As a local resident pointed out, 'I can't honestly say that we were scared of the UDA . . . No, 'cause they did create more of an attitude where you could go and talk to them. Where the Catholics were more or less told what to do [by the IRA] and they hadn't a choice, that was never put that way to us' (in interview with the author).

In other Belfast neighbourhoods, however, the relationship between the UDA and local communities has not been as 'idyllic': a UDA ex-combatant, for instance, recognized that in North Belfast 'it'd be fair to say [that] under some leadership it became the community under the paramilitaries – and I mean under the boot' (in interview with the author). This absence of a centralized structure and strong leadership is reflected in the nature of the organization's memorial activity, whereby the commemorative effort lacks the coherency observed with regard to the other main paramilitary organizations in Northern Ireland. Since the late 1990s, the UDA has, in fact, attempted to elaborate several motifs that possessed historical depth; however, they have failed to achieve widespread support in terms of symbolic longevity and relevance.

Tiptoeing through History in Search of Illustrious 'Forefathers'

Whereas the UVF had 'its own mystique' and historical heritage – in the words of the late PUP leader David Ervine (Wood 2006: 7) – the 'fatherless' UDA has struggled to elaborate and secure an original self-defining 'myth of origin' or 'Golden Age' on which to base a credible narrative of historical and ideological legitimacy. Unlike the UVF who had in the 1913 UVF an 'obvious' illustrious genealogy, the UDA has been unable to evoke a similarly powerful historical lineage and has 'had to create an elaborate iconography to locate itself within the Loyalist tradition' (Jarman 1997: 217), resorting to obscure heraldic connections that some academics are fascinated to trace down but that, in general, lie outside of public awareness. The organization's emblem is, for instance, a redesign of the Ulster coat of arms that was adopted by Ulster Unionism during the Home Rule crisis;[3] and its motto *Quis Separabit* ('Who will separate [us]') 'was first used on the insignia of the Knights of the Most Illustrious Order of St Patrick, founded in 1783 by George III; it was later taken up by the Ulster Unionist Convention in Belfast in 1892, and became the motto of the Royal Irish Rifles, who fought at the Somme' (Jarman 1997: 218).

As Jarman (1992: 157–58) points out, this 'official' heraldic design – that presents the UDA shield superimposed on the Ulster flag and the Union Jack – is interpreted by the organization as a warrant of its legitimacy, in that 'it aims to . . . stress the natural and unassailable link between Britain and Ulster, but if this union is in doubt the two over-lapped flags are protected by the shield of the UDA'. If we exclude the use of King Billy, an iconic figure that pertains more generally to the

Protestant tradition and is not the exclusive 'heritage' of the UDA, the UDA's commemorative activity has been predominantly centred around events and individuals linked to the recent Troubles.[4] However, since 'a worthy and distinctive past must be rediscovered and appropriated . . . in order to create a convincing representation of the "nation"' and a group's 'national' identity (Smith 1997: 36), from the late 1990s – perhaps as a reaction to the intensification of UVF commemorative activity around the 36th Ulster Division and the Somme – there have been an ever-increasing number, if confused and sporadic, of commemorative 'experiments' by the UDA to anchor its claim of historical legitimacy deeply into the past.

According to Harrison's theorization of political symbolism (1995), four prototypical forms of symbolic conflict can be detected in intragroup competitions for what Bourdieu (1990: 112–21) has termed 'symbolic capital'. Groups seeking to establish or accentuate their distinctiveness from each other can generate a distinct set of symbolic representations of their unique identity in what Harrison (1995: 260–63) defines as 'innovation contests'. They can also attempt to strengthen the relative rank of their symbols of identity on some scale of value or worth such as prestige, legitimacy or sacredness, either by promoting the reputation of one's own symbols or attempting to diminish the status of other groups' symbols in the case of 'valuation contests' (ibid.: 256–58). Alternatively, a group can try to displace its competitors' symbols of identity with its own symbols in an 'expansionary contest' (ibid.: 263–65). More pertinent to the UDA case, a group can try to appropriate the symbolic inventory of other groups, starting a 'proprietary contest' for the monopoly or partial control over the symbolic property of some important collective symbols (ibid.: 258–60). From the mid-1990s onwards, some UDA murals, for instance, have attempted to establish a direct connection between the organization and a mythical 'Golden Age' embodied by the hero Cuchulainn, traditionally a 'symbolic property' of Irish nationalism.[5] Largely based on the works of Adamson (1974, 1982; Adamson, Hume and McDowell 1995) that in the mid-1980s stimulated a debate within the UDA on questions of identity and history (McAuley and McCormack 1990: 156–59), Cuchulainn is interpreted as belonging to the autochthonous inhabitants of Ireland, the 'Cruthin', that were driven out of Ireland by invasions of the Celts, and stands as the ultimate defender of Ulster against the attack of the forces of the Celtic King and Queen of Connaught. Given the stronger degree of appropriation that the Irish Republican movement can claim over the image of Cuchulainn, this proprietary contest has, however, failed to originate a permanent association of the symbolic capital emanated by this mythical figure with the UDA. The choice of 'symbolic property' to challenge might seem strange or overly ambitious, in that the UDA has aimed to distinguish itself from its traditional opponents – the Irish Republican movement – by attempting to appropriate a symbol belonging to that same group they wish to distance themselves from. However, it might appear less bizarre if considering that this 'fatherless' organization needs to establish an original genealogy and a credible narrative, not only in opposition to Irish Republicanism but also to mark itself off ideologically from the stronger – in terms of symbolic capital – UVF.

In more recent years, the UDA has turned its 'symbolic radar' inwards towards the Loyalist tradition and has challenged the UVF's 'exclusivity' over the Somme – and more generally over the First World War – in an attempt to partake of the symbolic capital associated with it. Interestingly, the UVF came, in turn, to gain a degree of ownership over this symbolic capital against mainstream Unionism. One might ask: why was the symbolic appropriation of the Somme by the modern UVF successful, unlike the symbolic appropriation of the image of Cuchulainn by the UDA? The reason lies in the credibility that society affords these accretive exercises: the modern UVF waged an insightful proprietary contest in 1966 when it appropriated the name and symbols of the original UVF and the 'symbolic capital' that came with them. Over time this appropriation was sanctioned by civic society, for instance, when the Northern Ireland Parades Commission allowed the use of UVF 1912 flags (produced and used by the modern UVF) on the basis that they had some historical validity (Bryan 2010).[6] As will be discussed in the next part of this chapter, the UDA has tried to claim proprietary rights over the 'commemorative density' of the Somme to create a sense of history and tradition for itself that can be relied upon, especially at times of political and strategic changes. This exercise of ideological and political accretion reached its epitome on Remembrance Sunday 2007 at the Sandy Row Memorial Garden, when the Ulster Freedom Fighters were officially disbanded by the UDA leadership during a commemorative service for the Commonwealth's dead from the two world wars, including the soldiers who died at the Somme. During the ceremony, the UDA experimented with more potential symbolic appropriation, attempting to link itself to the Ulster Defence Union (UDU), an organization established in 1893 to resist Gladstone's second Home Rule Bill that drew widespread support from men of every creed and class within Ulster Unionism. An earlier inconsequential attempt to link the UDA to the UDU was made in 2000 in a mural in the Lower Shankill that depicted an 1893 UDU member, a 1972 UDA member and a modern-day UFF member in a historical continuum (Fig. 8.1).

Figure 8.1 UDA/UDU mural
Source: Viggiani 2005

According to Smith (1997: 56), the heroic epoch 'chosen' as a group's 'Golden Age', upon which a credible narrative of historical and ideological legitimation can be built, must be able to 'kindle the imagination of large numbers of the population' and must possess '"mythic" quality, that is, it must contain a widely believed tale or tales of a heroic or sacred past that can serve present needs and purposes'. The similarities between the appropriation of the UDU by the UDA and of the original UVF by the modern UVF are obvious: both the original UVF and the UDU had drawn their members from mainstream Ulster Unionism and had widespread public support; but as a paramilitary organization that has no political voice and whose mass support is declining, the UDA is attempting to 'borrow' legitimacy and conquer a wider place in the Protestant/Unionist history in the hope that their brand new 'forefathers' will prove as powerful as the original UVF have been for the modern UVF. Since this new historical association with the UDU is still in its infancy, it is difficult to ascertain whether it will acquire historical longevity and symbolic relevance, and be collectively 'embraced' as the UDA's 'Golden Age'. To this author's knowledge, it has so far only been pursued through the display of UDU flags in some areas of Belfast and Derry/Londonderry during summer 2009, whereas no new permanent form of UDA memorialization presents any iconographic reference to the UDU.[7]

The Sandy Row Memorial Garden: Attempting to Appropriate the Myth of the Somme

Completed in November 2006 in City Way, a pedestrian passage off Sandy Row, the Sandy Row Memorial Garden was specifically built to provide the local community (and members of the local UDA brigade) with a fitting and appropriate place to gather on the occasion of the annual Remembrance Sunday service (Fig. 8.2). Before 2006, the people of Sandy Row would congregate in front of a full gable mural in memory of UDA South Belfast brigadier John McMichael and other fallen members of the 'A' Battalion, situated at the bottom of the street (McCormick 2001).[8] The garden came about as part of the regeneration scheme that had been ongoing in the area: following the publication of the Taskforce Report on Sandy Row on 25 January 2005,[9] the Sandy Row Community Forum (SRCF) – the key community agency for the regeneration and development of the area, based in the Sandy Row Community Centre – received grants from the Belfast City Council and the Big Lottery Fund for the delivery of three environmental improvements in the area.[10] Representing the culmination of over two years' work by the SRCF in partnership with Northern Ireland Housing Executive (NIHE), Groundwork Northern Ireland, Belfast City Council (BCC) and Philips Contractors, three community gardens were opened in the area in 2006: the Fairy Thorn Garden in Blythe Street; the Britannic Drive Community Garden and the McAdam Park outside the Sandy Row Methodist Church (Northern Ireland Housing Executive 2006a).

Although there is no official mention in any government documents of the memorial garden in City Way, local community workers have informed this author that the site was designated as surplus land by the Housing Executive and was, therefore, allocated for a community garden funded by donations from private individuals and businesses from the area. The memorial garden was built by a local builder and the headstone and memorial plaques were provided by Loyalist ex-prisoners and the South Belfast UDA brigade (interview with local community workers). Some interviewees have, however, affirmed that land was 'donated' by NIHE for the Sandy Row Memorial Garden and that public funding was used, for instance, for the clearing of the area and the provision of memorial benches. Despite a denial from the local authorities (NIHE,

Freedom of Information request RFI/402 2008a), it was not possible to clarify whether these incongruences are due to a degree of confusion among local residents as a result of different redevelopment projects in the area or whether the official 'toleration policy' described in Chapter 5 with regards to Troubles-related memorials has been applied by BCC and NIHE in the case of the City Way Memorial Garden.

Layout and Iconography

Like the majority of Loyalist memorials, the UDA memorial garden in Sandy Row is less elaborate and adorned than mainstream Republican memorials such as the Clonard Martyrs Memorial Garden. Enclosed by a plain black wrought-iron fence, the garden has its centrepiece in a minimalist headstone dedicated to the UDA South Belfast Brigade, featuring the organization's emblem and the symbols of its three sister groups: the Loyalist Prisoners' Aid (LPA), the UFF and the UDA's youth wing, the Ulster Young Militants (UYM). In addition to a smaller-scale replica

Figure 8.2 UDA/UFF 'A' Battalion, South Belfast Brigade Memorial Garden
Source: Viggiani 2007

of the mural in memory of local fallen members (see endnote 8), two plaques along the rear wall recite the Roll of Honour of the 'A Battalion', South Belfast Brigade, UDA, recording the date of death of each volunteer and reminding passers-by that 'these courageous men . . . gave their life for Ulster'. Like Republican forms of memorialization, Loyalist memorials recognize the individual sacrifice of modern volunteers. In UVF and UDA memorials, for instance, the names and dates of death of individual volunteers are often recorded. Yet, each death is subsumed and interpreted within an overarching narrative of symbolic national allegiance and collective sacrifice to defend, in the Loyalist case, Northern Ireland's position within the United Kingdom.

The most notable element of the garden, however, is a permanent placard in memory of the dead of the First and Second World War, positioned above the central headstone, which reads: 'Only by remembering these men, and others like them, can we ever repay their memory'. While the Loyalist interpretation of the conflict is not directly expressed in the Sandy Row Memorial Garden, the symbolic national allegiance with Great Britain is clearly articulated through the depiction of a wreath of red poppies on the placard and the use of the Union Jack, the Ulster flag and the Scottish Saltire, permanently flown above the memorial. The silhouette of a battlefield at dawn provides a compelling background to the placard's inscription: as seen in the previous chapter, this stylistic device can be interpreted as an evocation of the Battle of the Somme.

As mentioned at the beginning of the chapter, the UDA has tried to challenge the UVF's 'exclusive' proprietary rights over the Battle of the Somme in its most recent memorials, although this exercise of symbolic accretion has not been too radical or ubiquitous: devoid of its own original 'Golden Age', the UDA has waged a 'proprietary contest' over the most powerful myth of origin available in the widespread Loyalist tradition in order to project a partisan narrative, parallel to that of the UVF, of historical legitimacy and national identification. This narrative cannot be considered 'sectional' in that it does not present a different 'reading' of the same past, nor does it act as a specification of the (UVF's) dominant narrative, as observed earlier with respect to the Republican scenario between the Provisional IRA and the INLA. Rather, it can be seen as an attempt by the UDA to appropriate part of the 'commemorative density' associated with a historical (and mythical) event taken to be a common 'asset' in the symbolic capital available to the wider Loyalist tradition. Shared by both groups, the (ideological) interpretation of this event is that the supreme sacrifice of Protestant Ulster at the Somme, embodied in the 36th (Ulster) Division, represents the ultimate testimony of its Britishness. In addition, the courage and patriotic spirit shown by past members of one's imagined community are evoked to galvanize those same qualities in the present generation, to foster a sense of intragroup cohesion handed down through time and, ultimately, to indicate historical continuity and the notion of a shared vision between the actions of present-day volunteers and the past sacrifices of a group's martyrs. Thus, similarly to those who gave their lives during the First and Second World War as a token of their Britishness and commitment to their nation, 'others like them' have paid a similar sacrifice on Ulster soil in the name of the same (imagined) nation.

If the association with the Somme is merely implied in the case of the Sandy Row Memorial Garden, it is accentuated and made explicit in the UDA-commissioned memorial garden in Roden Street (Fig. 8.3). Built on the site where a poorly drawn mural and minimalist headstone in memory of the UFF South Belfast Brigade once stood (UDA/UFF, South Belfast Brigade, Viggiani 2013), this artistically elaborate memorial garden was finished in the latter half of 2006 and establishes a more direct connection between the present UDA/UFF and the Somme. Enclosed within iron gates patterned with poppies, the memorial has as its centrepiece

Figure 8.3 UDA/UFF South Belfast Brigade Memorial Garden
Source: Viggiani 2007

the original headstone 'in memory of fallen comrades Ulster Freedom Fighters South Belfast Brigade'. On the rear wall above it, an abstract sculpture featuring red poppies and doves was, according to its caption, 'inspired by the poem "In Flanders Fields" by John McCrea – Ypres, Belgium 1915'. Most significantly, the iron sculpture on the right-hand side of the garden presents a series of overlaid poppies, each engraved with the name of a different fallen member of the South Belfast UDA/ UFF or with the words 'remember', 'reflect' and 'contemplate'. Thus, the dead of the First World War and the volunteers of the South Belfast Brigade who lost their lives as a result of the modern Troubles are remembered together, and the combination of iconographic and symbolic references to the Somme on the one hand and the modern UDA/UFF on the other attempts to blend the two together with no temporal distinction. It is worth noting, however, that unlike UVF commemorative sites, UDA memorials do not depict Battle Honours or make explicit mention of First World War iconic battles or military units.

From the list of individuals commemorated in the Sandy Row and Roden Street memorial gardens, it is evident that only members of local paramilitary group(s) are remembered. Unlike mainstream Republican memorials, it is uncommon for Loyalist memorials to mention the local Protestant civilians who died as a result of the Troubles, possibly because they directly mimic First World War monuments, which list each individual fallen soldier without mentioning non-military casualties, given that the war was mostly fought on battlefields.[11] A process of 'social amnesia' is also at play in the case of UDA forms of memorialization, in that intragroup assassinations go unacknowledged. In post-conflict Northern Ireland, moreover, paramilitary-related memorials act as a permanent statement of appropriation/repudiation of individuals by a specific organization. As the relative of a South Belfast UDA deceased volunteer pointed out in interview with the author,

> there was a lot of occasions where people were killed and were portrayed as that they were not involved in anything. We used to say that someone was 'claimed'. If it was somebody who wasn't claimed and then you found a few years later that their name appeared on the memorial . . . and that was paramilitary groups, organizations saying 'well that was my person, that was my man that I lost and I want them recognized' . . . I think that there has been times when that has put people on their back foot . . . well, hang on, you told me before that that wasn't the case. Or you have the other perspective where you have families who were very well aware of the involvement that their husband, their father had and don't like that there is a decision not to claim him because it's like you are pretending that there is no value, it didn't mean anything to you.

Thus, the names of Harry Black and Samuel 'Sammy' Hunt appear on the UDA 'A' Battalion Roll of Honour in the Sandy Row Memorial Garden, whereas at the time of their death it was denied that the men had any links with the organization (McKittrick et al. 2007: 647, 1268). Drawing on the quotation above, it is interesting to briefly examine here the input that family members of fallen volunteers have in the erection of local memorials to their loved ones.

Role of Families in the Memorial Process

As seen so far, memorial committees and various associations aligned to different political parties or paramilitary groups have taken on the role of 'memory makers' in Northern Ireland, sifting through the 'confusion' of the past and selecting who and what is remembered and forgotten on permanent memorials. Because of this unusual scenario, it is interesting to reflect upon the extent to which the families of the individuals commemorated have an input into the process of memorialization of their deceased loved ones. Research conducted for this study among the local population and relatives of commemorated individuals suggests that the degree of consultation with families is significantly more for Republican than Loyalist groups. According to the minutes of the first meeting of the Teach Na Fáilte Memorial Committee Belfast, for instance, the first issue to be addressed was to contact the next of kin of each of the twenty volunteers to be commemorated in Belfast, in order to obtain their approval for the committee's memorial programme (TNFMCB 6 June 2002). As confirmed by Noel Little's nephew in interview with the author, the families were kept fully informed about the wording and location of the plaques and the details of the unveiling ceremony, but the memorial committee took full responsibility for the physical completion of the plaque, the organization of fundraising events and the unveiling ceremony. Family members of Republican volunteers are also given a prominent role on the day of the unveiling ceremony, being asked to unveil the plaque, to read a brief statement before the main oration or to express their gratitude and perhaps voice personal memories of their deceased loved one at the social gatherings that customarily follow the ceremony.

Conversely, consultation with families of Loyalist fallen volunteers is significantly less. As the son of South Belfast UDA brigadier John McMichael, killed in a car-bomb attack by the Provisional IRA in 1987, admitted in the interview with the author, 'in the case of my father . . . people would, the UDA I guess, arrange for memorials to be erected – it's a local issue [and] there is never consultation with the family'. Surprisingly, he has never visited some of the memorials in memory of his father and has been made aware of commemorative events in his honour only by reading local newspapers. Although he understands the reasons why the UDA would want to remember John McMichael, given his very public profile and leadership position within the organization, and does not object to this practice, he recognizes that it is somewhat incongruous that the organization would hold the right to remember its members, without consultation with the families or consideration of any personal circumstances. As an example, he told how his stepmother and stepbrother have never been invited to the annual parade that occurs in Lisburn and ends at a plaque erected on a wall near the spot where John McMichael was killed, opposite the house where the family still lives: 'so they sit in their house and watch this happening' (interview with the author).

A typical predicament encountered during the course of fieldwork for this study was striking a balance between a paramilitary group's right to remember its members and the families' wishes and sensitivities. Whereas the approval of families is usually sought by Republican ex-prisoners prior to the erection of (more) recent memorials, some interviewees – both ex-prisoners and members of local communities pertaining to either side of the divide – expressed the opinion that, once enlisted in a paramilitary group, individuals enter the public sphere of soldiery and, therefore, the 'armies' for which they fought have the right to remember their sacrifice, even against the families' will. As a Loyalist ex-combatant explained,

> [commemoration] is not an individual choice, an individual decision. When you get somebody who is in that position, once you go into the public domain, then it no longer becomes a remit of an individual person or an individual family . . . and the group has the right to commemorate over the family. (Interview with the author)

Given the life of secrecy conducted by many volunteers, some felt that in many cases comrades may have been closer than families, who may have been deliberately kept unaware of militant involvement. Thus, a Republican ex-prisoner described this as a conundrum of 'competing rights' because

> those people who were members of organizations and died as part of the activities that they were involved in are owned both by their family and by their organizations; and sometimes maybe they were more identified even by the organization than their families, or the organization knew more about them than their families in some senses. (Interview with the author)

Focusing on the UDA Remembrance Sunday service in November 2007, the final part of this chapter explores how paramilitary-related commemorations assume a clear political nature for Loyalists and how present historico-political circumstances infuse their commemorative activities. It also investigates how commemorations create what this author defines as a political 'mesolevel', acting as a linchpin between the microlevel of the community and the macrolevel of the (symbolic) nation state.

Remembrance Day

Every year at 11 A.M. on the Sunday closest to 11 November (the 'eleventh hour of the eleventh day of the eleventh month'), ceremonies take place at local war memorials throughout the United Kingdom and Commonwealth countries to commemorate the cessation of hostilities on the Western Front during the First World War at 11 A.M. on 11 November 1918, and to remember British and Commonwealth soldiers who died in service – including those who died at the Somme.[12] First known as Armistice Day, it was renamed Remembrance Day in Commonwealth nations after the Second World War. In Belfast, while an official ceremony is held at the cenotaph in the City Hall grounds with the attendance of state, church and armed forces representatives, many unofficial commemorations take place throughout the city at different Loyalist memorials, often 'hosted' by Loyalist paramilitary groups, to pay homage to the Ulstermen and women who 'have been prepared to step forward and Volunteer for Crown and Country, in defence of our British way of life' (*Combat* [November/December] 2005: 12). As explained earlier, in 'paramilitarized time and space' these Ulstermen and women include both those who died abroad while enlisted in the British Army during the two world wars and those who paid the ultimate sacrifice in more recent times on Ulster soil in defence of the union with Great Britain. As Brown (2007: 717) points out, 'the symbolism of the day is direct: Loyalist paramilitarism and service in the British armed forces is to be deliberately run together across time, with sacrifice in either projected as co-terminate in legitimacy and value'.

In Sandy Row, two simultaneous events unfold: while the UVF Sandy Row Company, 2nd Battalion, gathers at their memorial next to the Sandy Row Community Centre (see endnote no. 2), the UDA South Belfast Brigade parades from the Donegall Road to the City Way memorial, stopping on the way at the Roden Street garden. In faithful imitation of official ceremonies, paramilitary-related Remembrance Sunday services follow a similar format: red poppy wreaths are laid by representatives of different brigades and battalions who pay their respects with military salute, followed by sympathizing groups and family members; at exactly 11 A.M. a minute's silence is observed, followed immediately by the 'Last Post'. In contrast to official ceremonies, however, the service culminates in a speech delivered by a member of the local paramilitary group or by a political representative – from the ranks of the Progressive Unionist Party (PUP) for the UVF; traditionally from the UDP and, in most recent years, from the Ulster Political Research Group (UPRG) for the UDA.[13] As seen in previous chapters, in the tradition of paramilitary-related commemorative activity in Northern Ireland, the main oration on Remembrance Sunday is also a strong political act. While the aim is to pay homage and remember past members of the Ulster Protestant imagined community who died in conflicts from the First World War onwards, there are more contemporary meanings and messages that make this occasion as much about the present and future of a collectivity as about its past: as Brown (2007) points out, the speech is used to re-inforce the security of the union with Great Britain and to express an unwavering sense of Britishness; to foster military discipline and trust in the leadership; and, ultimately, to negotiate difficult political messages about the peace process and to help to transform Loyalism, both militarily and politically.

'What the World Needs Now Is Love, Sweet Love': 2007 UDA Remembrance Sunday

To the surreal sound of this famous Carpenters' song blaring through the speakers, several hundred people who had gathered at the City Way Memorial Garden on 11 November 2007 left with the knowledge that they had just witnessed history. From midnight, 'all active service units of the Ulster Freedom Fighters [would] . . . stand down with all military intelligence destroyed and . . . all weaponry . . . put beyond use' (UDA 2007).[14] The statement, read by Colin Halliday of the UPRG, was preceded by a powerful symbolic demonstration of this major strategic shift when, after the one-minute silence, the UFF flag was furled away into a plastic sheath to signify that 'their job is done and hopefully they'll never have to come back to do what they did before' (McDonald 2007). However, several times in the UDA statement and in the main speech – given by South Belfast brigadier Jackie McDonald – that followed, the assembled crowd was reassured that, although 'the Ulster Defence Association believes that the war is over', 'the UDA is not going away' and that 'we, the members of the Ulster Defence Association 2007, reaffirm our commitment to maintaining the Union' (UDA 2007; McDonald 2007). Similar to the modern UVF's rhetoric in relation to the original UVF, the same commitment, national allegiance and 'true' spirit of modern UDA volunteers are interpreted as stretching back through the centuries in an unbroken thread to the 'forefathers' of the Ulster Defence Union:

> our members have from 1893 went forward and paid the ultimate sacrifice and gave their lives in the defence and freedom of small nations on Flanders fields at the Somme during the First World War, in Burma, Africa, Europe and the Middle East during WWII. We continue that struggle for freedom of small nations in the present theatres of war in Afghanistan and Iraq. (UDA 2007)

Thus, the UDA leadership has attempted to articulate a 'brand new' and original genealogy for the organization and, implicitly, the name of Ulster is added to the list of small nations for whose freedom Ulster Protestants have fought since the dawn of time.

As seen in previous chapters for Republican groups, main orations at commemorative events are paramount at times of strategic change to foster intragroup cohesion and mediate a transformation of the very same paramilitary groups. Thus, on 11 November 2007, among the 'ghostly national imaginings' of the past, the new direction of the UDA was announced: 'the Ulster Defence Association is now committed to supporting the building of communities and encourages all members to participate at all levels of regeneration and social development' (UDA 2007). As part of the transition 'from paramilitarism to old comrades' organizations' (Brown 2007) and to a role of 'community workers' (see also Chapter 9), it was decided that 'the UDA will remain the parent organization but will establish an umbrella organization titled the Ulster Defence Union to facilitate the retirement of members and the needs that will affect them'; in addition, 'all Ulster Young Militants will be redirected towards education, personal development and community development'. The statement concluded with the reassuring reiteration that 'above all we must stick together and let no one separate us' (UDA 2007). As Gary McMichael points out, while there is no doubt at commemorative events that '[paramilitary leaders] are actually talking with their membership . . . and spend 90 per cent of their time concerned with trying to hold together their own people' (interview with the author), it is interesting to note how a political message aimed at the local community can be delivered concurrently. The final section of this chapter examines how macro (national) politics and micro (community) politics are played out at commemorative events.

'Awakening the Sleeping Giant': Macro and Micropolitics at Commemorations

As mentioned in Chapter 4, paramilitary-led forms of memorialization can be ascribed to the 'vernacular' dimension of memory. Throughout this book, however, this author has argued that, while memorials still pertain to a microlevel of remembrance, they act as a gateway to a wider interpretative level, linking each casualty listed to a macrolevel *national* 'imagined community'. Here, it will be illustrated how a similar process can be at play during commemorative ceremonies and how they can combine issues pertaining to the sphere of community politics while still opening up a communication channel for national political messages to be delivered.

Although the permanent disbandment of the UFF was the 'breaking news' of the 2007 Remembrance Day ceremony, the UDA's statement dealt with the issue in its 'Action 2' section, half way through the official announcement. The first topics of importance brought to people's attention by the leadership were their confidence in the 'new democratic dispensation that will lead to permanent political stability' and an incitement to the Loyalist community to register to vote and develop ways of getting their political voices heard (UDA 2007). Feeling that 'the majority of Unionist politicians are unable to defend our rights at present but [recognizing] that politics in the new assembly are very much in transition', the clear call from the leadership was to abandon the marginalization in which the Protestant working class lives and to participate more actively in the political life of the province, so that 'our communities can become equals in the new political dispensation and shared future, achieving a lasting and sustainable peace' (ibid.). This stance on 'state' politics was forcefully reiterated in the speech given by Jackie McDonald, during which he openly expressed support for the then Northern Ireland First Minister Ian Paisley's political conduct, because

> he had to do it. I know a lot of people aren't happy; he has to make progress; we have to have an Assembly; we have to have devolved government, whatever the price, we have to have it, we have to move on. I supported when he did it; I knew he would do it before he did, and I still support him; I still agree with what he is doing. (McDonald 2007)

After a brief mention of the controversy about funding between the UDA and the then Social Development minister, Margaret Ritchie,[15] the brigadier went on to launch his call to 'awaken the sleeping giant':

and say the folks on the hill [Stormont minister, as the Northern Ireland Assembly sits in Stormont Castle, situated on top of a hill] don't wanna listen to us and they wanna do their own thing and they wanna play politics; let them! . . . we'll do it ourselves; we're awakening the sleeping giant . . . We have to register to vote and vote for somebody from within our ranks, within our own estates, within our own community. And let that Loyalist voice take it to the hill and speak on our behalf. (ibid.)

Thus, commemorative events such as Remembrance Sunday services are often used to connect people at grassroots level with the political developments 'up in the hill' and can act as a communication channel for political messages pertaining to the macrolevel of 'state' or 'national' politics – and, in some cases, as electoral propaganda rallies. As a community representative explained:

it is important for people from particular organizations to give this sort of speeches, because . . . they put it in more plainer terms . . . They are getting it over to the people, because there's a lot of propaganda and news reports, but we are hearing it from the horse's mouth so to speak. And the people who is doing them speeches, people in this community would listen to something they say quicker than, say, what a mainstream Unionist party person would say . . . because they have been where we have, they can see it from our point of view; they have been directly involved in the conflict . . . so they know what they are talking about.

However, commemorations are concurrently occasions where the leadership, both political and paramilitary, can contend with issues pertaining to the microlevel of politics, taking a position on matters that, being part of their everyday lives, closely affect the local communities. During the 2007 Remembrance Sunday service, the focus was on criminality, specifically drug dealing: 'Action 4' of the UDA's statement gave 'a general order to all members not to be involved in crime or criminality', coldly stating that 'people [who have been involved in drug dealing] must be rooted out and never be allowed to breath [sic] in our ranks' (UDA 2007). Jackie McDonald reiterated this firm condemnation in his speech, inviting the community to 'shop' the drug dealers:

we have to get rid of the criminality as the statement says. The drug dealers must go. If they can't shoot them, shop them, I'm telling ya. Don't think anybody is an informer, if they tell the PSNI where the drugs are or where the drug dealers are, because it's our kids that suffer. (McDonald 2007)

While this is clearly a message aimed at the membership, laying out internal parameters of discipline and cohesion, it concurrently has a significant effect on the local community, challenging long-established attitudes among residents and setting the ground for community workers to tackle the issue more effectively in the streets of Sandy Row. As one community worker admitted in interview with the author,

> because that platform was used for such a public statement, people like myself can actually begin to quite easily kind of challenge those behaviours that are still going on on the ground with the back-up of the very public statement that was made. So, the statement about going to the police if you know about drug dealers and things like that, we can reinforce, we can take the lead from that and reinforce it on the ground, when we hear if there's drugs being sold or whatever. It's good for the likes of community representatives like myself who are trying to deal with the issues on the ground, but you may not have felt that you could tackle them as effectively, because there wasn't that public statement from the leadership of the organization.

As memorials 'open up' a national dimension by linking individual deaths to a wider interpretative framework or overarching narrative, acting as a linchpin between the sacrifice paid by local individuals and communities and the broader 'national' struggle, a similar process can be detected in the case of commemorative events. As has been illustrated above, main orations are the arena where both macro (national or state) politics and micro (community) politics are played out. While opening up an understanding of and communication channel with the greater 'Politics' of the state, political messages given at commemorations can simultaneously affect local communities' behaviours and set out the parameters for community 'politics', creating a political 'mesolevel' that the leadership – whether of a political party or a paramilitary group – can control to convey a difficult political message in times of transition.

This chapter has investigated how the 'fatherless' UDA has struggled to establish a legitimizing historical genealogy for itself and how, initially, it attempted to appropriate the UVF's 'rightful' heritage of the Somme and then, since 2007, it has 'proposed' the Ulster Defence Union as its historical 'forefathers'. The UDA 2007 Remembrance Sunday service in Sandy Row illustrates how paramilitary-related commemorative events are occasions when community politics are played out, but how they simultaneously act as a gateway to a symbolic national dimension and the macrolevel of state politics. This chapter is the last of the four case study chapters: having examined how the four main paramilitary groups in Northern Ireland have attempted to project a credible narrative about the conflict in post-conflict Northern Ireland, Chapter 9 now turns to the 'memory receivers', focusing on the complex relationship they have with the paramilitary groups that live, operate and 'make' memory among them. Based on a door-to-door survey in four areas – Clonard, Turf Lodge, Woodvale and Sandy Row – the next chapter investigates the extent to which local communities have 'bought into' these narratives, and discusses their perceptions and attitudes with regard to memorials and commemorations in their areas.

Notes

1. This famous mural was replaced with a portrait of William III in 2012, as part of a plan of economic regeneration for the area. See 'Sandy Row Loyalist Mural Being Replaced with William of Orange Painting' (2012).
2. The UVF erected a memorial next to the Sandy Row Community Centre to remember the 1912 Ulster Volunteer Force South Belfast Battalion, which features the three stones that formed the crest above the front entrance of the now demolished Brewery Buildings. They depict a crown, the (red) hand of Ulster and the crest of the city of Belfast and they are thought to be the last surviving artefacts from the UVF's initial mobilization in Belfast in 1912 (UVF, South Belfast Battalion 1912, Viggiani 2013).
3. The UDA emblem is 'a white shield with a red cross and the Red Hand of Ulster . . . centred on a white star. In each quadrant created by the cross are the logos of the four [sister] organizations: UDA, UDF [Ulster Defence Force], UFF and UPA [Ulster Protestant Action]. Underneath is the Latin inscription *Quis Separabit* and partially covered by the shield are the Ulster Flag and the Union Jack' (Jarman 1992: 157).
4. An exception was constituted by a series of historical murals in the so-called Hammer estate in the Lower Shankill, depicting the Siege of Derry/Londonderry and the 1641 (Catholic) rebellion in Ireland (wrongly dated 1600); see Rolston (2003a: 52–53). They were removed in 2012.
5. The murals were located in the Lower Newtownards Road, Belfast and Lincoln Courts, Waterside, Derry/Londonderry, but they no longer exist. An example still exists in Highfield Drive, Belfast. In 2006, a memorial stone in memory of the fallen volunteers of 'A' Company, West Belfast Brigade, Ulster Defence Association/Ulster Freedom Fighters was added to this mural (UDA/UFF, 'A' Company, West Belfast Brigade, Viggiani 2013). A more recent example appeared in the 'Hammer' area in the Lower Shankill in the summer of 2012.
6. Set up in 1998 to monitor parades in Northern Ireland, the Northern Ireland Parades Commission is clear in excluding the display of paramilitary flags such as UDA flags.
7. On the display of UDU flags in Derry/Londonderry, see 'UDU Flags "Must Come Down" – MLA' (2009) and 'UDU Flags "Not Paramilitary"' (2009).
8. In agreement with the local paramilitaries, the mural was removed in 2006 in order for the owner of the property to secure a mortgage, which had previously been refused because of the painting on the side of the house. A smaller replica of the mural adorns the right-hand sidewall of the memorial garden in City Way; it was added to the original structure in November 2007.

9. The Taskforce, addressing the needs of working-class Protestant communities, was established in April 2004 by the then Minister for Social Development, John Spellar MP, and was composed of senior civil servants recruited from different governmental departments. Within this initiative, the Sandy Row Project Team was specifically set up to carry out 'a focused piece of work targeted on the Sandy Row area . . . [to] examine the delivery and effectiveness of public services in the area and identify scope for improvement . . . [to] consider the need and focus for specific initiatives in relation to access to employment, skills training, adult literacy and youth intervention; and [to] identify measures to promote community development and community cohesion, particularly leadership training' (NIDSD 2004).

10. Specifically, a grant of £39,954 from Belfast City Council under the Neighbourhood Economic Development Programme (NEDP), Phase 2 and 3 (Belfast City Council, Freedom of Information request E521/00 2008) and £1.3 million through the 'Big Lottery Fund Transforming Your Space' initiative (Northern Ireland Housing Executive, Freedom of Information request RFI/440 2008b).

11. For a history of the process of 'democratization' with regard to war dead names in military graveyards and on war monuments across Europe, see Mosse (1990: 80–106).

12. It is worthwhile to note that, while Remembrance Day is the official day in memory of all British and Commonwealth soldiers who died on active service during the two world wars and subsequent conflicts, the Battle of the Somme is specifically commemorated on 1 July. For a detailed history of Remembrance Sunday commemorations, see Gregory (1994) and King (1998). For the memorial activity around the Somme in Northern Ireland, see Jarman (1999), Bryan (2000: 56–68), Graham and Shirlow (2002) and Brown (2007).

13. After the dissolution of the UDP in November 2001, ex-UDP members Sammy Duddy, Frank McCoubrey, Jim Wright, Frankie Gallagher and Tommy Kirkham formed the UPRG to act as a political advisory body to the UDA (Wood 2006: 298–99). In October 2006, Kirkham left the group to create a new body under the name of 'Beyond Conflict'. This breakaway was reflected in the military ranks, with the UDA South East Antrim Brigade announcing a split from the mainstream organization. See 'UDA Group "Wants £8m to Disband"' (2006).

14. For the full UDA 2007 Remembrance Day Statement, see 'Ulster Defence Association Remembrance Day Statement, 11 November 2007' (2007).

15. In March 2007, the then Social Development minister, David Hanson, announced that the Northern Ireland Office was to grant £1.2m to the three-year Conflict Transformation Initiative (CTI) project drawn up by the UPRG with the aims of moving the UDA away from violence and crime, and of encouraging redevelopment in Loyalist communities. The government, however, stipulated that funding would be withdrawn if the UDA did not end all violent and criminal activity, including extortion rackets and drug dealing. Following clashes between UDA factions in Carrickfergus and Bangor during summer 2007, the then SDLP Social Development minister, Margaret Ritchie, announced that funding would be withdrawn within sixty days if the UDA did not engage meaningfully with the Independent International Commission on Decommissioning and start to decommission its weapons (Kearney 2007).

Chapter 9

DISSECTING CONSENSUS

'Memory Receivers' and the Narrative's 'Hidden Transcript'

⋙•⋘

> I go to a remembrance service and it's just not about
> them names on the wall; I have people in my head
> that when I am at that commemoration, their name
> might not be said aloud there, but it's been shouted in
> my head very, very much.
> – Loyalist respondent in interview with the author

The focus of this book so far has been the investigation of the practical means, symbolic systems and ideological reasons behind the erection of memorials to the casualties of the Troubles in many areas of Belfast. Attention has been given primarily to those organizations – specifically paramilitary groups – who have attempted to assert control over the past in order to project competing narratives of historical legitimation, national identification and political justification. Applying the theoretical approach to symbolism and community championed by Cohen (1985) and the critical distinction between 'public' and 'hidden transcript' posited by Scott (1990), this chapter attempts to shed light upon the other end of the spectrum of these discursive projections, on those 'communities' who periodically witness memorials being built a few yards away from their homes and parades passing through their streets – ultimately, the grassroots level and 'base support' who are the intended recipients of these constructed narrations of the past. The aim is to investigate the complex relationship between those this author has termed throughout the book 'memory makers' and 'memory receivers', and to uncover the extent to which such narratives are accepted by the latter, based on the views of a hundred local Belfast residents. Although the survey cannot claim universal statistical representativeness, it first provides a form of 'casting-out-nines' proof of the degree of acceptance and ownership of these memorial projects among the general population, and is a way of measuring the power of penetration and adoption of these collective narratives; second, it represents one of the first analyses of the 'issue of reception' of visual representations and embodiments of collective memory of the Troubles in Northern Ireland.

Recalling the observations in Chapter 4, collective narratives about the past can be regarded as 'ideological hat stands' able to subsume within themselves a variety of individual experiences and interpretations of that past, generating a perceived commonality of belief among its adherents. Their core constituents are a series of symbols or symbolic frameworks, which are shared but ultimately 'interpreted' in discrete ways by different people or by the same individual at different moments in time. This possibility of attaching one's own personal meaning to a commonly accepted symbol is precisely what allows the collectivity that shares a discursive framework or collective narrative to 'gloss over' the full range of specific meanings. Members of a collectivity 'share the symbol, but do not necessarily share its meaning', and it is exactly 'because symbols are malleable in this way [that] they can be made to "fit" the circumstances of the individual' (Cohen 1985: 15, 18). As illustrated by the case studies in the previous chapters, this is readily evident when examining the process of interpretation of memorials to the casualties of the conflict in Northern Ireland. Each individual death is afforded its unique relevance, and its ontological distinctiveness is acknowledged; each interpretation of that death is inevitably skewed by the idiosyncratic experience that the agent of the interpretative process has of the events or the individuals commemorated. Through a careful use of shared symbolic repertoires, however, those deaths are inevitably linked to a wider interpretative framework and subsumed within an overarching collective narrative of resistance and 'national' struggle championed by the different paramilitary groups. Thus, individuality and commonality are in most cases reconciled. Paradoxically, the process at play is similar for Republican and Loyalist memorialization, with the difference that 'claimed' individual deaths are incorporated into opposing, distinctive collective narratives of the past.

Paraphrasing Cohen, Jenkins (2004: 112) affirms that participation in a common symbolic domain, that is, sharing with others a similar 'sense of things', constitutes 'community membership'. Cohen (1985: 12) defines the word 'community' as 'the members of a group of people [who] (a) have something in common with each other, which (b) distinguishes them in a significant way from the members of other putative groups'. The idea of community is, therefore, 'relational', in that it is based upon the differentiation of one group of people from other social groups, and the concept of 'boundary' assumes great relevance as the discriminating element that 'marks the beginning and end of a community . . . and encapsulates the identity of the community'; community itself is not a structural entity but a symbolic construct, 'existing in the minds of the beholders' (ibid.). The narrative(s) through which collective memory finds expression are at the core of this process of community membership 'creation', in that they provide a common symbolic domain that acts as a 'mask of similarity which all [community members] can wear, an umbrella of solidarity under which all can shelter' (Jenkins 2004: 110). Differences of opinion and semiotic interpretation among members of the same community are inevitable, but the adherence to a shared framework of recollection and remembrance masks these differences, constructing 'a semblance of agreement and convergence' and emphasizing 'the boundary between members and non-members' (ibid.: 113). This boundary is not material or geographic, but symbolic, and can be interpreted as the demarcating line between different symbolic domains – in other words, as marking the beginning and end of different collective narratives shared by a particular social group or community. Ultimately, narratives about a collective past are intended by their promoters to be a community's 'consistent face to the outside world' (ibid.), what Cohen (1985: 74) defines as 'the public face and "typical" mode' of the community – that is, 'the sense [members of a community] have of its perception by people on the other side'.

If in Northern Ireland a 'narrative boundary' can traditionally be traced between Republican and Loyalist narratives of the conflict, this chapter attempts to expose the interpretative discrepancies and tensions within each group and to explore what Cohen (1985) terms 'the private face and idiosyncratic mode' of the community – in other words, the community members' own sense of the community and participation in its common symbolic domain 'as refracted through all the complexities of their lives and experiences'. Since memorials can be considered as expressions and reifications of these narratives, a qualitative analysis of community members' opinions of them can facilitate an understanding of the extent to which individuals do actually share and accept these sets of symbols.

Before exploring the variety of reactions towards processes of memorialization, it is worthwhile drawing attention to the fact that the term 'community' can have an elusive nature and has multiple meanings that depend upon the identity and motivation of the term's user and the circumstance of this usage.[1] During interviews with the promoters of memorial programmes, it was a common occurrence to hear that these initiatives were carried out 'with the full support of the community' or represented 'the will of the entire community'. When used by the so-called 'memory makers', the very term 'community' becomes a key constituent of the narratives of legitimation that they are trying to promote, and must, therefore, be accepted with a hint of reservation. As Jenkins (2004: 112) suggests,

> 'Community' is itself a symbolic construct upon which people draw, rhetorically and strategically. Claims to act in the best interests of the 'community' or to represent the 'community' are powerful. We're all supposed to be in favour of 'community': it's a feel-good word carrying a powerful symbolic load, hence its political uses . . . 'Community' is ideological: it not only says how things are, it says how they *should* be . . . Hence its rhetorical potency in ethnically divided situations such as Northern Ireland. (Italics in the original)

Thus, in Northern Ireland the idea of community and of 'communal championing' often conceals 'identity politics' and it is used as a mechanism of social and ideological control (Bauman 2001: 2–6).

In his work *Domination and the Arts of Resistance*, Scott (1990) postulates a useful analytical distinction between 'public transcript' and 'hidden transcript' in any power relation. The 'public transcript' is 'the *self*-portrait of dominant elites as they would have themselves seen' (ibid.: 18); in ideological terms,

> the discourse of the public transcript is a decidedly lopsided discussion. While it is unlikely to be merely a skein of lies and misrepresentation, it is, on the other hand, a highly partisan and partial narrative. It is designed to be impressive, to affirm and naturalize the power of dominant elites, and to conceal or euphemize the dirty linen of their rule.

Most importantly, 'the capacity of dominant groups to prevail . . . in defining and constituting what counts as the public transcript [is] . . . no small measure of their power' (ibid.). If one considers dominant groups in a wider sense to encompass not only ruling authorities, but also social groups who have control in defining what constitutes memory and have power over its reification and interpretation, it is possible to regard the different narratives projected by paramilitary groups in Northern Ireland as parallel, yet opposing, 'public transcripts' of the Troubles. As seen in the previous chapters, both Republican and Loyalist narratives of the conflict are partisan and historically selective, and tend to sustain each group's respective claim of ontological necessity and ideological legitimation, while 'forgetting' elements that might discredit or oppose such claims. Moreover, if we examine the relationship between dominants and subordinates in the public performance of power relations, 'with rare, but significant exceptions the public performance of the subordinate will, out of prudence, fear, and desire to curry favour, be shaped to appeal to the expectations of the powerful' and 'any analysis [of these performances] based exclusively on the public transcript is likely to conclude that subordinate groups endorse the terms of their subordination and are willing, even enthusiastic, partners in that subordination' (Scott 1990: 2–4). Thus, if we look at the number of people who, for instance, stand at the side of the street watching memorial parades go by their estates, or local residents who donate money towards the erection of a memorial during door-to-door collections without further investigation into their feelings and motivations, we might well conclude that local memorial initiatives 'represent the will of the entire community' and 'have its full and unconditional support', as promoters passionately claim.

As Scott (1990: 4) points out, however, 'we cannot know how contrived or imposed the performance is unless we can speak, as it were, to the performer offstage, out of this particular power-laden context'. Researchers interested in investigating the subordinates' – or in the case of Northern Ireland, the memory receivers' – 'true' motives and opinions need to gain 'a privileged peek backstage or a rupture in the performance' from where to uncover the 'hidden transcript', that is 'the discourse that takes place "offstage", beyond direct observation by power holders', consisting of 'speeches, gestures and practices that confirm, contradict, or inflect what appears in the public transcript' (ibid.: 4–5). It is in the confidentiality and anonymity of a 'backstage survey' with the local population during their everyday lives, away from power-laden contexts such as commemorations or memorial unveiling ceremonies, that this study has sought to uncover the hidden transcript of power relations over memory in Northern Ireland. Before reflecting upon the findings, however, it is important to further investigate the social and historical relationship between the groups at the opposite ends of the spectrum of this cognitive and communicative process – the paramilitary groups who 'formulate', 'encode' and 'transmit' memory, and the local communities who 'receive' and 'decode' it.

Paramilitary Groups and Local Communities:
A Complex Relationship

According to Burton (1978: 2), the phenomenon of political violence cannot be understood unless it is examined within the historical and social context from which it stems. This argument reflects the opinion, often voiced among those interviewed for this study, that paramilitaries in Northern Ireland are not 'dropped into' the community, but are an intrinsic part of it, a force – whether necessary, desired or destructive – operating from within; communities, therefore, should not be considered as passive spectators, but as an integral element that shapes the dynamics of political violence (Cavanaugh 1997: 46). Many studies have been carried out on the relationship between paramilitary groups and local communities in Northern Ireland (Boyle, Chesney and Hadden 1976; Burton 1978; Darby 1986; Sluka 1989; R. White 1989; Bell 1990; Feldman 1991; Silke 1998); here, it is sufficient to lay out the general terms of this relationship.

In the absence of national state legitimacy and of a perceived 'impartiality' of the traditional law-enforcement mechanisms (both security forces and legal system), paramilitaries in Northern Ireland came to fill the void in the spheres of 'defence' and 'social control' in the areas they controlled (Burton 1978: 128). In her ethnographic study on political violence, Cavanaugh (1997: 39) has found that 'security-related fears' and 'a sense of being collectively rather than individually threatened' from hostile out-groups were the main reasons for militant involvement, with many combatants ascribing their decision to engage in political violence to a sense of 'social responsibility' to defend and protect their communities; whereas Republicans were most affected by 'organized and unorganized state repression', Loyalist violence was 'most affected by Republican violence and activated when Loyalists [felt] threatened' (Cavanaugh 1997: 45). These security-related fears and a sense of collective victimization were shared by the wider Republican and Loyalist communities, creating, especially at the height of the conflict, an interdependency between paramilitaries and community members: paramilitary groups depended on their communities 'for protection, discretion and financial support' (Cavanaugh 1997: 49), whereas communities depended on paramilitaries to maintain security and guarantee protection from what Knox and Monaghan (2002: 10) have termed 'political' crimes, most notably real or perceived threats of an ethnic/sectarian nature from out-groups. It is important to note, however, that throughout the conflict 'communal reactions to paramilitants in both Republican and Loyalist communities were often contradictory, temporal and, in many cases, dependent on political movements' (Cavanaugh 1997: 46); communal support was conditional, and varied from active to passive support 'with some gradations of grey within each grouping' (ibid.) – however, as a Catholic resident, non-supportive of the Republican movement, recalls in interview with the author, open criticism was very rarely voiced for fear of reprisal or out of a sense of respect.

In addition, paramilitaries came to fulfil the need for intracommunal order and control against 'normal' crime in the areas they controlled. Since the state and its organs were seen as either 'active participants' in the conflict or as ineffective, the usual channels through which to tackle 'normal' crime were closed off, especially for the Catholic population, and local communities turned to so-called 'informal justice mechanisms' – that is to say, 'acts committed outside the boundaries of the formal criminal justice system [which] usually involve collective violence' to deal with offences such as burglary, theft, rape and drug dealing (Knox and Monaghan 2002: 11). Republican paramilitary groups assumed the role of 'informal policing' of their own areas from the beginning of the Troubles, justifying their actions by claiming the absence of a legitimate police service: the RUC/PSNI was, in fact, a force almost entirely composed of Protestant members and was seen as harassing Catholics with unwarranted house searches and arrests. It was considered to be as acting as an agent of the British government, in many cases allegedly in collusion with Loyalist paramilitary groups (Knox and Monaghan 2002: 71).[2] Conversely, the Loyalist community did recognize the RUC/PSNI as the official, legitimate police force of Northern Ireland, but considered it ineffectual, 'part of a system of criminal justice which cannot react quickly enough and exact retribution deemed appropriate by victims of crime' (ibid.).[3]

With the cessation of a permanent state of conflict, the role of paramilitaries as 'defenders' of their own areas from external attacks ceased to be prominent, and many interviewees remarked on the fact that now they had peace, there was no need for paramilitaries anymore. The role of paramilitaries as 'community police', however, is less clearly defined. Notwithstanding the endorsement of the Police Service of Northern Ireland by Sinn Féin in January 2007, some Catholic respondents believed there is still a need for 'informal justice' and expressed quite nostalgic views of the days when the IRA patrolled the streets of West Belfast, maintaining order and social control.[4] As an elderly Catholic woman affirmed,

> I used to pray for peace, but peace is worse. Everyone is bored now and
> turns to vandalism. I never thought I would say this, but I wish the IRA

was out again because we have no law and order anymore in the area. On sunny days, everyone was out in the parks, but now everyone is afraid to go because of the gangs of youth drinking there.

Though not an opinion widely voiced, it is understandable given the increase in attacks on elderly residents in West Belfast and a general rise in anti-social behaviour among the local 'hoods'.[5] In contrast, some Loyalist respondents expressed fear that should paramilitaries disappear completely, the societal void left would soon be filled by criminal gangs that the police alone would be unable to control.

Following the provisions of the Good Friday/Belfast Agreement, and facilitated by a series of governmental and EU funding schemes, politically motivated ex-prisoners and ex-combatants have tried to negotiate a new role for themselves within their own communities and in the wider Northern Irish society, embarking upon community-based activities and so-called conflict transformation initiatives. In their study on the role of former prisoners in post-conflict Northern Ireland, Shirlow and McEvoy (2008: 107–10) reported that 81.3 per cent of Republican respondents and 46.7 per cent of Loyalist respondents had been involved in community work since their release from prison, most notably in initiatives aimed at reducing interface violence and in youth and community safety/restorative justice schemes. In addition, politically motivated ex-combatants who organized around ex-prisoners' groups or local residents' associations have attempted to 'empower' their communities, establishing drop-in centres where community members can seek advice on housing, benefits, employment, legal matters, education, and physical and psychological health. More broadly, former prisoners and ex-combatants can be seen to be playing three conflict-transformation roles:

> in practical community development work within [their respective] communities . . . in direct conflict-related work, such as projects designed to reduce sectarian violence at interface areas . . . [and] in the creation of personal, communal and social narratives linked to the transition from conflict-exploring issues such as communal attitudes to truth recovery, commemoration and "dealing with the past". (Shirlow and McEvoy 2008: 123)

However, the relationship that Republican and Loyalist ex-combatants have now with their respective communities presents significant differences. Because of a general political mobilization of the Republican community around prisoner-related issues during the Troubles and the fact that imprisonment for politically motivated reasons impacted on a more significant share of the Catholic population, 'the status of former [politically motivated] prisoner is more likely to be seen as a "badge of honour"', denoting an activist who was imprisoned by the British state for his or her part in the war and who now continues the 'struggle' by other means (Shirlow and McEvoy 2008: 139). Around 70 per cent of Republican ex-combatants found it 'easy to fit in' their community after 1998 and 'there are high levels of community expectation upon former Republican prisoners that they will take on leadership roles at all levels' (Shirlow and McEvoy 2008: 84, 139). Conversely, Loyalist ex-combatants have experienced higher levels of isolation and social stigma within Loyalist communities, given the lack of a 'history of political prisoners or the eulogising of the "law-breaking"' that Republicans have and the attitudes of condemnation and criminalization of 'middle' Unionism (Shirlow and McEvoy 2008: 138). In particular, Loyalist ex-combatants feel that they are treated with loathing and mistrust by their community and that they are all demonized by the criminal activities of a small percentage of Loyalists, to the extent that 'it's come to the stage now that many [Loyalist] ex-POWs are afraid to build an extension, buy a new car or own their own house because they'll be stigmatized as drug dealers, criminals or gangsters' (Shirlow and McEvoy 2008: 84, 139). These contrasting community attitudes towards ex-combatants are mirrored in the findings on local residents' opinions about the memorial activity promoted by the different paramilitary groups, in particular the erection of memorials to the casualties of the Troubles in their areas.

Coexisting in Ambivalence: Memorials and Local Residents

If we take as valid the 'public transcript' of memorialization of the Troubles that can be inferred from conversations with the promoters of various memorial projects, support for and ownership of these initiatives is widespread among the local population – both for Republicans and Loyalists. The survey conducted in four areas of Belfast found a higher acceptance of memorial projects among Catholic residents than Protestants: 78 per cent of Catholic respondents (rising to 96 per cent in the staunchly Republican area of Clonard), as opposed to 54 per cent of Protestant, agreed with the erection of memorials in their areas. These findings mirrored the attitude towards visual displays of identity observed by the Northern Ireland Life and Times surveys (NILT), where 83 per cent of Catholics as opposed to 78 per cent of Protestants stated that they do not 'feel annoyed' when seeing, respectively, Republican and Loyalist murals, kerb paintings or flags (NILT 2008: REPMUR2, LOYMUR2).

When asked to elaborate upon the motivation of their agreement, 35 per cent of respondents (both Catholic and Protestant) affirmed that they believe memorials are a fitting tribute to the people from the area that died during the conflict, and 21 per cent that they are symbols of local history and community identity and memory. However, some respondents voiced a certain degree of cynicism and ambivalence in relation to the degree of 'communal agreement' found in their areas: they recognized that many residents might not support these initiatives, but acquiesce 'to the hidden power of quite powerful organizations locally' (interview with a Catholic Nationalist) because they feel they have no choice. As one Protestant resident summed it up, echoing the differential power relationship necessary for a group to prevail in defining what counts as 'public transcript', 'you have to go with the flow whether you like it or not, because it doesn't matter if you say "no", these memorials will go up anyway'.

With regard to the level of opposition against these memorials, only 3 per cent of respondents were able to recall an instance when dissent was openly voiced, whereas 86 per cent of respondents stated that there had not been any resistance in their area (11 per cent of respondents did not know or could not remember). When asked if this was to be ascribed to a real or perceived fear of paramilitary retaliation, 32 per cent of Protestant and 14 per cent of Catholic respondents answered affirmatively. One Protestant resident recalled how one summer he had confronted some local youths who were painting the kerbstones red, white and blue for the upcoming marching season; forbidding them to paint the section of the kerb running in front of his house, he had expected to have his property vandalized in return for his 'affront'. An interesting comment was made by a female Catholic respondent who believed that local residents do not openly challenge the erection of memorials in their area because, rather than being afraid of local paramilitaries, any opposition would result in social stigma and cause them to be ostracized by the rest of the community. Similarly, one Catholic male respondent confessed that he volunteered his skills as a builder when the local memorial was being built not because he was supportive of the Republican cause, but because he was afraid of losing local building contracts if he was not seen to be making a contribution. These insights seem to reflect the observation made in Chapter 4 in relation to criticism and opposition to the official or dominant narrative, and confirm the existence of a variety of internal mechanisms of social control that absorb potential challenges to the narrative from within. Conversely, 68 per cent of Catholic and 58 per cent of Protestant respondents did not believe that the lack of protest by local residents against the construction of memorials was due to fear of paramilitary intimidation; some pointed at the lack of vandalism against memorials and the high attendance at fundraising events and ceremonies at the commemorative site as a proof and measurement of the local community's genuine support for these initiatives.

Consultation and 'Ownership'

An issue related to the level of community support for memorial projects is that of consultation and perceived 'ownership' of the memorial. In general terms, consultation with the local communities is a more common occurrence in Republican than Loyalist areas, with 40 per cent of Catholics as opposed to 20 per cent of Protestants stating that they had been consulted by local ex-prisoners or paramilitaries before the erection of memorials. These percentages, however, would seem not to corroborate the claim made by the promoters of these memorials that consultation with the local communities is widespread and represents a key phase in the process, as, of those surveyed, 54 per cent Catholics and 76 per cent Protestants claimed that their opinion was not sought. In particular, the least degree of consultation with the local community was registered in Turf Lodge, with only 13 per cent of surveyed residents having been consulted; Woodvale and Sandy Row followed, both with 20 per cent, whereas the highest level of consultation was found in Clonard, with 62 per cent of local residents having been informed before the memorial garden was built. To a certain degree, the different types of memorial initiatives examined may explain this difference, with the erection of a memorial plaque (Turf Lodge) perhaps necessitating less consultation than the building of a memorial garden (Clonard).

If we examine issues of perceived 'ownership' of permanent commemorative structures by local communities, the claim often made by promoters that memorials – especially memorial gardens – are the outcome of a 'community effort' and the assumption that local residents consider them as 'people's gardens' because of their direct involvement in the fundraising and building processes were somewhat weakened by the findings of the survey. Community involvement was significantly higher in Republican than Loyalist areas, with 40 per cent of Catholic respondents, as opposed to 8 per cent of Loyalist respondents, having contributed either financially or materially towards the erection of memorials. In particular, 74 per cent of Clonard residents provided financial or material support for the construction of the memorial garden in Bombay Street: 40 per cent of those who provided support made a financial contribution; 40 per cent either donated building materials or volunteered their skills; 10 per cent participated in door-to-door collections; and 10 per cent provided refreshments for the builders. It is important to specify, however, that the lower percentage of support in Loyalist areas is not entirely a reflection of Protestant residents' unwillingness to participate directly in memorial projects in their areas, but may in part be ascribed to the lack of fundraising initiatives, with some residents stating that they would have made a financial contribution if a door-to-door collection had been organized.

Cohabiting the Same Space

The differing degrees of 'ownership' and direct communal involvement observed above are reflected in the spatial perception that local residents have of memorials and, particularly in relation to memorial gardens, the use that they make of these sites on a day-to-day basis. Regular 'acknowledgement' of these memorials is somewhat similar in Republican and Loyalist areas, with 68 per cent of Catholic and 60 per cent of Protestant respondents affirming that they notice local memorials on their daily commute to work, school and/or local shops. This percentage rose to 78 per cent in Clonard, perhaps given the size of the memorial garden in Bombay Street, as opposed to 56.5 per cent in Turf Lodge, where some residents admitted to having never noticed the plaque in memory of Bunting and Little.

Surprisingly, only 40 per cent of Woodvale residents noticed on a daily basis the three very colourful full-gable-wall UVF murals, whereas 80 per cent of Sandy Row residents regularly acknowledged the presence of their local memorial garden, situated in a side street away from the busy main Sandy Row road. This can perhaps be attributed to the fact that a memorial garden is seen more as a 'communal space' than a mural; also, murals can often appear in the space of only a few hours and are seen as the work of single artists rather than the orchestrated efforts of a group of people. Although some residents believed the number of memorials in Belfast is too high or disagreed with the presence of a memorial in their area, no Catholic respondent and only two Protestant respondents mentioned any feelings of intimidation by these displays of identity, similar to the findings by the NILT survey, where 9 per cent of Catholics and 11 per cent of Protestants stated that they 'feel intimidated' when seeing murals, kerb paintings or flags (NILT 2008: REPMUR, LOYMUR).

When asked whether they considered these sites as 'sacred space', 36 per cent of Catholics and 32 per cent of Protestants answered that they considered memorials as hallowed and sanctified as graveyards and churches, to the extent that some respondents blessed themselves or stopped to say a prayer when passing them. Conversely, more than half of respondents – 54 per cent Catholics and 62 per cent Protestants – did not attach religious or pseudo-religious sacredness to these sites: of this group, 20 per cent of interviewees (both Catholic and Protestant) considered memorials to be respectful spots, at times inspiring reverence, whereas 32 per cent attached no spiritual or personal meaning to these sites. Some of the respondents for whom memorials had no significance at all recognized, however, that their perception might have been different had they known or been related to any of the individuals commemorated.

Local residents in Clonard and Sandy Row were asked whether the memorial gardens in their areas were used on other occasions and for different purposes than periodical commemorative ceremonies.[6] Seventy per cent of respondents in Clonard and 28 per cent of respondents in Sandy Row answered affirmatively, indicating the presence of tourists as the most common occurrence (42 per cent and 29 per cent of respondents, respectively). A minority of Catholic residents (15 per cent) complained about the number of tourists these sites attracted, labelling the numerous political tours organized by ex-prisoners as mere 'money-making' exercises that do not bring to life the actual history of the place. Interestingly, the second most popular use was for family members, friends and ex-comrades to stop at the garden to reflect and meditate (31.5 per cent of Clonard and 28 per cent of Sandy Row residents). Conversely, 22 per cent of Clonard and 64 per cent of Sandy Row interviewees stated that memorial gardens are not frequented on a daily basis by local residents, the most common reason indicated (67 per cent and 81 per cent, respectively) being that these landmarks become part of the territory and people become somewhat accustomed to them. As one Catholic respondent admitted, 'I know it sounds awful, but [the memorial] is like that tree there; I don't notice it every time I pass it, because it's there, it becomes part of the area'.

When asked if the memorials in their areas had ever been vandalized, 90 per cent of Protestant and 82 per cent of Catholic residents did not recall any such instances. Interestingly, the majority of total respondents (55 per cent of Protestants and 83 per cent of Catholics) ascribed this to a general sense of respect and reverence towards these sites, regardless of one's own religious or political affiliation, whereas 44 per cent of Protestants and only 10 per cent of Catholics believed this to be the result of fear of paramilitary retaliation. As one Republican interviewee affirmed, 'it's wrong to vandalize [memorials], no matter who puts them up, the UDA, the UVF. I disagree wholeheartedly; it's like wrecking graves. That was somebody's son, somebody's daughter ... the man is dead, the girl is dead; they do no harm. You are only lowering yourself [if you vandalize memorials]'. Conversely, 14 per cent of Catholic and 10 per cent of Protestant residents recalled episodes of vandalism against the memorials: these attacks were predominantly of a sectarian nature in Republican areas (86 per cent of Catholic respondents), especially in Clonard, whereas in Loyalist areas acts of vandalism were mainly the result of antisocial behaviour by the local youth or young neighbouring gangs (80 per cent of Protestant respondents), reflecting the persisting 'symbolic rivalry' between the UVF and the UDA after the violent feud in 2000 between these two organizations. The most common attacks were the 'paint bombing' of plaques and murals, and causing general damage to components such as plinths and plants.[7]

Reasons behind Memorialization

The second part of the survey attempted to verify the extent to which the eight most common reasons quoted by the 'memory makers' as the rationale behind memorialization were, in fact, held to be true by the 'memory receivers'.[8] Although some crossovers between answers and, indeed, between underlying motives have been observed, these motivations have been grouped under the following four subcategories: social memory, territorialization, historical change and politico-ideological exercise (see Table 9.1 for a general overview).

Table 9.1 Rationale for memorialization

Rationale for Memorialization	Agree		Disagree		Do not know	
	Cath	Prot	Cath	Prot	Cath	Prot
Social memory						
Form of remembrance	88%	88%	8%	8%	4%	4%
Form of education	54%	30%	36%	60%	10%	10%
Territorialization						
Territorial marker	42%	64%	40%	26%	18%	10%
Historical change						
Sign that conflict is over	32%	28%	52%	56%	16%	16%
Keep paramilitaries busy	40%	44%	38%	26%	22%	30%
Community anchor	52%	52%	26%	38%	22%	10%
Politico-ideological exercise						
Portraying a one-side story	38%	58%	34%	34%	28%	8%
Political platform	50%	26%	40%	56%	10%	18%

Source: Viggiani 2013

Social Memory

Unsurprisingly, 88 per cent of both Catholic and Protestant respondents believe that memorials are built to remember the local dead who lost their lives as a direct result of the conflict. This reflects the genuine desire to pay a fitting permanent tribute to deceased comrades and friends expressed by ex-prisoners and ex-combatants in the previous chapters. Among the 8 per cent of both Catholic and Protestant respondents who did not agree that this was a rationale behind memorials, 25 per cent were of the opinion that people in Northern Ireland did not need memorials to remember what had happened during the thirty years of conflict, whereas 37.5 per cent pointed to the fact that some of the individuals commemorated were not from the area where the memorial was located and, therefore, had been included on plaques or murals solely because of the ex-prisoners' or ex-combatants' will.[9]

As social memory is inextricably linked to the transmission of shared values and beliefs to the younger generation, a strictly related issue concerned the latent educational function of these memorials. A majority of Catholic respondents, 54 per cent, as opposed to 30 per cent of Protestant respondents, believed that memorials have an active role in educating the younger generation. As seen in Chapters 5 and 6, this can be explained in light of the fact that memorials are considered a key facet of the numerous local history projects promoted by Republican groups in order to articulate a 'history from below' that granted recognition to the so far unheard voices of Republican communities and allowed them to 'set the historical record straight'. In addition, it might be seen as echoing the long-standing Irish Republican tradition of transmitting Irish/Republican history in jails (English 2003). In general terms, three different points of view seemed to prevail in relation to the educational function of memorials: firstly, they were seen as 'catalysts' of local history, stirring curiosity in the minds of young people and, in some cases, prompting further clarification from older family members and neighbours on the events and individuals commemorated; secondly, they were seen as 'danger signals', warning young people to learn from the mistakes of the past in order to avoid further waves of violence and death; finally, they were eyed with a certain degree of worry by the older generations as 'advertising billboards', glorifying paramilitary culture and calling to join the ranks, or at least to become actively involved in political or cultural activities linked to ex-combatants' and ex-prisoners' groups. As one Protestant respondent summed up,

> murals glorify paramilitaries and they might be perceived differently by young people than by adults. Young people might think 'I would like to be on that wall'. [Memorials] advertise these organizations. If something is

advertised, it means that it's present, and perhaps it's something that you can or should join.

Interestingly, 36 per cent of Catholic and 60 per cent of Protestant respondents did not think that memorials had any impact on the younger generation, quoting the typical apathy of teenage years and the fact that young people are accustomed to seeing memorials in their areas as the main reasons for this opinion.

Territorialization

Unsurprisingly, more Protestant than Catholic respondents (64 per cent and 42 per cent, respectively) considered memorials to be territorial markers. As seen in Chapter 3, forms of memorialization have assumed an enhanced function of spatial demarcation within Loyalism after the 2000 feud between the UDA and the UVF, to the extent that one Protestant resident described, rather colourfully, Loyalist paramilitary groups as acting 'like dogs pissing on a wall'. In contrast, the lower percentage of Catholic respondents interpreting memorials as marking out different paramilitary groups' 'areas of influence' can be explained in light of the fact that the INLA never achieved a sufficient degree of public support to challenge the Provisional IRA's territorial predominance of symbolic displays. It is worthwhile noting that, regardless of whether or not it was perceived that these memorials performed a demarcating function, many respondents observed that memorials in Northern Ireland possess an intrinsic divisive function and perpetuate ethnic segregation and sectarianism, mirroring the wider opinion that freedom from displays of sectarian aggression has definitely not been achieved or at best has only been partially achieved in Northern Ireland (NILT 2008: TARGET2A). As one Protestant respondent stated, 'memorials split the community and turn people into bigots'.

On the contrary, 40 per cent of Catholic and 26 per cent of Protestant interviewees did not believe that territorial demarcation was an intended rationale behind memorials. While the former group pointed to the inclusive nature of Republican commemorative sites, where civilians are commemorated alongside volunteers and political activists, the latter group remarked that, in their opinion, Loyalist memorials had been mainly erected to commemorate the casualties of the two world wars.

Historical Change

As investigated in Chapter 3, memorials in Northern Ireland have either been interpreted as a public recognition of the end of the Troubles or as a perpetuation of the conflict through symbolic means. Among the local population, 32 per cent of Catholics and 28 per cent of Protestants believed memorials to be a way of drawing a line under the past, a way of recognizing the end of the conflict by means of presenting to the world a definitive list of casualties. Conversely, 52 per cent of Catholics and 56 per cent of Protestants did not believe that the erection of conflict-related memorials was a clear sign that the 'war' was over. This high percentage is largely due to many respondents misinterpreting the question to mean whether they thought the conflict was really over: 17 per cent of total respondents openly expressed doubts about the precarious nature of peace in Northern Ireland or held a completely pessimistic view that the conflict is not over.

The 'social displacement' experienced by ex-prisoners and ex-combatants after the cessation of a permanent state of conflict represented a related issue. Earlier chapters have explored how memorial projects have been deployed as a way of maintaining discipline, camaraderie and political engagement among previously active members of paramilitary groups: 44 per cent of Protestant and 40 per cent of Catholic residents agreed with the statement that memorial projects 'give paramilitaries something to do now that we have peace'. One Protestant respondent interpreted the relationship between ex-prisoners/ex-combatants and local community as a mutual exchange of support, in the absence of a successful reintegration process of the former group into normal society: 'they can't get any job. We donate to them and that's their wages. In return, they volunteer to look after memorials and organize our commemorations'. Although not a widespread reason of concern, a minority of respondents (6 per cent of total interviewees) did voice their dissatisfaction with the lack of official support mechanisms (mostly the absence of educational and vocational training courses) for the reintegration of ex-combatants into society, and praised ex-prisoners' groups for having autonomously filled that void with minimal assistance from the government or sympathizing political parties.

When asked about the role that commemorative sites play on a wider societal level as 'identity anchors' (see Chapter 3), the majority of respondents (52 per cent of both Catholics and Protestants) agreed that memorials play an important role, especially at times of political transformation, in that they act as a reminder – and a reassurance – of a community's identity, its past and shared values, while the community attempts to make sense of a radically changing world and to renegotiate that same identity and those same values. As one Protestant resident explained in relation to his community:

for so long the Loyalist community was told by Paisley 'no, no, never' and then, just because politically it suits that party and Sinn Féin to come together . . . after thirty years, nearly forty years of violence, to just expect that ingrained fear, the life you haven't chosen [to disappear], you can't expect that . . . that's forty years, that's two generations, so you have to give it another two generations at least to begin to move on.

Similarly, a Catholic respondent recognized that

this is a time now of great soul-searching for the Republican community in terms of political changes and in terms of things that they are having to accept: the IRA officially ending its campaign, even though it had been over for years, just that statement 'those days are over, totally'; weapons dealt with; acceptance for the PSNI – they were massive changes for the Republican community.

Memorials and other forms of remembrance, therefore, become psychological anchors to the past at times when, as a result of shifting historical circumstances, communities struggle to reconcile their shared meaning and interpretation of that past with the new political or social context they are moving to or find themselves in. As one Republican activist explained,

you have a population who were in the midst of a very deep conflict, who are moving into a new period, and so what are their anchors? Their anchors have to be to some extent the past. It becomes, in a sense, a cult of the dead. It has to be about how you place the death of those who died in active service and those civilians who died within the context of where you're moving to.

Politico-ideological Exercise

The last section of the survey aimed to investigate the extent to which the 'memory receivers' are aware of the attempt by the 'memory makers' to project legitimizing political and ideological narratives through commemorative activity. Among Protestant respondents, 58 per cent recognized that memorials tend to portray a one-sided version of the conflict; as one interviewee summed up, '[memorials] can only do so; they can't do both sides'. Interestingly, only 38 per cent of Catholic respondents were of this opinion, which can perhaps be explained in light of the perceived higher 'inclusiveness' of the Provisional movement's narrative of the conflict. As seen in Chapter 5, the narrative projected by the Provisional IRA attempts to give full recognition to the sacrifice of every individual

– including civilians – while subsuming his or her death within an over-arching framework of *communal* national struggle; thus, the version of the conflict portrayed in Provisional IRA's memorials might be perceived as being the Catholic community's version of the conflict, rather than the version promoted by one specific paramilitary group. On the contrary, 34 per cent of both Protestant and Catholic respondents did not believe that memorials portray a partisan version of the conflict: while some respondents doubted that memorials are erected as a way of 'debating' the conflict or 'taking sides', a minority of interviewees stated that memorials – especially those in memory of the casualties of the two world wars – were designed for everyone and are open to members of the other community if they wish to visit them.

When asked about the interrelation of memory and politics at play during commemorative events, 50 per cent of Catholic and 26 per cent of Protestant respondents believed that one of the rationales behind the erection of memorials was to provide power holders (paramilitary leadership, members of affiliated political parties and other activists) with a platform from which to deliver political speeches on specific occasions. The more coherent, substantial and publicized calendar of Republican commemorations developed over the years compared to that of Loyalist organizations could perhaps explain the higher percentage of Catholic responses. In contrast, 40 per cent of Catholics and 56 per cent of Protestants lamented the 'interference' of politics during commemorative events, remarking, among other comments, that 'these are the only times when politicians are here' or that 'politicians are all liars'.

During fieldwork, two distinct points of view were observed with regards to the interrelation between memory and politics at commemorations in Belfast; though clearly not a question of establishing a 'universal truth', rather a matter of accepting the coexistence of mutually exclusive views – at times even within the same individual – for the purpose of this book it is worthwhile to document how they are expressed at the two extremes of the spectrum. On the one hand, there is condemnation of the process of 'hijacking' commemorations for political 'point scoring'. Many interviewees – in particular local residents and family members, and to a lesser degree Republican and Loyalist activists – were of the opinion that these events should mainly be about remembering individuals for who they were as men and women, their achievements in life, their role as husbands and wives, fathers and mothers, sons and daughters; political messages should, instead, be communicated at electoral rallies and political meetings, or reserved for designated commemorations – for example, Easter Sunday for Republicans when a message from the military and political leadership is traditionally delivered. Many recognized that expressing political messages while 'actually [trying] to hang on to a person who was dead twenty-five years ago' was a way of 'shielding from criticism', because 'nobody can speak for them' and nobody knows 'how they might feel about things today'. Ultimately, there was widespread agreement that, should the family wish so, politics should not play any part in commemorative events.

On the other hand, mainly ex-combatants and community activists stated that the commemorative and political dimensions cannot be divorced, as the individuals commemorated were political people, soldiers who died for their politics; it would be a fallacy, therefore, to remember the person and not what they died for. In addition, echoing what was examined in Chapter 8, they believed that announcing the politics for the year ahead at these events was beneficial in order to keep the community informed of the direction chosen by the leadership and 'to put [politics] in plainer terms to people than what somebody on TV would do' (interview with Loyalist community representative). It is interesting to note how this process of appropriation of the past for contemporary purposes is explained: it is not a case of simply affirming that dead volunteers would have supported the current position of the leadership, but a skilful process of setting the dead in the context of their historical times, then in the context of the broad politics of that period, and finally demonstrating the consistency of the group's politics that has brought a particular imagined community from that historical time to the present day, showing that the commitment and the ideology are unbroken. As a Republican ex-prisoner explained,

> if you are going to remember volunteers who died, well you also want to know what's the thinking of their comrades today and the leadership of the Republican movement and where they're at . . . I think the norm would be talking about the people at that time, either they were committed to the movement, the ideas of the movement; maybe show the values that they espoused . . . I think there is a thin line between saying they were committed volunteers, they went with whatever the army [IRA] was saying; you could draw a conclusion: well, if the army says we are now having a cease-fire, then, as committed volunteers, they would say 'ok, we are having it'.

Ex-combatants, political representatives and activists interviewed during the course of this book have often pointed to the high number of spectators lining the streets while parades pass by as a clear measurement of support for their paramilitary group or political movement. Examining the 'hidden transcript', however, only 22 per cent of Catholic residents who regularly attend commemorative events (54 per cent of total Catholic respondents) and 31 per cent of Protestant residents (out of 38 per cent of total Protestant respondents who regularly attend commemorations) affirmed that their participation was specifically driven by the desire to show support for paramilitary groups or associated politics and political movements. The most common reason mentioned to attend commemorative events – 67 per cent of Catholics and 53 per cent of Protestants – was individual involvement or interest, whether to pay tribute to friends or neighbours now gone, or simply out of curiosity to see what was happening on one's doorstep. Another attraction posited by these events was its social element, with 11 per cent of Catholics and 16 per cent of Protestants stating that they enjoyed a day out with friends and neighbours, and that commemorative events were a great opportunity to catch up with people who might have now left the area.

Conversely, opposition to paramilitary groups and associated politics emerged as the most common reason among the 46 per cent of Catholic and 62 per cent of Protestant respondents who did not attend any commemorative events, with 34.5 per cent of Catholics and 58 per cent of Protestants quoting it as their main reason; 22 per cent of Catholics and 32 per cent of Protestants declared they had no interest at all in these events, while 39 per cent Catholics and 10 per cent Protestants quoted individual reasons for not attending, such as physical disabilities, absence from the area or unawareness of when such events were taking place. In addition, some residents – most notably in Woodvale (16 per cent of total respondents in the area) – openly complained about the degree of drinking and littering on the streets and about the fact that the area is cordoned off to traffic as a result of the commemorative parades.

In conclusion, communal attitudes towards memory and memorialization in post-conflict Northern Ireland are complex and varied, and internal tensions tarnish the 'mask of similarity' that the different groups present as their consistent face to the outside world. Through a 'backstage' survey of local residents' views and opinions about memorial activity in their areas, this book has attempted to uncover the 'hidden transcript' of power relations over memory and to account for idiosyncratic differences and interpretative discrepancies that are 'glossed over' and left unexplored in any analysis that exclusively focuses on the 'public transcript'. In some instances, the survey results have significantly weakened some common claims made by the 'memory makers' and promoters of memorial projects. While this survey does not claim to be a comprehensive investigation from which to make universal generalizations, it does call for a problematization of the very term 'community' when used by power holders and will hopefully serve as a reference point for future researchers when facing claims such as 'with the full support of the community'.

Notes

1. For a further problematization of the term 'community' in the Northern Irish context, see Bryan (2006) and Shirlow and Murtagh (2006).
2. It is important to note, however, that in more recent times support for the RUC among the Catholic population has grown significantly, to the extent that 62 per cent of Catholics affirmed that the police dealt fairly with everyone in situations of 'normal crime' (Secretary of State for Northern Ireland 1996).
3. For a thorough analysis of informal justice mechanisms in Northern Ireland, see Thompson and Mulholland (1995), Brewer, Lockhart and Rodgers (1998), McEvoy and Mika (2001, 2002), Knox (2002), Knox and Monaghan (2002), and McEvoy and Eriksson (2008).
4. For Sinn Féin's endorsement of the RUC/PSNI, see 'SF Ard Fheis Backs Policing Motion' (2007). For opposition to this endorsement among Republicans, see the Republican Network for Unity's website (formerly the 'Ex-POWs and Concerned Republicans against RUC/PSNI' group).
5. See, for instance, the attacks by local youths who caused the death of West Belfast residents Harry Holland and Frank 'Bap' McGreevy ('Stabbing Victim on Life Support' 2007; 'Funeral for Man Beaten to Death' 2008).
6. This question was not asked to residents in Woodvale or Turf Lodge given the nature of the memorials taken as the case study in those areas (three commemorative murals and a plaque, respectively).
7. Acts of vandalism were, for instance, perpetuated against the Provisional IRA plot in Milltown Cemetery (McCann 2007) and the McCurrie/Neill Memorial Garden on the Newtownards Road (East Belfast Historical and Cultural Society 2002: 64–66).
8. Mentioned by at least two 'memory makers' in interviews with the author.
9. For example, UVF volunteer Trevor King was originally from the Springmartin area in West Belfast, but he is commemorated in one of the murals in Disraeli Street.

Chapter 10

THE MEMORY OF THE DEAD

Seeking Common Ground?

≫•≪

> Historical events properly understood, especially in a
> divided society, can be a source of inspiration for the
> living . . . Let not our children accuse us of distort-
> ing history, thereby perpetuating division, when we
> have the chance of establishing a new beginning. Let
> us seek to ensure that the history we bequeath to our
> children enhances all of their lives.
> – Alex Maskey, 'The Memory of the Dead'

With these words, the newly elected first Sinn Féin Mayor of Belfast,
Alex Maskey, concluded his speech on 26 June 2002 in Belfast City Hall,
during which he announced Sinn Féin's decision to 'take a difficult walk
into history' (Gibney 2002) in an attempt 'to seek to identify a common
ground which we can willingly share so that our commemorations, at this
level [of democratically elected government], of those who lost their lives
can be a unifying source and a calming influence on the course of future
political developments' (Maskey 2002). A few days later, on 1 July 2002,
ten Sinn Féin councillors, including Maskey, walked the short distance
from Belfast City Hall to the cenotaph in its grounds to lay a wreath to
the dead of the First World War on the occasion of the 86th anniversary
of the Battle of the Somme. In almost a century, 'no one else in republican
Ireland had ever walked the distance or even thought about walking the

distance': two hundred yards and the mould of nationalist and republican history was broken (Gibney 2002).

Notwithstanding the high symbolic significance of this gesture and others that followed in more recent years, memory still remains a divisive issue in Northern Ireland;[1] despite recommendations for an inclusive memorial to all the casualties of the conflict made by Bloomfield (1998) and, more recently, by the Consultative Group on the Past (2009), paramilitary memorials still remain the only material embodiment of the history of the Northern Irish conflict. The 'history' they tell is scripted by competing agents adamant to see their opposing 'stories' about the collective past articulated and legitimized, in order to win the higher moral ground in the ideological and political contest for the status of victimhood.

As exemplified by many studies that took place in different historical and geographical settings (see Chapter 1), war memorials are used, together with other cultural artefacts and practices, by nation states and governing authorities to project official constructions of power and ideology based on a 'sanitized' version of a shared past that define and sustain the collective identity, symbolic continuity and social cohesion of the nation's 'imagined community'. Invented traditions, myths of the war experience and national 'Golden Ages' are carefully selected from the communal past and manufactured into politically strategic narratives in order to perpetuate the 'sacredness' of human sacrifice in name of the 'motherland' or 'fatherland' of the nation and, ultimately, to provide historical, ideological and political legitimacy to the ruling establishment. The contribution this book makes to the study of collective memory and the politics of memorialization comes, instead, from the analysis of a scenario where, in the absence of state-sponsored narratives about a shared national past, other societal agencies – in Northern Ireland's case, paramilitary groups and their related political manifestations – have tried to fill this void, thus attempting to exert the 'right' of nation making that comes with the process of setting the canon of public collective memory.

Similar to state memorialization, non-state memorials can define and sustain the collective identity, symbolic continuity and social cohesion of 'imagined communities' of a national nature; in situations of political unrest and conflict between two 'traditions' or ethnic groups, as in Northern Ireland, these national 'imagined communities' are opposing and often mutually exclusive. And like other 'divided societies' such as Cyprus where, for instance, the two sections of the population identify themselves with the nation states of Turkey and Greece respectively, the national identification established and promoted by paramilitary narratives in Northern Ireland is of an 'outward-looking' nature, symbolically projected outside the geographical boundaries of the territory on which contested identity struggles occur. Since the existence of the Northern Irish nation state is rejected by a section of the population and since, throughout its history, Northern Ireland as a political entity has been understood in relation to external nation states (Ireland and the United Kingdom), Republican and Loyalist narratives of the conflict, in fact, underpin two opposing projected national identifications, Irish and British, with which the two imagined communities – Catholic/Nationalist/Republican and Protestant/Unionist/Loyalist, respectively – can identify.

Sifting through the confusion of the past, non-state memorialization can also establish direct symbolic lineages between modern agencies of memory articulation and glorious 'ancestries of resistance' or noble 'Golden Ages', from which to borrow historical, political and ideological legitimacy and, in societies where political violence has been used as the dominant mechanism of engagement, justification for such use of violence. Thus, in Northern Ireland, the 'martyrs' of the Easter Rising and the heroes of the Somme lend their legitimacy to their 'progenies', vouchsafing for the ontological, historical and ideological raison d'être of the modern paramilitary groups and their political manifestations. The actions of these groups during the conflict lose the unmistakable randomness of sectarian violence to become legitimate episodes in the century-long history of resistance against the British occupation of Ireland or of defence of the union of Northern Ireland with Great Britain.

In situations where a political entity is devoid of a recognized contemporary establishment and there are oppositional non-state agents who are seeking to form a future establishment such as Northern Ireland, memory assumes an even further political significance: the past becomes, in fact, a highly strategic asset when leaderships have to negotiate changes in political and ideological strategy, without incurring accusations of 'selling out' from base supports and electorates. Developing Halbwachs' theorization of the importance of the present in the formation and permutation of a group's collective memory, the case study of Northern Ireland has shown how collective narratives of the past prove to be extremely adaptable to shifting sociopolitical circumstances, moulding themselves to present needs and necessities while maintaining an 'illusion' of historical continuity. Chapter 7, for instance, examined how the message given by the UVF leadership at three annual commemorations in the Woodvale area has dramatically changed over the years, adapting to and facilitating the acceptance of the permutations of the political scenario in Northern Ireland, while still evoking the same 'ghostly national imaginings' of the 1913 UVF volunteers. The use of the past for contemporary political endorsement can, at times, reveal surprising connotations, as in the case of the commemoration to mark the fiftieth anniversary of the deaths of volunteers Seán Sabhat and Feargal O'Hanlon that took place on 1 January 2007 in County Fermanagh: during his speech, Sinn Féin's leader Gerry Adams (2007a) remarked how he was 'very aware of the irony', but saw 'no contradiction' in honouring two IRA volunteers who lost their lives in attempting to blow up a police barracks, while at the same time promoting Sinn Féin's new policy on the policing issue, that included the acceptance of and support for the PSNI, sanctioned by the Ard Chomhairle only three days before the commemorative event.

It has been noted how these non-state groups disagree on the past and essentially the future, yet all use a selective version of the past to try and change present-day contemporary feelings or biases in their own relative group to manipulate support towards their own political goals. As the examples of non-state forms of memorialization in Northern Ireland exemplify, memorialization can help to facilitate the political path to power of movements that once covered an oppositional or peripheral space into civic society, such as paramilitary or 'terrorist' groups, and can act as a way for their narratives to transcend their oppositional status and become official or quasi-official narratives.

Finally, this analysis of war memorialization of the Troubles has brought about some interesting reflections on the vastly investigated relation between individual and collective memory. Individuals engage with collective memory and its material representations such as memorials based on their particularistic experience of the past. Their cognitive and interpretative act, however, always occurs in the social environment they inhabit. Like ideological hat stands, collective memories curtail the number of possible interpretations of a given past and are able to accommodate within themselves a variety of 'mnemonic hats', due to a selective use of the past and the multivocal nature of the symbols they employ: thus, they provide shared social frameworks within whose elastic boundaries individual recollections take place and are subsumed. As demonstrated in Chapter 5, for instance, this process of 'mnemonic collectivization' is evident not only in relation to the acts of remembering of living individuals, but also in relation to the subject matter of these acts: in Northern Ireland's case, individuals who lost their lives as a result of the conflict are recognized and accounted for, but their particularistic deaths are subsumed within a narrative of communal 'martyrdom' or 'supreme sacrifice' in the name of a wider collectivity. Memorials, thus, can be seen as acting as a linchpin between the individual and collective level, both in terms of the act of remembering and the remembered subject.

At Last, a Common Ground in Northern Ireland?

As Ashplant, Dawson and Roper (2000) have documented, multiple narratives of the same past are common in any given society. The role of dominant or hegemonic 'memory maker' is usually reserved for the state or ruling establishment, while other social minority groups can attempt to project sectional or oppositional narratives which specify or challenge the dominant one. This book has investigated, instead, a most interesting scenario where, in the absence of state-sponsored narratives about the (recent) past, four parallel non-state narratives are concurrently present. A political struggle over memory ensues, as different groups compete to give public articulation and gain recognition for their 'version' of the past and competing national identifications, which results in the coexistence of multiple narratives of the same past, each interlinked in a relation of dominance/opposition to each other and within wider societal dimensions. The political weight achieved by these narratives is often directly proportional to the political status of their articulating agents.

To summarize and place these four narratives in the context of the wider Northern Irish society, the Republican 'version' of the conflict has had more success than its Loyalist counterpart in terms of public visibility, acceptance and recognition (see, for instance, Chapter 9). This is directly proportional to the political weight of Republican agencies of articulation. As seen in the case study chapters (Chapters 5–8), multiple manifestations or versions branch out from each narrative strand, promoted by different groups within the wider Republican or Loyalist tradition. After years of political migration from a militant policy of armed struggle and resistance to a more mainstream agenda of equality and integration, Sinn Féin is today one of the most prominent political players in contemporary Northern Ireland.[2] Having carefully crafted throughout the years an enticing and media-attractive narrative of the conflict, the Provisional Republican's version of the past has become the dominant version for the Republican side, due to Sinn Féin's prominent position in government. Moreover, Sinn Féin has had an easier task of conquering the spotlight of Republican/Nationalist collective memory due to the absence of a pre-existent narrative, publicly expressed and promoted by the constitutional nationalist front. Although during the conflict the SDLP was the main political voice of the Catholic section of the population, the conditions to gain political power – and, therefore, public recognition of the SDLP's 'version' of the past – were historically premature. In addition, as the SDLP condemned the use of violence as a political means, no possible narrative of the conflict could have been told without admitting a degree of failure and inefficacy of constitutional nationalism. Even though further research is necessary, this author believes that a combined lack of public avenues for the expression of their version of history, due to the lack of political status, and weakness of 'story material' can account for the absence of nationalist memorials for the Northern Ireland conflict. Although at times oppositional, the narrative promoted by the Republican Socialist movement borrows some of the limelight associated with the Provisional Republican movement, in particular with regard to areas of symbolic crossover such as the 1981 hunger strike.

Conversely, Loyalist narratives of the conflict have not reached such widespread success in terms of public status or visibility. This is primarily due to the fact that Loyalism lacks political ascendancy in Northern Ireland, with the UVF-aligned Progressive Unionist Party securing only a handful of votes (0.20 per cent of first preferences in the 2011 Assembly election) and no organized political voice for the UDA. In addition, Loyalism competes in the public arena with the pre-existent mainstream Unionist narrative of the past, in relation to which Loyalism wants to concurrently establish a degree of connection and differentiation. As seen in Chapters 7 and 8, both the UVF's and the UDA's narratives of the conflict portray Loyalism as the last true bulwark of loyalty to the Crown and defence of the Union, accusing mainstream Unionism of having 'sold out' to the political pressures of Irish Republicanism – but at the same time they attempt to partake of mainstream Unionism's historic 'Golden Age' (e.g. the myth of the Somme) and its respectability and legitimacy. Finally, Loyalism has historically failed to project a globally marketable and attractive narrative of the past. While a romanticized version of the (Provisional) Republican narrative has been successfully exported outside the geographical boundaries of Northern Ireland, gaining the sympathies and the moral, political and financial support of international audiences, Loyalism has been perceived outside Northern Ireland as a sectarian ideology, 'frozen' in the past and impermeable to compromise.

Notwithstanding many stand-offs and setbacks in the peace process, a return to a widespread use of political violence in Northern Ireland seems fortunately unlikely. Public symbolic acts of closure – such as the Bloody Sunday Inquiry chaired by Lord Saville (Saville, Hoyt and Toohey 2010) – continue to take place, at last giving the bereaved an opportunity to utter their grief and feel heard in an official framework. In this scenario, what is the future for the process of memorialization of the Troubles? The majority of interviewees recognized the importance of memorialization in the aftermath of the 1998 Agreement as a cathartic mechanism to exorcize the ghosts of the past; as a Republican ex-prisoner explained, it's a healthy process that people have documented [the past], they have made videos, they have written books, they have put up gardens. By doing that, it also means that there is something there that people can point to and say 'well, that's another issue being dealt with, that's another ghost exorcized'.

However, they also recognized that this process has had its heyday and has to be finite in order for a society to be able to move forward. With the disbandment of ex-prisoners' groups and the fact that almost every area in Belfast now has a memorial garden, the majority of respondents foresee a decline in memorial activity over the next few years, perhaps with small local commemorations giving way to more centralized, unified forms of remembrance. Despite the fact that paramilitary-related commemorative murals and memorials might remain, most interviewees agree that memorialization of the conflict will become less relevant in future generations 'because people don't remember or aren't connected to the same extent [to the past]' and 'memorials will become familiar, just part of the scenery like you'll see all over Ireland memorials to IRA men'.

As the relatively recent proliferation of memorialization from non-state actors has been used to both legitimize each group's historical use of violence and to set the course of their political future, will the time and space for a cross-community narrative of the conflict in the public arena ever materialize? In a survey conducted in 2000, 64 per cent of respondents expressed themselves in favour of a memorial to the victims of the Troubles in Northern Ireland (NILT 2000: MEMVICT); of these, 49 per cent agreed that this memorial should be for everybody killed during the conflict, whether paramilitaries, police or members of the public (NILT 2000: WHOMEM). Yet, no plans for such a memorial are under way nor has it been actively supported by any societal agency so far. The path towards not only its erection, but the possibility of it, seems complex and challenging if we consider that, to this day, the ideological and political differences between agencies of articulation pertaining to the same 'side of the divide' have yet to be overcome with the erection of a memorial to all the Republican or Loyalist deaths.

To speculate, a first step towards the prospect of an all-inclusive memorial to the casualties of the Troubles will have to incorporate a shift from the narration of the pain and loss endured to the recognition of the pain and loss inflicted, and all agencies of memory articulation will have to exchange legitimacy for responsibility for each other's status of victimhood. In realistic terms, as long as collective narratives of the past underpin opposing political claims, the prospect for such a memorial will be relegated to the world of 'wishful thinking'. For Northern Ireland to reach the point where a memorial to all the casualties of the Troubles is not only possible, but also beneficial, a brand new narrative of the past will have to be projected, a narrative that subsumes all components of Northern Irish society as equal actors in a shared past and, most importantly, that underpins a shared political goal that all parties involved can subscribe to and actively support for the future. Notwithstanding the many problems that persist for the erection of an all-inclusive memorial to the casualties of the Troubles, one has to wonder whether the status quo of non-state manifestations of memory may perhaps serve a greater function for bringing about a future political dispensation in Northern Ireland, as opposing groups use memorialization to wave in new viewpoints that, true, serve their own political goals, but are also moving people towards mutual compromise and a more common ground.

For now, next time you are wandering the streets of Belfast and you encounter one of the many memorials this book has introduced you to, pause for a minute and listen to the stories they have to tell.

Notes

1. Another significant gesture was the flying of the Irish tricolour alongside the Union Jack at a historic ceremony to remember Irish and British war dead in Derry/Londonderry in 2005 (Jackson 2005).
2. In the 2011 Northern Ireland Assembly election, Sinn Féin polled 26.9 per cent of total votes, making it the second major party in Northern Ireland after the Democratic Unionist Party (30 per cent). For full results, see Northern Ireland Elections (2011).

Appendix A: List of Memorials

No.	N/E/S/W Belfast	Type	Name	Location	Area	Date	Commissioned By	Pre-1969 Ref.
1	N	MEM	Ligoniel Casualties	Millview Court	Ligoniel	[Celtic cross: August 2004]	[PIRA]	X
2	N	MEM	McGurk's Bar Explosion	Junction of North Queen Street and Great George's Street	[New Lodge]	4 December 2001	Local Republicans	
3	N	MEM	PIRA – Ardoyne and Ligoniel Volunteers	Berwick Road	Ardoyne	20 April 1976	[PIRA]	X
4	N	MEM	PIRA – Ardoyne, Bone and Ligoniel Volunteers	Ardoyne Avenue	Ardoyne	1 September 2003	[PIRA]	X
5	N	MEM	PIRA – New Lodge Gairdin Cuimhneachain	Donore Court, off New Lodge Road	New Lodge	2004		
6 – No Longer Exists (NE)	N	MEM	UDA – E Company, 3rd Battalion Tiger's Bay, North Belfast Brigade	Cosgrave Heights, off Mervue Street	Tiger's Bay		[UDA]	
7	N	MEM	UDA/UFF – North Belfast Brigade	Junction of Brae Hill Park and Brae Hill Way, off Ballysillan Road	Ballysillan	10 June 2004	Ballysillan Garden Project	X
8	N	MEM	UDA – Glen Branagh	North Queen Street	Tiger's Bay		[UDA]	X

9	N	MEM	UVF – 3rd Battalion Mount Vernon, North Belfast	Junction of Mount Vernon Park and Mount Vernon Gardens	Mount Vernon		[UVF]	X
10	N	MUR	PIRA – Ardoyne, Bone and Ligoniel Volunteers	Ardoyne Avenue (+ Easter Lily mural)	Ardoyne	[2002?]	Coiste	
11	N	MUR	The New Lodge Six	Donore Court, off New Lodge Road	New Lodge	1 February 2003	[PIRA]	
12	N	MUR	UVF – D Company, 1st Battalion Ballysillan	Ballysillan Road	Ballysillan		[UVF]	X
13	N	PLA	INLA – Joseph Craven	Bawnmore Park, off Shore Road	Bawnmore	8 December 2002	Irish Republican Socialist Ex-Prisoners' Memorial Committee	X
14	N	PLA	Trevor Kell (Protestant civilian)	Hesketh Road	Ardoyne			
15	N	PLA	UDA – Hill McFarlane	Leroy Street, off Crumlin Road	Ballysillan		[UDA]	
16	N	PLA	McGurk's Bar Explosion	North Queen Street, underneath West Link passage	[New Lodge]	1 December 1996		
17	N	PLA	William Morgan (Protestant civilian)	North Queen Street	Tiger's Bay			
18	N	PLA	UDA – Bill Reynolds	Ligoniel Road	Ligoniel			
19	E	MEM	James McCurrie Robert Neill Memorial Garden	Lower Newtownards Road	Ballymacarrett	2003	[UDA] East Belfast Historical and Cultural Society	

No.	N/E/S/W Belfast	Type	Name	Location	Area	Date	Commissioned By	Pre-1969 Ref.
20	E	MEM	UVF – Long, Cordner, Seymour and Bennett	Fraser Pass, off Ballymacarrett Road	Ballymacarrett	Spring 2003	Pitt Park Company, East Belfast Battalion, UVF	X
21	E	MEM	Short Strand Casualties	St Matthew's Chapel	Short Strand			
22	E	MEM	UDA – 4th Battalion Castlereagh, East Belfast Brigade	Kenbaan Street, off Beersbridge Road	Ballymacarrett	2000	[UDA]	
23	E	MEM	UDA – East Belfast Brigade	Dee Street	Ballymacarrett/Sydenham		[UDA]	
24	E	MEM	UVF – 2nd Battalion Willowfield, East Belfast Regiment (1914–18)	Cherryville Street, off Woodstock Road	Ballymacarrett	1 July 1997	UVF East Battalion	X
25	E	MUR	UVF – Long, Cordner, Seymour and Bennett	Island Street	Ballymacarrett		[UVF]	X
26	E	MUR	PIRA – B Company, 3rd Battalion, Belfast Brigade	Mountpottinger Road	Short Strand	1 May 2005	Short Strand Memorial Committee	
27	E	MUR	RHC – C Company	Lower Newtownards Road	Ballymacarrett		[RHC]	
28	E	MUR	UVF	Castlereagh Road	Castlereagh		[UVF]	X
29	E	MUR	UVF – 36th Ulster Division	Clonduff Drive	Castlereagh		[UVF]	X
30	S	MEM	PIRA – South Belfast Volunteers	Stanfield Place	The Market	29 October 2000	[PIRA]	

31	S	MEM	Sean Graham Bookmaker's Shooting	Junction of Ormeau Road and Hatfield Street	Lower Ormeau	5 February 2002		X
32	S	MEM	UDA/UFF – South Belfast Brigade	Roden Street	The Village	new one: 2007	[UDA/UFF]	X
33	S	MEM	UVF – A Company, 2nd Battalion, South Belfast	Walnut Street	Donegall Pass	Autumn 2000	UVF Volunteers of Donegall Pass	
34	S	MEM	UVF – B Company, 2nd Battalion, South Belfast	Moltke Street	The Village		[UVF]	X
35	S	MEM	UVF – South Belfast Battalion (1912)	Sandy Row	Sandy Row		[UVF]	X
36	S	MUR	UVF/RHC – Hanna, McCrea and Mehaffy	Broadway	The Village		[UVF/RHC]	X
37	S	PLA	OIRA – Joe McCann	Joy Street	The Market	13 April 1997	[OIRA]	
38	S	PLA	INLA – Power, Power, O'Reilly and Gargan	Junction of Friendly Street and Steward Street	The Market	11 May 2003	Irish Republican Socialist Ex-Prisoners' Memorial Committee	X
39	S	PLA	FIANNA – Jim Templeton	Lower Ormeau Road	Lower Ormeau	1 November 1998	[PIRA]	X
40	W	MEM	1798 Rebellion	Roddy McCorley's, Glen Road	Andersonstown	19 November 1995	Roddy McCorley Society	X

No.	N/E/S/W Belfast	Type	Name	Location	Area	Date	Commissioned By	Pre-1969 Ref.
41	W	MEM	1981 Hunger Strikers	Junction of Falls Road and Glen Road	Andersonstown	4 July 2006	Riverdale Sinn Féin Cumann and Andersonstown '81 Committee	
42	W	MEM	Andersonstown Garden of Remembrance	South Link	Andersonstown	3 November 1996	Local Republicans	X
43	W	MEM	Ballymurphy Gairdin Cuimhneachain	Divismore Way, off Springfield Road	Ballymurphy	27 November 2005	Former POWs from the Greater Ballymurphy area	X
44 - NE	W	MEM	Celtic Cross	Locan Street	Falls			
45	W	MEM	Clonard Martyrs Memorial Garden	Bombay Street	Clonard	20 August 2000	Greater Clonard Ex-Prisoners' Association	X
46	W	MEM	PIRA – Kieran Doherty	Commedagh Drive	Andersonstown	29 July 2001	[PIRA]	
47	W	MEM	Falls Garden of Remembrance	Lower Falls Road	Falls	24 June 2001	Falls Cultural Society	X
48	W	MEM	Hunger Strikers	Twinbrook Road	Twinbrook	7 May 2006	[National Hunger Strike Commemoration Committee]	

No.		Type	Name	Location	Area	Date	Organization	
49	W	MEM	Hunger Strikers	Roddy McCorley's, Glen Road	Andersonstown	5 May 2001	[National Hunger Strike Commemoration Committee]	
50	W	MEM	Hunger Strikers	Beechmount Avenue	Falls	August 2006		
51	W	MEM	Hunger Strikers 1917–81	Roddy McCorley's, Glen Road	Andersonstown			X
52	W	MEM	Ann Carol Kelly (Catholic civilian)	Aspen Park	Twinbrook	24 May 1998	Local community	
53	W	MEM	Julie Livingstone (Catholic civilian)	Junction of Lenadoon Avenue and Stewartstown Road	Andersonstown		Young people of Leicester	
54	W	MEM	IRA County Antrim Plot	Milltown Cemetery	Upper Falls	1966	Belfast National Graves Association	X
55	W	MEM	IRSP/INLA Communal Plot 1	Milltown Cemetery	Upper Falls		IRSM	X
56	W	MEM	IRSP/INLA Communal Plot 2	Milltown Cemetery	Upper Falls	1999/2000	IRSM	X
57	W	MEM	OIRA Communal Plot	Milltown Cemetery	Upper Falls	1972	Workers Party	
58	W	MEM	PIRA Communal Plot	Milltown Cemetery	Upper Falls	new: 7 December 2003	Belfast National Graves Association	X
59	W	MEM	Workers Party Communal Plot	Milltown Cemetery	Upper Falls		Workers Party	X

No.	N/E/S/W Belfast	Type	Name	Location	Area	Date	Commissioned By	Pre-1969 Ref.
60	W	MEM	PIRA – A Company, 1st Battalion, Belfast Brigade	Junction of Shaws Road and Rosnareen Road	Andersonstown		[PIRA]	
61	W	MEM	PIRA – A Company, 2nd Battalion, Belfast Brigade	Beechmount Avenue	Falls	4 June 2006	Mid-Falls Commemoration Committee	X
62	W	MEM	PIRA – B Company, 1st Battalion, Belfast Brigade	Bingnian Drive, off Glen Road	Andersonstown	8 June 2003	Andersonstown Ex-Prisoners' Association	X
63	W	MEM	PIRA – Volunteers of the Greater Lenadoon Area	Roddy McCorley's, Glen Road	Andersonstown	6 May 2000	Local Republicans	X
64	W	MEM	PIRA – Volunteers of the Greater New Barnsley Area	New Barnsley Gardens, off Springfield Road	New Barnsley	27 June 1999	[PIRA]	X
65	W	MEM	PIRA – Volunteers of Twinbrook and Poleglass	Twinbrook Road	Twinbrook	August 1998	Teeling Group	X
66	W	MEM	Shankill Memorial Park	Shankill Road	Shankill	16 August 1992		X
67	W	MEM	Springhill Massacre Memorial Garden	Westrock Drive	Ballymurphy	4 May 1999	Upper Springfield Development Trust	
68	W	MEM	UDA – C Company, 2nd Battalion, West Belfast Brigade	Boundary Way	Shankill	1998	Former C Company personnel	
69	W	MEM	UDA/UFF – A Company, West Belfast Brigade	Highfield Drive	Springmartin		[UDA/UFF]	X

No.								
70	W	MUR	PIRA – Bryson and Mulvenna	Ballymurphy Road	Ballymurphy	3 June 2001	[PIRA]	
71	W	MUR	PIRA – Delaney, Campbell, Clarke, Parker and Sloan	Glenalina Road	Ballymurphy		[PIRA]	X
72	W	MUR	PIRA – Kieran Doherty	Slemish Way, off Andersonstown Road	Andersonstown		[PIRA]	
73	W	MUR	PIRA – McCracken, Dougal, McWilliams and Stone	Springhill Drive	Ballymurphy		[PIRA]	
74	W	MUR	PIRA – O'Neill, Quigley, McCormick and Magee	Glenalina Road	Ballymurphy		[PIRA]	
75	W	MUR	PIRA – O'Rawe, McCrudden and Jordan	Divismore Way, off Springfield Road	Ballymurphy		[PIRA]	X
76	W	MUR	PIRA – A Company, 2nd Battalion, Belfast Brigade	Beechmount Avenue	Falls		[PIRA]	X
77-NE	W	MUR	PIRA – A Company, 2nd Battalion, Belfast Brigade and SF MidFalls Cumann	Amcomri Street	Falls	2003	Coiste Cuimhneachain Ard na Bhfea	X
78	W	MUR	PIRA – Volunteers from the Greater Ballymurphy Area	Ballymurphy Road	Ballymurphy	12 May 1985	Local Republicans	X
79	W	MUR	PIRA – Stone, Tolan, McGrillen and Kane	Ballymurphy Crescent	Ballymurphy		[PIRA]	
80	W	MUR	UVF – Bill Campbell	Northland Street	Shankill	11 July 1997	[UVF]	X
81	W	MUR	UVF – Trevor King	Disraeli Street	Woodvale	1994?	[UVF]	X
82	W	MUR	UVF – King, Marchant and Hamilton	Spier's Place, off Shankill Road	Shankill	July 1995	[UVF]	X

No.	N/E/S/W Belfast	Type	Name	Location	Area	Date	Commissioned By	Pre-1969 Ref.
83	W	MUR	UVF – McIntyre, Wadsworth, Chapman, McGregor and Hannah	Emerson Street, off Shankill Road	Shankill	Autumn 2002	[UVF]	X
84	W	MUR	UVF – Brian Robinson	Disraeli Street Glenwood Street	Woodvale	1989?	[UVF]	X
85	W	MUR	UVF – 4 Platoon, A Company, 1st Battalion, Belfast		Shankill		[UVF]	X
86	W	MUR	WDA (UDA/UFF) – B Company	Ohio Street	Woodvale		[UDA/UFF]	
87	W	MUR	YCV – Samuel Rockett	Disraeli Street	Woodvale	23 August 2001	[YCV/UVF]	X
88	W	MUR	Republican Volunteers and Activists	Beechview Park, off Whiterock Road	Ballymurphy	26 March 2005	[Ogra SF]	X
89	W	MUR	Rubber Plastic Bullets Victims	Islandbawn Street, off Falls Road	Falls	11 September 2005	Troops Out Movement and Relatives For Justice	
90	W	MUR	Shankill Atrocities	Shankill Road	Shankill	2003	Kinner family	
91	W	PLA	INLA – Bunting and Little	Junction of Downfine Gardens and Gransha Park, off Glen Road	Turf Lodge	13 October 2002	Irish Republican Socialist Ex-Prisoners' Memorial Committee	X

92	W	PLA	INLA – Ferguson and O'Neill	Whiterock Drive	Ballymurphy	23 February 2003	Irish Republican Socialist Ex-Prisoners' Memorial Committee	X
93	W	PLA	INLA – Kearney and Campbell	Junction of New Barnsley Parade and Springfield Road	New Barnsley	19 January 2003	Irish Republican Socialist Ex-Prisoners' Memorial Committee	X
94	W	PLA	INLA – Loughran, Campbell, McLarnon, McCann, Tumelty, Gallagher and Dornan	Junction of Albert Street and Christian Place	Divis/Falls	6 April 2003	Irish Republican Socialist Ex-Prisoners' Memorial Committee	X
95	W	PLA	McLarnon, McCabe and Doherty	Linden Street, off Lower Falls Road	Falls	26 July 2001	Lower Falls/Clonard 1980/81 Memorial Committee	
96	W	PLA	INLA – McNamee and Daly	Andersonstown Road	Andersonstown	6 July 2003	Irish Republican Socialist Ex-Prisoners' Memorial Committee	X

No.	N/E/S/W Belfast	Type	Name	Location	Area	Date	Commissioned By	Pre-1969 Ref.
97	W	PLA	IRSP – Seamus Costello	Costello House, Falls Road	Falls		IRSP	
98	W	PLA	IRA – Sean Doyle	Brittons Drive	Ballymurphy	23 March 2003	[PIRA]	X
99	W	PLA	IRA – Tom Williams	Bombay Street	Clonard	1992	Belfast National Graves Association	X
100	W	PLA	PIRA – Crossan, McCann, Lewis and Johnston	Clonard Street	Clonard	10 March 2002	Greater Clonard Ex-Prisoners' Association	
101	W	PLA	PIRA – Kieran Doherty	Commedagh Drive	Andersonstown		[PIRA]	
102	W	PLA	PIRA – Pearse Jordan	Hugo Street	Upper Falls		[PIRA]	X
103	W	PLA	PIRA – Kavanagh and Carberry	Upper Falls Road	Upper Falls		Coiste Cuimhneachain Ard na Bhfea and Uibh Eachach	
104	W	PLA	PIRA – Joe McDonnell	McDonnell Street, off Lower Falls	Divis/Falls	25 April 2001	[PIRA]	
105	W	PLA	PIRA – Finbarr McKenna	Crocus Street, off Springfield Road	Falls	2? May 2002	Greater Clonard Ex-Prisoners' Association	
106	W	PLA	FIANNA – John Dempsey	Divis Drive, Falls Bus Depot	Turf Lodge	5 May 2003	Republicans from Turf Lodge	

No.	Type		Name/Description	Location	Area	Date	Organisation	
107	PLA	W	FIANNA – Neil McCrory	Beechmount Avenue	Falls	February 2005	[PIRA]	X
108	PLA	W	SF – Loughran, McBride and O'Dwyer	Sinn Féin Office, Falls Road	Falls		[SF]	
109	PLA	W	SF – Pat McGeown	Sinn Féin Office, Falls Road	Falls		[SF]	
110	PLA	W	SF – O'Dwyer, Loughran and McBride	Sinn Féin Office, Falls Road	Falls	2 February 2002	[SF]	
111	PLA/ME	W	UVF – Brian McCallum	Ainsworth Avenue, off Woodvale Road	Woodvale	25 June 1994	[UVF]	X
112	PLA	W	Rooney and McCabe	Divis Tower	Divis/Falls		SF	
113	PLA	W	Kelly's Bar Explosion	Junction of Springfield Road and Whiterock Road	Whiterock	13 May 2004		
114	PLA	W	Thomas Johnston (Protestant civilian)	North Boundary Street	Shankill			
115	PLA	W	Falls and Clonard Casualties	Clonard Street	Clonard			
116	PLA	W	Equality for the Irish Language	Falls Road	Falls	28 July 2006	[SF]	
117	MEM	N	PIRA – Vol. Scullion and Republican Activists and Civilian Casualties	Junction of Plunkett Court and Kildare Street	Carrick Hill		[PIRA]	X
118	MEM	N	UDA/UFF/UYM – North Belfast Brigade	Mervue Street/Hogarth Street	Tiger's Bay	November 2007	[UDA]	
119	MEM	N	PIRA – Volunteers and Civilians from the Greater Bone, Ballybone and Rosapenna Area	Louisa Court	Ardoyne		[PIRA]	X

No.	N/E/S/W Belfast	Type	Name	Location	Area	Date	Commissioned By	Pre-1969 Ref.
120	N	MEM	PIRA – Bawnmore Memorial Garden	Bawnmore Park, off Shore Road	Whitewell		[PIRA]	X
121	N	MEM	16th Irish Division and 36th Ulster Division	Junction of Mount Vernon Park and Mount Vernon Gardens	Mount Vernon	2007/2008	[UVF]	X
122	N	MUR	PIRA – Larry Marley	Junction of Ardoyne Avenue and Havana Gardens (+ An Gorta Mor mural)	Ardoyne		[PIRA]	
123	N	PLA	UDA – Fulton and Goatley	York Road	Tiger's Bay		[UDA]	
124	E	MEM	Deceased Members of the Loyal Orange Institution of Ireland	'Schomberg House', Cregagh Road	Castlereagh/Cregagh		Orange Order	
125	S	MEM	UDA/UFF/UYM – A Battalion, South Belfast Brigade	City Way	Sandy Row	November 2006	[UDA]	X
126	S	MEM	UDA/UFF – South Belfast Brigade	Hornbeam Walk	Seymour Hill/Derriaghy	19 January 2008	[UDA]	
127	S	PLA	Gary Whittley (Protestant civilian)	Donegall Road	Sandy Row		[UDA]	
128	S	MUR	UDA – Robert Dougan	Blythe Street	Sandy Row	2007	Dougan family	
129	W	MEM	Hunger Strikers	Junction of Stewartstown Road and Upper Dunmurry Lane	Suffolk		[PIRA]	

No.		Type	Description	Location	Area	Date	Attribution	
130	W	MEM	Harbinson Plot	Milltown Cemetery	Upper Falls	1912		X
131	W	MEM	PIRA – Volunteers of the Greater Turf Lodge Area	Junction of Norglen Road and Monagh Crescent	Turf Lodge		[PIRA]	X
132	W	MEM	Teeling Family and 1798 United Irishmen	Junction of Stewartstown Road and Upper Dunmurry Lane	Suffolk	1998	People of Twinbrook and Poleglass	X
133	W	MEM	The Bayardo Bar Bombing	Shankill Road	Shankill	2008	Bayardo Somme Association	
134	W	MEM	UVF – B Company and UDA – B Company Woodvale	Disraeli Court	Woodvale	Late 1980s	[UVF/UDA]	
135	W	MEM	PIRA – Black and Ryan and SF – Ferguson and Keenan	Pantridge Road	Poleglass	2007	[PIRA]	X
136	W	MUR	Brian Stewart (Catholic civilian)	Norglen Road	Turf Lodge		Brian's family and friends	
137	W	MUR	UDA – Stevie McKeag	The Hammer	Lower Shankill		[UDA]	X
138	W	MUR	James Connolly	Rockmount Street	Upper Falls			X
139	W	MUR	Hunger Strikers	Iveagh Street	Upper Falls			
140	W	PLA	PIRA – Shaw and Lynch	Junction of Springfield Road and Crocus Street	Falls		Greater Clonard Community	
141	W	PLA	SF – Maire Drumm	Sinn Féin Office, Falls Road	Falls	2007?	[SF]	X
142	W	PLA	Angela Gallagher (Catholic civilian)	Iveagh Drive	Upper Falls	10 September 2007		

No.	N/E/S/W Belfast	Type	Name	Location	Area	Date	Commissioned By	Pre-1969 Ref.
143	W	PLA	FIANNA – John Dempsey	Norglen Road	Turf Lodge	5 May 2003	[PIRA]	
144	W	PLA	FIANNA – Gerard McAuley	Junction of Bombay Street and Waterville Street	Clonard	9 March 2003	Greater Clonard Ex-Prisoners' Association	
145	W	PLA	IRA – Pat and Dun Duffin	Clonard Gardens	Clonard	23 April 2001	Greater Clonard Ex-Prisoners' Association	X
146	W	PLA	PIRA – Frankie Ryan and Patricia Black	Woodside Park	Poleglass	3 September 2000	[PIRA]	X
147	W	PLA	FIANNA – Sean O'Riordan	Cawnpore Street	Clonard	23 March 2002	Greater Clonard Ex-Prisoners' Association	
148	W	PLA	IRA – Sean Gaynor	Colinview Street	Clonard	22 September 2002	Greater Clonard Ex-Prisoners' Association	X
149	W	PLA	PIRA – Danny O'Neill	Oranmore Street	Clonard	11 January 2004	Greater Clonard Ex-Prisoners' Association	

150	W	PLA	PIRA – Fox, Bailey, Campbell and Marlowe	Iveagh Street	Upper Falls	29 February 2004	Coiste Cuimhneachain Ard na Bhfea and Uibh Eachach	X
151	W	PLA	Falls Curfew's Civilian Casualties	Falls Road	Falls			
152	W	PLA	PIRA – Joe McDonnell	Lenadoon Avenue	Lenadoon	June 1968	Coiste	
153	W	PLA	James Connolly	Falls Road	Falls			
154	W	PLA	Shankill (Frizzell's Fish Shop) Bombing	Shankill Road	Shankill			
155	W	PLA	Deceased Protestants and Members of the Security Forces in the Greater Shankill Area	Bray Street	Woodvale	12 November 1996	Orangemen of North and West Belfast	
156	W	PLA	Balmoral Furniture Showrooms Bombing	Shankill Road, on Shankilll Leisure Centre	Shankill	2008		
157	W	PLA	The Bayardo Bar Bombing	Shankill Road	Shankill	2008		

Appendix B: Emblems and Flags

36th Ulster Division (Shield): Union Jack in the upper left quadrant; a harp under a crown in the upper right quadrant; the Red Hand of Ulster and nine shamrocks in the lower quadrant.

Belfast City (Crest): bell in the upper left part; series of triangles pointing downwards in the upper central part; sailing vessel in the lower part.

Connaught Province (Shield): black eagle on a white background and white arm holding a knife on a blue background.

Fianna Na H-Éireann (Flag): orange sunburst on a blue field.

Irish National Flag (Tricolour): green, white and orange vertical stripes.

IRSM (Emblem): rifle in a clenched left-hand fist with a red star in the background.

Leinster Province (Shield): gold harp on a green background.

LPA (Emblem): Red Hand of Ulster entwined in barbed wire under a crown.

Munster Province (Shield): three gold crowns on a blue background.

PAF (Emblem): triangular emblem with the Red Hand of Ulster on a light blue background and the name around the yellow rim.

RHC (Emblem): Red Hand of Ulster with gold wings against an irregular yellow four-point star and the name around the rim.

Scottish National Flag (St Andrew's Cross): white saltire [in heraldry, an X-shaped ordinary, i.e. a diagonal cross] on a navy blue field.

Starry Plough (Emblem and Flag): seven white stars forming the eponymous constellation on a light blue field.

UDA (Emblem): 'red cross on a white shield, with the Red Hand [of Ulster] in a six-point star in the centre. The initials appear over the shield in a scroll, and their motto "Quis Separabit" ("Who Shall Separate Us") similarly underneath. Each quadrant contains the symbol of one of the four groups within the organisation [UDA, UFF, LPA and UDF] . . . The UDA emblem has a Red Hand on a blue field under a crown . . . Usually the UDA shield is flanked by the Union Jack and the Ulster flag, although sometimes the Scottish flag replaces one of these' (Jarman 1997: 217–18).

UFF (Emblem): 'simple clenched red fist' (Jarman 1997: 217–18).

Ulster (Province, 9 Counties) Flag: red cross on a yellow field. Red Hand of Ulster enclosed in a white shield in the centre.

Ulster (Government of Northern Ireland, 6 Counties) Flag: red cross on a white field. Red Hand of Ulster enclosed within a six-pointed star positioned in the centre under a crown.

Ulster Province (Shield): red cross on a yellow background. Red Hand of Ulster enclosed in a white shield in the middle.

United Irishmen (Flag): gold harp on a green field.

United Kingdom Flag (Union Jack or Union Flag): juxtaposition of the flag of England (a red cross with a white background, known as St George's Cross), the flag of Scotland and the flag of Ireland (a red saltire with a white background, known as St Patrick's Cross).

UVF (Emblem): 'upright, gold-coloured oval with the Red Hand of Ulster in the centre and the words "For God and Ulster" around the rim' (Jarman 1997: 217–18).

UVF (Flag): purple with the Union flag or the 6 County Ulster flag in the upper left quadrant.

UYM (Emblem): red fist on a white background with the motto 'Terrae Filius' ('Son of the Earth') below it, and the name around the light blue rim.

YCV (Emblem): green shamrock with the letters 'Y', 'C' and 'V', one on each leaf.

YCV (Flag): white with a green shamrock and the Red Hand of Ulster in the centre.

BIBLIOGRAPHY

Newspapers, Journals and Periodicals

Andersonstown News
An Phoblacht/Republican News
Belfast Telegraph
Blanket
Coiste.comm
Combat
Daily Ireland
Daily Mirror
Greater Clonard Ex-Prisoners' Association Bulletin
Guardian
Independent
Irish Independent
Irish News
Irish Republican News
Irish Times
News Letter
New Ulster Defender
North Belfast News
Observer
Purple Standard
Saoirse/Irish Freedom
Spotlight
Starry Plough
Sunday Life
Sunday Times
Sunday Tribune
Ulster
Ulster Star
Volunteer

Newspaper, Journal and Periodical Articles

Although not all directly cited in the text, a list of primary sources and supporting material collected during the years of research for this book is included here, in the hope that it could be a useful starting point for researchers and readers interested in the topic.

'1st Belfast Battalion Ulster Volunteer Force Remember Volunteer Brian Robinson, Killed in Action – 2 Sept 1989'. 2001. *Combat*, special edn [Christmas]: 7.

'95 Anniversary – Ulster Day'. 2007. *The Purple Standard* 4 [September]: 1.

'An Act of Remembrance'. 2002. *Combat* 8 [September]: 4–5.

'A Tribute to a Volunteer'. 1999. *Combat*, September: 9–10.

'A Tribute to Brian'. 1992. *Combat*, October: 12.

'Barracks Mural Completed'. 2008. *Spotlight – Quarterly Bulletin of Andersonstown Irish Republican Socialist Party* 1: 1.

'Bunting and Little Are Commemorated at Turf Unveiling'. 2002. *Andersonstown News*, 14 October: 2.

'Bunting Has a Private Funeral'. 1980. *Belfast Telegraph*, 18 October: 1.

'Butcher on Parade'. 2003. *Sunday Life*, 20 July 2003: 6.

'Cameron's Comments "The 1st of July"'. 2007. *The Purple Standard* 2 [May/June]: 1.

'Clonard Commemoration Events'. 2002. *Greater Clonard Ex-Prisoners' Association Bulletin* 2(3) [March/April]: 1.

'Clonard Commemoration Weekend'. 2006. *Greater Clonard Ex-Prisoners' Association Bulletin*, [February]: 1.

'Clonard Exhibition. Can You Help?'. 2001. *Greater Clonard Ex-Prisoners' Association Bulletin* 1(4) [April]: 4.

'Clonard History Project'. 2001. *Greater Clonard Ex-Prisoners' Association Bulletin* 1(6[8]) [August]: 2–3.

'Clonard Martyrs Commemorative March'. 2005. *Greater Clonard Ex-Prisoners' Association Bulletin* [July/August]: 1.

'Clonard Martyrs Honoured'. 2003. *Greater Clonard Ex-Prisoners' Association Bulletin* 3(3) [March]: 1.

'Clonard Martyrs Memorial Garden'. 2001. *Greater Clonard Ex-Prisoners' Association Bulletin* 1(6[8]) [August]: 4.

'Clonard Memorial Garden Fundraiser'. 2005/2006. *Greater Clonard Ex-Prisoners' Association Bulletin* [December/January]: 4.

'Daly Sympathy over Robinsons'. 1989. *Belfast Telegraph*, 5 September, 6th edn: 1.

'Deaths'. 1989. *Belfast Telegraph*, 4 September: 2.

'Deceased Ex-POWs'. 2002. *Greater Clonard Ex-Prisoners' Association Bulletin* 2(6) [August]: 3.

'Dial a Drink or Trouble'. 2001. *Greater Clonard Ex-Prisoners' Association Bulletin* 1(3[2]) [February]: 4.

'Editorial'. 1989. *Combat*, 25 September: 1.

'Fallen Volunteers Remembered. Teach na Failte Memorial Project Goes from Strength to Strength'. 2003. *The Starry Plough*, August/September: 7–8.

'Feud Tension High as Victim Is Buried'. 2000. *Belfast Telegraph*, 26 August: 1.

'Feud Victim Is Given Paramilitary Sendoff'. 2000. *Irish News*, 28 August: 4.

'First Battalion "B" Company – Ulster Volunteer Force in Memory of Volunteer Brian Robinson'. 2002. *Combat* 9 [October]: 9–10.

'First Belfast Battalion "B" Company, Ulster Volunteer Force Memorial Parade in Memory of Volunteer Brian Robinson'. 2005. *Combat* 31 [September/October]: 10–11.

'Forever Remembered Volunteer Samuel Rockett'. 2003. *Combat* 17 [October]: 10.

'Greater Clonard Community Council'. 2001. *Greater Clonard Ex-Prisoners' Association Bulletin* 1(4) [April]: 2.

'Heart of the Empire'. 1994. *Combat*, July: 6.

'Honour Ireland's Dead on Easter Sunday'. 2003. *Greater Clonard Ex-Prisoners' Association Bulletin* 3(4) [April]: 1.

'Hundreds at UVF Member's Funeral'. 1989. *Belfast Telegraph*, 5 September, 6th late edn: 1.

'Hungerstrike 25 Anniversary'. 2006. *Daily Ireland*, 9 May: 1–12.

'In Eternal and Precious Memory of Volunteer Brian Robinson Fifteenth Anniversary'. 2004. *Combat* 24 [September/October]: 8–10.

'In Honour of Volunteer Samuel Rockett, 1st Battalion – B Company. Murdered by Cowards, 23rd Day of August 2000'. 2001. *Combat* 2 [October]: 14.

'In Loving Memory of Lieutenant Colonel T.J. King'. 2002. *Combat* 8 [September]: 5.

'In Memory of a Young Soldier. Volunteer Samuel Rockett. 1st Battalion "B" Company, Ulster Volunteer Force'. 2002. *Combat* 9 [October]: 12.

'In Memory of Lieutenant Colonel Trevor James King'. 2006. *Combat* 37 [June/July]: 7.

'In Memory of Lieutenant Colonel Trevor King, First Belfast Battalion "B" Company'. 2003. *Combat* 16 [August/September]: 11.

'In Memory of Vol. Samuel Rockett "Murdered by Cowards"'. 2005. *Combat* 31 [September/October]: 16.

'In Memory of Volunteer Brian Robinson 1st Battalion Belfast – "B" Company. Ulster Volunteer Force'. 2003. *Combat* 17 [October]: 7–9.

'In Memory of Volunteer Samuel Rockett 1st Belfast Battalion "B" Company, Young Citizen Volunteers'. 2006. *Combat* 38 [August/September]: 18.

'In Memory of Volunteer Samuel Rockett'. 2007. *The Purple Standard* 4 [September]: 14.

'James Trevor King, His Only Crime Was Loyalty'. 1994. *Combat*, September: 5.

'Joe Craven Plaque Unveiled in Bawnmore'. 2003. *The Starry Plough*, February/March: 6.

'Joint UDA/UVF Ceremony'. 1988/89. *Ulster*, December/January: 17.

'Leading Loyalist and Gun Victim Lose Fight for Life'. 1994. *Irish News*, 11 July: 1.

'Lest We Forget [Brian Robinson Memorial Parade]'. 1995. *Combat*, September: 7.

'Lest We Forget [Trevor King Memorial Parade]'. 1995. *Combat*, September: 8.

'Lest We Forget. The Following Oration Was Given at the Graveside of Colin Craig'. 1994. *Combat*, July: 7.

'Lest We Forget'. 1994. *Combat*, September: 4.

'Lest We Forget'. 1996. *Combat*, December: 4.

'Lest We Forget'. 1997a. *Combat*, Christmas issue [December]: 14.

'Lest We Forget'. 1997b. *Combat*, October: 13.

'Lest We Forget'. 1998. *Combat*, December: 8.

'Lest We Forget'. 1999. *Combat*, September: 11.

'Lieutenant Colonel Trevor James King Memorial Parade'. 2008. *The Purple Standard* 10 [July]: 11–12.

'Lisburn Pays Tribute to John McMichael'. 1992?. *New Ulster Defender* 1(3) [Autumn]: 21.

'Lodge Death Notice Clarified'. 1989. *Belfast Telegraph*, 6 October: 9.

'London Loyalists Remember Our Dead'. 2005. *Combat* 32, Remembrance Day and Christmas special issue [November/December]: 8.

'Memorial Day in Honour of Lieutenant Colonel Trevor King'. 2005. *Combat* 30 [August]: 9–10.

'Memorial Parade in Memory of Volunteer Lieutenant Colonel Trevor King Tenth Anniversary'. 2004. *Combat* 23 [July/August]: 8–9.

'More Volunteers Remembered in Ongoing Program of Erecting Memorials'. 2003. *The Starry Plough*, February/March: 6.

'Murdered by the Enemies of Ulster'. 2001. *Combat*, special edn, January: 13.

'Oration Given at the Graveside of Brian Robinson'. 1989. *Combat*, August: 13.

'Order Defends Attendance at UVF Funeral'. 1989. *Sunday Life*, 24 September: 31.

'Order to Probe Maverick Lodge'. 2000. *Irish News*, 6 September: 11.

'Outrage at Orange Tribute to UVF Killer'. 2000. *Irish News*, 4 September: 1.

'Pals Gunned down in Street Terror'. 1994. *Irish News*, 17 June: 1.

'Parade Is "Sick" Says Brother of UVF Victim'. 2000. *Irish News*, 5 September: 1.

'Plaque to Murdered IRSP Men Unveiled'. 2002. *Irish News*, 14 October: 10.

'Private Funeral for Little'. 1980. *Belfast Telegraph*, 17 October: 4.

'Remembering 1969'. 2001. *Greater Clonard Ex-Prisoners' Association Bulletin* 1(2[1]) [January]: 2–3.

'Remembrance Day Orations – "Lest We Forget". 1st Belfast Battalion'. 2005. *Combat* 32, Remembrance Day and Christmas special issue [November/December]: 12–13.

'Ronnie Bunting & Noel Little Remembered in Belfast Unveiling'. 2002/2003, *The Starry Plough*, December/January: 6.

'Shankill Band Parade'. 1990. *Combat*, 31 August: 13.

'Shankill on Edge for March'. 2000. *Belfast Telegraph*, 2 September: 1.

'Shankill Shooting: Man Dies'. 1989. *Belfast Telegraph*, 9 July: 1.

'Sincerity Test for Orangeism'. 2000. *Irish News*, 4 September: 7.

'Sponsored Walk'. 2003. *Greater Clonard Ex-Prisoners' Association Bulletin* 3(6) [June]: 3.

'The Death of a Volunteer'. 1989. *Combat*, August: 11–12.

'The Following Oration Was Delivered by a Loyalist Community Representative at the Lieutenant Colonel Trevor King Memorial Mural'. 2007. *The Purple Standard* 3 [July/August]: 16.

'The Following Oration Was Given at the Graveside of Trevor King in Roselawn Cemetery'. 1994. *Combat*, September: 3.

'The Memorial Garden'. 2002. *Greater Clonard Ex-Prisoners' Association Bulletin* 2(6) [August]: 2–3.

'Third Man Shot Dead in Loyalist Feuding'. 2000. *Irish News*, 24 August: 1.

'Thirtieth Anniversary Remembered'. 2002. *Greater Clonard Ex-Prisoners' Association Bulletin* 2(2) [January/February]: 1.

'Toddler Hit on by Stone'. 2000. *Irish News*, 22 August: 11.

'Two Shot Dead in North Belfast'. 1989. *Belfast Telegraph*, 2 September, 6th edn: 1; 6th late edn: 2.

'UDP's Warning of Further Bloodshed'. 2000. *Belfast Telegraph*, 24 August: 1.

'Ulster Pays Tribute. Lieutenant Colonel Trevor King. Memorial Parade & Service, 7th July, 2001'. 2001. *Combat* 1 [August]: 7.

'Unveiling of Clonard Street Plaque'. 2002. *Greater Clonard Ex-Prisoners' Association Bulletin* 2(3), March/April: 1.

'UVF Victim Had No Political Connections'. 1989. *Irish News*, 4 September: 1.

'Violence Fears over UVF Shankill Parade'. 2000. *Belfast Telegraph Extra*, 2 September: 2.

'Vol. Brian Robinson Parade – 1993'. 1993. *Combat*, November: 13.

'Vol. Brian Robinson Parade – 1994'. 1994. *Combat*, September: 10.

'Volunteer Brian Robinson Memorial Parade 2nd September 2007'. 2007. *The Purple Standard* 4 [September]: 9–11.

'Volunteer Brian Robinson Memorial Parade 3rd September 2006'. 2006. *Combat* 38 [August/September]: 12.

'Volunteer Danny O'Neill to Be Honoured'. 2004. *Greater Clonard Ex-Prisoners' Association Bulletin* 4(1) [January]: 3.

'Volunteer Samuel Rockett Murdered by Cowards – 23rd August 2000'. 2004. *Combat* 24 [September/October]: 4.
'Wall Murals – An Intricate Part of Loyalist Culture'. 2008. *The Purple Standard* 6 [November]: 13.
'We Shall Remember Them'. 1994. *Combat*, July: 8.
'We Shall Remember'. 1995. *Combat*, September: 5.
'We Will Remember Them'. 2000. *Combat*, special edn [October]: 2.
'Wrangle over Bunting Funeral Arrangements'. 1980. *Belfast Telegraph*, 16 October: 1.
'Youth Urged to Forget "Manufactured Cardboard Heroes"'. 2003. *The Starry Plough*, February/March: 7.
Barnes, C. 2007. 'Shrines Attacked from Tour Coach', *Andersonstown News*, 3 November: 1, 3.
Byrne, C. 2007. 'The Day the Paramilitaries Called a Halt to Violence . . .', *Irish Independent*, 12 November: 23.
Cox, R. 2003. 'Loyalist Bands Ignore Commission's Order', *Andersonstown News*, 30 June: 4–5.
McCaffrey, B. 2003. 'Parade Passes off Peacefully', *Irish News*, 30 June: 7.
McCambridge, J. 2007. 'Sleeping Giant Awakes to the Sound of a Carpenters Ballad', *Belfast Telegraph*, 12 November: 4.
McKernon, A. 2003. 'Face of a Butcher', *North Belfast News*, 12 July: 4.
Murray, G. 2002. 'Remembering Our Fallen Volunteers', *Starry Plough*, August/September: 10.
Rowan, B. 2007. 'What Happens Next Is the Important Bit', *Belfast Telegraph*, 12 November: 2–3.
Rusk, D. 2006. 'Commemoration Stirs Memory', *Irish News*, 14 August: 5.
Sheahan, F. 2007. 'Loyalists Lay down Their Guns for Peace', *Irish Independent*, 12 November: 1, 22.
Simpson, C. 2008. 'UVF-linked Band Gets Lotto and Ulster-Scots Body Cash', *Irish News*, 12 May: 1

Parliamentary Acts, Reports, Official Media Releases and Policy Documents

Belfast City Council. 2007. 'Sandy Row Revival Strategy Launched', 24 May. Retrieved 20 July 2013 from http://www.belfastcity.co.uk/news/news.asp?id=891&month=5.
Bloomfield, K. 1998. '"We Will Remember Them": Report of the Northern Ireland Victims Commissioner Sir Kenneth Bloomfield KCB'. Belfast: Stationery Office Northern Ireland. Retrieved 14 July 2013 from http://www.ofmdfmni.gov.uk/bloomfield_report.pdf.
Brown, K. 2008. 'Artefacts Audit. A Report of the Material Culture of the Conflict in and about Northern Ireland'. Belfast: Healing Through Remembering.
Bryan, D., and G. Gillespie. 2005. 'Transforming Conflict: Flags and Emblems'. Belfast: Institute of Irish Studies, Queen's University Belfast.
Bryan, D., and C. Stevenson. 2006. 'Flags Monitoring Project 2006. Preliminary Findings'. Belfast: Institute of Irish Studies, Queen's University Belfast. Retrieved 14 July 2013 from http://www.ofmdfmni.gov.uk/flags-monitoring.pdf.
Bryan, D., C. Stevenson and G. Gillespie. 2007. 'Flags Monitoring Project. 2007 Report'. Belfast: Institute of Irish Studies, Queen's University Belfast. Retrieved 14 July 2013 from http://www.ofmdfmni.gov.uk/flagsreport2007-2.pdf.
———. 2008. 'Flags Monitoring Project 2008/09. Interim Report Covering 2008 with Comparative Figures from 2007 and 2006'. Belfast: Institute of Irish Studies, Queen's

University Belfast. Retrieved 14 July 2013 from http://www.ofmdfmni.gov.uk/flags_monitoring_project_2008_report__pdf_218kb_-2.pdf.

Bryan, D., C. Stevenson, G. Gillespie and J. Bell. 2010. 'Public Display of Flags and Emblem in Northern Ireland. Survey 2006–2009'. Belfast: Institute of Irish Studies, Queen's University Belfast. Retrieved 14 July 2013 from http://www.qub.ac.uk/schools/IrishStudiesGateway/FileStore/Filetoupload,196779,en.pdf.

Community Relations Unit, Office of First Minister and Deputy First Minister. 2005. 'A Shared Future. Policy and Strategic Framework for Good Relations in Northern Ireland'. Belfast: OFMDFM. Retrieved 14 July 2013 from http://www.ofmdfmni.gov.uk/asharedfuturepolicy2005.pdf.

Consultative Group on the Past. 2009. 'Report of the Consultative Group on the Past'. Belfast: Consultative Group on the Past. Retrieved 14 July 2013 from http://cain.ulst.ac.uk/victims/docs/consultative_group/cgp_230109_report_sum.pdf.

Copete, J. n.d. 'The Experiences that Make Us What We Are. Dealing with the Legacy of the Past in Post-Settlement Northern Ireland'. Retrieved 21 June 2010 from http://www.humanrights-observatory.net/revista1/copete.pdf.

Fitzgerald, S. 2006. 'Healing Through Remembering. Commemoration Sub Group'. Belfast: Healing Through Remembering.

Hamber, B., D. Kulle and R. Wilson. 2001. 'Future Policies for the Past. Report 13'. Belfast: Democratic Dialogue.

Healing Through Remembering. 2002. 'The Report of the Healing Through Remembering Project'. Belfast: Healing Through Remembering.

HMSO. 1922. 'Civil Authorities (Special Powers) Act (Northern Ireland), 1922'. London: HMSO. Retrieved 14 July 2013 from http://cain.ulst.ac.uk/hmso/spa1922.htm.

———. 1954. 'Flags and Emblems (Display) Act (Northern Ireland), 1954'. London: HMSO. Retrieved 14 July 2013 from http://cain.ulst.ac.uk/hmso/fea1954.htm.

Kelly, G. and B. Hamber. 2005. 'Reconciliation: Rhetoric or Relevant? Report 17'. Belfast: Democratic Dialogue.

Kgalema, L. 1999. 'Symbols of Hope. Monuments as Symbols of Remembrance and Peace in the Process of Reconciliation'. Retrieved 14 July 2013 from http://www.csvr.org.za/index.php/publications/1676-symbols-of-hope-monuments-as-symbols-of-remembrance-and-peace-in-the-process-of-reconciliation.html.

Institute of Irish Studies, Queen's University Belfast. 2006. 'St Patrick's Day Outdoor Event 2006. Monitoring Report'. Retrieved 14 July 2013 from http://www.qub.ac.uk/schools/IrishStudiesGateway/FileStore/Filetoupload,125533,en.pdf.

Leonard, J. 1998–1999. 'How Conflicts Are Commemorated in Northern Ireland.' Belfast: Central Community Relations Unit. Retrieved 14 July 2013 from http://cain.ulst.ac.uk/ccru/research/qub/leonard97.htm.

Nagle, J. 2006. 'Healing Through Remembering. Commemoration Sub Group'. Belfast: Healing Through Remembering.

Naidu, E. 2004. 'Symbolic Reparations: A Fractured Opportunity'. Retrieved 14 July 2013 from http://www.csvr.org.za/docs/livingmemory/symbolicreparations.pdf.

Northern Ireland Assembly, Research and Library Service. 2002. 'Measures of Deprivation: Noble V Robson'. Retrieved 14 July 2013 from http://archive.niassembly.gov.uk/research_papers/research/0202.pdf.

Northern Ireland Department for Social Development. 2004. 'Taskforce – Addressing the Needs of Working Class Protestant Communities. Sandy Row Project Team: Executive Summary'. Retrieved 14 July 2013 from http://www.dsdni.gov.uk/sandy_row_executive_summary.doc.

————. 2005. 'Spellar Considers Sandy Row Proposals', media release. Belfast: 18 March.

————. 2005. 'David Hanson Announces Sandy Row Progress', media release. Belfast: 4 August.

Northern Ireland Housing Executive. 1998. 'Economic Appraisal. Sandy Row, Belfast'. Belfast: Northern Ireland Housing Executive.

————. 2006a. 'Sandy Row's Fairy Thorn Good for Another Hundred Years!', media release. Belfast: 27 February.

————. 2006b. 'Official Opening of Sandy Row Environmental Improvement Scheme', media release. Belfast: 15 June.

Northern Ireland Office. 1998. 'The Belfast Agreement'. Retrieved 14 July 2013 from https://www.gov.uk/government/publications/the-belfast-agreement.

Northern Ireland Statistics and Research Agency, Department of Finance and Personnel. 2005. 'Northern Ireland Multiple Deprivation Measure 2005'. Norwich: The Stationery Office. Retrieved 14 July 2013 from http://www.nisra.gov.uk/deprivation/archive/NIMDM2005FullReport.pdf.

Purbrick, L. 2007. 'Without Walls: A Report on Healing Through Remembering's Open Call for Ideas for a Living Memorial Museum of the Conflict in and about Northern Ireland'. Belfast: Healing Through Remembering.

Royal Ulster Constabulary GC Foundation. 2004. 'Report for the Period 1st April 2003 to 31st March 2004'. Belfast: PSNI Publications.

Saville, M., W. Hoyt and J. Toohey. 2010. 'Report of the The Bloody Sunday Inquiry'. Retrieved 14 July 2013 from http://webarchive.nationalarchives.gov.uk/20101103103930/http:/report.bloody-sunday-inquiry.org/.

Secretary of State for Northern Ireland. 1996. 'Foundations for Policing'. Retrieved 14 July 2013 from http://cain.ulst.ac.uk/issues/police/docs/ffp1996.htm.

Southern Africa Reconciliation Project. 2005. 'Memorialisation and Reconciliation in Transitional Southern African Societies'. Retrieved 14 July 2013 from http://www.csvr.org.za/docs/livingmemory/memorialisatioreconciliation.pdf.

'Ulster's Solemn League and Covenant (1912)'. Ref. D627/429/95. Belfast: Public Record Office for Northern Ireland (PRONI).

United Kingdom Parliament, Publications and Records, Lords Publications. 2006. 'Lords Hansard Text for 11 January (60111w05)'. Retrieved 14 July 2013 from http://www.publications.parliament.uk/pa/ld200506/ldhansrd/vo060111/text/60111w05.htm.

Viggiani, E. 2007. 'Flags Monitoring Project 2006/07. Case Study: Sandy Row and South Belfast'. Belfast: Institute of Irish Studies, Queen's University Belfast.

Electronic Media

'A-Bomb Dome'. 2000. *Hiroshima Peace Memorial Museum Website*. Retrieved 20 July 2013 from http://www.pcf.city.hiroshima.jp/virtual/VirtualMuseum_e/tour_e/ireihi/tour_38_e.html.

'Ballymurphy Murals Unveiled'. 2002. *An Phoblacht*, 30 May. Retrieved 20 July 2013 from http://www.anphoblacht.com/contents/8818.

'Belfast 1981 Victims Remembered'. 2001. *An Phoblacht*, 2 August. Retrieved 20 July 2013 from http://republican-news.org/archive/2001/August02/02belf.html.

'Call Made to Remove INLA Monument'. 2007. *BBC News*, 21 March. Retrieved 20 July 2013 from http://news.bbc.co.uk/1/hi/northern_ireland/6474153.stm.

'Clashes in Dublin over Loyalist March'. 2006. *RTE News*, 25 February. Retrieved 20 July 2013 from http://www.rte.ie/news/2006/0225/loyalist.html.

'Clonard Rally Attacked'. 2000. *An Phoblacht*, 24 August. Retrieved 20 July 2013 from http://republican-news.org/archive/2000/August24/24clon.html.

'Conditions of Award of Battle Honours for the Great War 1914–1919'. 1996–2010. *The Regimental Rogue*. Retrieved 20 July 2013 from http://regimentalrogue.com/battle honours/firstworldwar-btlhnrs.htm.

'Continuity IRA Shot Dead Officer'. 2009. *BBC News*, 10 March. Retrieved 20 July 2013 from http://news.bbc.co.uk/1/hi/northern_ireland/7934426.stm.

'D Company Honours Its Fallen'. 2001. *An Phoblacht*, 28 June. Retrieved 20 July 2013 from http://www.anphoblacht.com/contents/7617.

'DUP Want INLA Statue Removed from Cemetery'. 2007. *Belfast Telegraph*, 11 April. Retrieved 20 July 2013 from http://www.highbeam.com/doc/1P2-10763612.html.

'Enniskillen Bomb Memorial'. 2010. *'Remembering': Victims, Survivors and Commemoration in Post-Conflict Northern Ireland*. Retrieved 20 July 2013 from http://cain.ulst.ac.uk/cgi-bin/AHRC/monuments.pl?id=827.

'First Victim of "Troubles" Commemorated'. 2009. *An Phoblacht*, 23 July. Retrieved 20 July 2013 from http://www.anphoblacht.com/contents/20397.

'Fitting 50th Anniversary Tribute to Sabhat and O'Hanlon'. 2007. *An Phoblacht*, 4 January. Retrieved 20 July 2013 from http://www.anphoblacht.com/contents/16242.

'Funeral for Man Beaten to Death'. 2008. *BBC News*, 22 March. Retrieved 20 July 2013 from http://news.bbc.co.uk/1/hi/northern_ireland/7308807.stm.

'Historic Ballymurphy Mural Project'. 2002. *An Phoblacht*, 23 May. Retrieved 20 July 2013 from http://www.anphoblacht.com/contents/8791.

'Huge Crowds Turn out to Honour the Hunger Strikers'. 2006. *An Phoblacht*, 17 August. Retrieved 20 July 2013 from http://www.anphoblacht.com/contents/15616.

'Irish Republican Socialist Movement Roll of Honour'. 2000. *Irish Republican Socialist Movement Website*. Retrieved 20 July 2013 from http://www.irsm.org/fallen/roll.html.

'Massacre Memorial Vandalised'. 2004. *BBC News*, 29 August. Retrieved 20 July 2013 from http://news.bbc.co.uk/1/hi/northern_ireland/3610144.stm.

'Memorial for "Troubles" Victims'. 2003. *BBC News*, 7 August. Retrieved 20 July 2013 from http://news.bbc.co.uk/1/hi/england/staffordshire/3131489.stm.

'Mickey Devine Remembered'. 2001. *An Phoblacht*, 23 August. Retrieved 20 July 2013 from http://www.anphoblacht.com/contents/7801.

'Mural Giving Shankill a New Image'. 2005. *BBC News*, 13 October. Retrieved 20 July 2013 from http://news.bbc.co.uk/1/hi/northern_ireland/4335872.stm.

'Northern Ireland Census 2011: Religion and Identity Mapped'. 2011. *The Guardian News Datablog*. Retrieved 20 July 2013 from http://www.guardian.co.uk/news/datablog/2012/dec/12/northern-ireland-census-2011-religion-identity-mapped.

'Palace Barracks Memorial Garden'. 2002–10. *Palace Barracks Memorial Garden Website*. Retrieved 20 July 2013 from http://www.palacebarracksmemorialgarden.org/Intro.htm.

'Parade to Mark Anniversary of McMichael's Death'. 2007. *Ulster Star*, 19 December. Retrieved 20 July 2013 from http://www.lisburntoday.co.uk/news/local-news/parade-to-mark-anniversary-of-mcmichael-s-death-1-1639868.

'Real IRA Was behind Army Attack'. 2009. *BBC News*, 8 March. Retrieved 20 July 2013 from http://news.bbc.co.uk/1/hi/northern_ireland/7930995.stm.

'RUC GC Garden'. n.d. *Royal Ulster Constabulary George Cross Foundation Website*. Retrieved 20 July 2013 from http://www.rucgcfoundation.org/garden.htm.

'Saddam Statue Toppled in Central Baghdad'. 2003. CNN.com, 9 April. Retrieved 20 July 2013 from http://edition.cnn.com/2003/WORLD/meast/04/09/sprj.irq.statue/.

'Sandy Row Loyalist Mural Being Replaced with William of Orange Painting'. 2012. *BBC News*, 25 June. Retrieved 20 July 2013 from http://www.bbc.co.uk/news/uk-northern-ireland-18578998.

'SF Ard Fheis Backs Policing Motion'. 2007. *Irish Republican News*, 28 January. Retrieved 20 July 2013 from http://republican-news.org/current/news/2007/01/sf_ard_fheis_backs_policing_mo.html.

'Shots Fired at Cell Death Funeral'. 2009. *BBC News*, 8 October. Retrieved 20 July 2013 from http://news.bbc.co.uk/1/hi/northern_ireland/foyle_and_west/8296322.stm.

'Stabbing Victim on Life Support'. 2007. *BBC News*, 12 September. Retrieved 20 July 2013 from http://news.bbc.co.uk/1/hi/northern_ireland/6990853.stm.

'Tallinn Tense after Deadly Riots'. 2007. *BBC News*, 28 April. Retrieved 20 July 2013 from http://news.bbc.co.uk/1/hi/world/europe/6602171.stm.

'The "Bronze Night" Cost Estonia over 4mn Euro'. 2007. *Regnum*, 27 July. Retrieved 20 July 2013 from http://www.regnum.ru/english/862457.html.

'Three Heroes Honoured'. 2002. *An Phoblacht*, 7 March. Retrieved 20 July 2013 from http://republican-news.org/archive/2002/March07/07beec.html.

'Tribute to Murdered Officers'. 2003. *BBC News*, 23 September. Retrieved 20 July 2013 from http://news.bbc.co.uk/1/hi/northern_ireland/3130566.stm.

'UDA Group "Wants £8m to Disband"'. 2006. *BBC News*, 2 October. Retrieved 20 July 2013 from http://news.bbc.co.uk/1/hi/northern_ireland/5400470.stm.

'UDU Flags "Must Come Down" – MLA'. 2009. *BBC News*, 22 June. Retrieved 20 July 2013 from http://news.bbc.co.uk/1/hi/northern_ireland/foyle_and_west/8112230.stm.

'UDU Flags "Not Paramilitary"'. 2009. *Derry Journal*, 23 June. Retrieved 20 July 2013 from http://www.derryjournal.com/politics/UDU-flags-39not--.5390039.jp.

'UVF Calls End to Terror Campaign'. 2007. *BBC News*, 3 May. Retrieved 20 July 2013 from http://news.bbc.co.uk/1/hi/northern_ireland/6618371.stm.

'UVF Statement in Full'. 2007. *BBC News*, 3 May. Retrieved 20 July 2013 from http://news.bbc.co.uk/1/hi/northern_ireland/6618365.stm.

Belfast City Council Elections. 1993–2011. '2011 Results'. Retrieved 20 July 2013 from http://www.ark.ac.uk/elections/lgbelfast.htm.

Breen, M. 2006. 'Terrorist Statue in City Graveyard Sparks Outrage', *Belfast Telegraph*, 11 June. Retrieved 20 July 2013 from http://www.belfasttelegraph.co.uk/imported/terrorist-statue-in-city-graveyard-sparks-outrage-28319086.html.

CAIN. 2009–12. *"Remembering": Victims, Survivors and Commemoration in Post-Conflict Northern Ireland*. Retrieved 20 July 2013 from http://cain.ulst.ac.uk/victims/index.html.

Cohen, P. 2012. 'Construction Frozen in a Fight over Financing', *The New York Times*, 2 June. Retrieved 20 July 2013 from http://www.nytimes.com/2012/06/03/arts/design/sept-11-memorial-museum-construction-is-frozen-over-financing.html?_r=2.

Frampton, M. 2007. 'Policing and the Day Sinn Fein Thought Would never Come', *Parliamentary Brief Online*, 8 March. Retrieved 20 July 2013 from http://www.zoominfo.com/CachedPage/?archive_id=0&page_id=1971105248&page_url=//www.thepolitician.org/articles/policing-and-the-408.html&page_last_updated=2008-07-26T08:41:16&firstName=Martyn&lastName=Frampton.

Friel, L. 2001. 'We Shall Overcome', *An Phoblacht*, 1 March. Retrieved 20 July 2013 from http://www.republican-news.org/archive/2001/March01/01clon.html.

Gibney, J. 2002. 'A Difficult Walk into History', *An Phoblacht*, 4 July. Retrieved 20 July 2013 from http://republican-news.org/archive/2002/July04/04diff.html.

Jackson, G. 2005. 'Tricolour and Union Jack Fly United in Peace', *Independent*, 7 November. Retrieved 20 July 2013 from http://www.independent.ie/national-news/ tricolour-and-union-jack-fly-united-in-peace-229451.html.

Kearney, V. 2007. 'How UDA Cash Carrot Was Pulled', *BBC News*, 16 October. Retrieved 20 July 2013 from http://news.bbc.co.uk/1/hi/northern_ireland/7047547.stm.

Lane, F. 2002. 'Proud To Be Here', *An Phoblacht*, 18 April. Retrieved 20 July 2013 from http://republican-news.org/archive/2002/April18/18tirg.html.

McCann, N. 2007. 'Vandals Damage Republican Graves', *BBC News*, 27 February. Retrieved 20 July 2013 from http://news.bbc.co.uk/1/hi/northern_ireland/6400379. stm.

McCormick, J. 1996–2013. *A Directory of Murals in Northern Ireland*. Retrieved 20 July 2013 from http://cain.ulst.ac.uk/mccormick/.

———. 2001. 'Album No. 34, Photograph No. 1160', *A Directory of Murals in Northern Ireland*. Retrieved 20 July 2013 from http://cain.ulst.ac.uk/mccormick/photos/no1160. htm#photo.

McCrory, M.L. 2007. 'Plaque Unveiled to Child Shot Dead by IRA in 1971', *Irish News*, 10 September. Retrieved 20 July 2013 from http://www.nuzhound.com/articles/irish_ news/arts2007/sep10_plaque_unveiled_child_shot_IRA_1971.php.

McDonald, H. 2004. 'Remember the Horrors. Murals Commemorate the Glorious Troubles, Not the Reality', *The Observer*, 22 August. Retrieved 20 July 2013 from http://www.guardian.co.uk/politics/2004/aug/22/northernireland.northernireland.

McNeill, C., and E. Moulton. 2007. 'Bus Tour Is Driven off Falls Road', *Belfast Telegraph*, 2 November. Retrieved 20 July 2013 from http://www.belfasttelegraph.co.uk/news/local- national/bus-tour-is-driven-off-falls-road-28397538.html.

Maher, K. 2009. 'Rebirth of the Reel IRA. Do Films on the Troubles Illuminate or just Inflame?', *The Times*, 11 April. Retrieved 20 July 2013 from http://www.thetimes. co.uk/tto/arts/film/article2431207.ece.

Northern Ireland Elections. 2007. 'Northern Ireland Assembly Elections 2007'. Retrieved 20 July 2013 from http://www.ark.ac.uk/elections/fa07.htm.

———. 2011. 'Northern Ireland Assembly Elections 2011'. Retrieved 20 July 2013 from http://www.ark.ac.uk/elections/fa11.htm.

Northern Ireland Life and Times Survey (NILT). 2000. 'Module: Political Attitudes, Variable: MEMVICT'. Retrieved 20 July 2013 from http://www.ark.ac.uk/nilt/2000/ Political_Attitudes/MEMVICT.html.

———. 2000. 'Module: Political Attitudes, Variable: WHOMEM'. Retrieved 20 July 2013 from http://www.ark.ac.uk/nilt/2000/Political_Attitudes/WHOMEM.html.

———. 2003. 'Module: Political Attitudes, Variable: IDBRIT-IDNONE'. Retrieved 20 July 2013 from http://www.ark.ac.uk/nilt/2003/Political_Attitudes/ID.html.

———. 2004. 'Module: Political Attitudes, Variable: MEMVICT2'. Retrieved 20 July 2013 from http://www.ark.ac.uk/nilt/2004/Political_Attitudes/MEMVICT2.html.

———. 2008. 'Module: Community Relations, Variable: LOYMUR'. Retrieved 20 July 2013 from http://www.ark.ac.uk/nilt/2008/Community_Relations/LOYMURAL.html.

———. 2008. 'Module: Community Relations, Variable: LOYMUR2'. Retrieved 20 July 2013 from http://www.ark.ac.uk/nilt/2008/Community_Relations/LOYMUR2.html.

———. 2008. 'Module: Community Relations, Variable: REPMUR'. Retrieved 20 July 2013 from http://www.ark.ac.uk/nilt/2008/Community_Relations/REPMURAL. html.

———. 2008. 'Module: Community Relations, Variable: REPMUR2'. Retrieved 20 July 2013 from http://www.ark.ac.uk/nilt/2008/Community_Relations/REPMUR2.html.

———. 2008. 'Module: Community Relations, Variable: TARGET2A'. Retrieved 20 July 2013 from http://www.ark.ac.uk/nilt/2008/Community_Relations/TARGET2A.html.

Republican Network for Unity. n.d. *Phoblachtáigh do Aontiú / Republican Network for Unity Website*. Retrieved 20 July 2013 from http://www.republicanunity.org/.

South Belfast Friends of the Somme Association. n.d. *South Belfast Friends of the Somme Association Website*. Retrieved 20 July 2013 from http://www.belfastsomme.com/.

Spain, M. 2002. 'The Tírghrá Commemorative Event. Honouring the Families of Our Fallen', *An Phoblacht*, 11 April. Retrieved 20 July 2013 from http://republican-news. org/archive/2002/April11/11tirg.html.

Special EU Programmes Body. n.d. 'SEUPB - What Is the PEACE III Programme?' Retrieved 20 July 2013 from http://www.seupb.eu/programmes2007-2013/peaceiii programme/overview.aspx.

Surowiecki, J. 1998. 'The Luck of the Irish. In the Movies, IRA Terrorists Become Dashing Heroes', *Slate*, 22 January. Retrieved 20 July 2013 from http://www.slate.com/articles/ news_and_politics/high_concept/1998/01/the_luck_of_the_irish.html.

Viggiani, E. 2006. *Public Forms of Memorialisation in Belfast*. Retrieved 20 July 2013 from http://cain.ulst.ac.uk/viggiani/menu.html.

———. 2013. *Talking Stones*. Retrieved 20 July 2013 from http://northernirelandmem orials.com/.

Whelan, P. 2001. 'Bombers Attack Clonard Commemoration', *An Phoblacht*, 15 March. Retrieved 20 July 2013 from http://www.anphoblacht.com/contents/7285.

Primary Sources

Pamphlets and Booklets

Adamson, I. 1974. *The Cruthin: The Ancient Kindred*. Newtownards: Nosmada Books.

———. 1982. *The Identity of Ulster: The Land, the Language and the People*. N.p.: Donard Press.

Adamson, I., D. Hume and D. McDowell. 1995. *Cuchulain the Lost Legend: Ulster the Lost Culture*. Belfast: Ulster Young Unionist Council.

Ardoyne Commemoration Project. 2002. *Ardoyne: The Untold Truth*. Belfast: Beyond the Pale.

Beechmount Commemoration Committee. 1998. *Green River: In Honour of Our Dead*. Belfast: Beechmount Commemoration Committee.

Coiste na n-Iarchimí. 1999a. *Working for the Republican Ex-Prisoner Community*. Belfast: Coiste na n-Iarchimí.

———. 1999b. *Legal Issues Facing Political Ex-Prisoners*. Belfast: Coiste na n-Iarchimí.

Conflict Transformation Initiative. 2006. *A New Reality? Loyalism in Transition*. Belfast: Farset Community Think Tanks Project.

Crothers, J. 1998. *EPIC Research Document No. 2: Reintegration – The Problems and the Issues*. Belfast: EPIC.

East Belfast Historical and Cultural Society. 2002. *Murder in Ballymacarrett: The Untold Story*. Belfast: East Belfast Historical and Cultural Society.

Falls Cultural Society. 2001. *Garden of Remembrance: June 24th 2001*. Belfast: Falls Cultural Society.

Greater Clonard Ex-Prisoners' Association. 2001. *Clonard Martyrs Memorial Garden: In Memory of Our Dead*. Belfast: Greater Clonard Ex-Prisoners' Association.

———. n.d. *Clonard Martyrs Memorial Garden*. Belfast: Greater Clonard Ex-Prisoners' Association.

National 1981 Hunger Strike Commemoration Committee. 2006. *A Generation Remembers: Cuimhíonn Glúin; 25th Anniversary Commemorative Programme of Events*. Belfast: National 1981 Hunger Strike Commemoration Committee.

National Graves Association. 1985. *Belfast Graves*. Dublin: An Phoblacht/Republican News Print.

———. 1994. *Belfast Graves – Vol. 2*. Dublin: National Graves Association.

———. n.d. *Antrim's Patriot Dead 1797–1953*. Belfast: National Graves Association.

New Lodge Commemoration Committee. 1993. *New Lodge Massacre*. Belfast: New Lodge Commemoration Committee.

Ó Coinn, S. 2002. *Our Patriot Dead: Short Strand 1972–2002; 30th Anniversary Commemoration Book*. Belfast: Sean Martin/Sean Treacy Cumann.

Power, T. 1998. *The Ta Power Document: An Essay on the History of the Irish Republican Socialist Movement*. Belfast: Irish Republican Socialist Party.

Quinn, R.J. 2004. *The Rising of the Phoenix. Éirí na Féinics. The Battle of St Matthew's and the Events Surrounding the Historic Weekend of June 27th 1970 on the Springfield and in Ardoyne*. Belfast: Belfast Cultural and Local History Group.

Sandy Row Women's Group. 2006. *One Hundred Years in the Shadow of the City Hall. Memories of the Sandy Row Women's Group*. Belfast: Sandy Row Women's Group.

Sinn Féin. 2006. *1916 Éirí amach na Cásca: 90th Anniversary*. Dublin: Sinn Féin.

Springhill Massacre Committee. 1999. *The Springhill Massacre: Belfast's Bloody Sunday*. Belfast: Springhill Community House.

Teach na Fáilte Memorial Committee Belfast. 2004. *Republican Socialist Ex Prisoners*. Belfast: Teach na Fáilte Memorial Committee Belfast.

Tírghrá Commemoration Committee. 2002. *Tírghrá: Ireland's Patriot Dead*. N.p.: Republican Publications.

Turf Lodge Commemoration Committee. 2006. *Greater Turf Lodge Book of Memories*. Belfast: Turf Lodge Commemoration Committee.

Twinbrook and Poleglass Commemoration Committee. 1999. *Unforgotten Sacrifice: A Tribute to Fallen Comrades*. Belfast: Sinn Féin Office Mairead Farrell House (Stewartstown Road).

Ulster Defence Association / New Ulster Political Research Group. 1979. *Beyond the Religious Divide: Papers for Discussion – March 1979*. Belfast: NUPRG.

Ulster Defence Association / Ulster Political Research Group. 1987. *Common Sense: Northern Ireland – An Agreed Process*. Belfast: UPRG.

Ulster Volunteer Force Regimental Association. 2006. *The Fallen and the Brave: In Memory of Family, Friends and Comrades*. Belfast: Ulster Volunteer Force Regimental Association.

Speeches and Orations (including fieldnotes)

Adams, G. n.d. 'An Address to the IRA'. Retrieved 17 July 2013 from http://www.sinnfein.ie/contents/15207.

———. 1994a. 'Comments by Gerry Adams MP, 1 March 1994'. Retrieved 17 July 2013 from http://www.sinnfein.ie/contents/15190.

———. 1994b. 'Address by Sinn Féin President Gerry Adams MP, 27 October 1994'. Retrieved 17 July 2013 from http://www.sinnfein.ie/contents/15200.

————. 2006a. 'Speech by Gerry Adams, then President of Sinn Féin, at the Easter Commemoration, Belfast, (Sunday 16 April 2006)'. Retrieved 17 July 2013 from http://cain.ulst.ac.uk/issues/politics/docs/sf/ga160406.htm.

————. 2006b 'Speech by Gerry Adams, then President of Sinn Féin, at a Republican Commemoration Marking the Twenty-fifth Anniversary of the Death of Bobby Sands, Hackballscross, County Louth (5 May 2006)'. Retrieved 17 July 2013 from http://cain.ulst.ac.uk/issues/politics/docs/sf/ga050506.htm.

————. 2007a. 'Speech by Gerry Adams, then President of Sinn Féin, at an Event to Commemorate Seán Sabhat and Feargal Ó hAnnluain, County Fermanagh, 1 January 2007'. Retrieved 17 July 2013 from http://cain.ulst.ac.uk/issues/politics/docs/sf/ga010107.htm.

————. 2007b. 'Extracts from Speech by Gerry Adams, then President of Sinn Féin, to an Easter commemoration, Dublin (8 April 2007)'. Retrieved 17 July 2013 from http://cain.ulst.ac.uk/issues/politics/docs/sf/ga080407.htm.

Gallagher, W. 2000. 'Irish Republican Socialist Party. Ard Comhairle Address. Unveiling of National Hunger Strike Memorial and North West Monument Republican Socialist Plot, Derry/Londonderry City Cemetery (5 March 2000)'.

Harkin, T. 2003. 'Speech Delivered by IRSP Ard Comhairle Member Terry Harkin at the Unveiling of a Plaque to Commemorate Mickey Kearney and Patrick Campbell, Two INLA Volunteers Killed on Active Service, Belfast (20 [sic – 19] January 2003)'. Retrieved 17 July 2013 from http://www.irsm.org/statements/irsp/current/030120.html.

Hutchinson, B. 2007. 'Speech at Commemoration in Memory of UVF Volunteer Brian Robinson, Disraeli Street, Belfast (1 September 2007)'.

Kelly, G. 2007. 'Speech by Sinn Féin Ard Comhairle Member Gerry Kelly at Easter Commemoration, Milltown Cemetery, Belfast (8 April 2007)'.

McAliskey, B. 2002. 'Speech at the Launch of a Commemorative Plaque Dedicated to Ronnie Bunting and Noel Little, Turf Lodge, Belfast (13 October 2002)'. Access to speaker's notes granted by Gerard Murray of the IRSP/INLA Belfast Teach Na Fáilte Memorial Committee.

McDonald, J. 2007. 'Speech at UDA Remembrance Sunday Commemoration, Sandy Row, Belfast (11 November 2007)'.

McGarrigle, E. 2003. 'Speech at the Unveiling of a Teach na Failte Memorial to the Memory of INLA Volunteer Hugh Ferguson and Comrade Hugh O Neill by Eddie McGarrigle, Belfast (24 May [sic – 23 February] 2003)'. Retrieved 17 July 2013 from http://www.irsm.org/statements/irsp/current/030322.html.

McMonagle, M. 2007. 'Speech by IRSP Ard Comhairle Member Martin McMonagle at Easter Commemoration, Milltown Cemetery, Belfast (8 April 2007)'.

Maskey, A. 2002. 'The Memory of the Dead: Seeking Common Ground. Speech by Alex Maskey MLA Mayor of Belfast, Belfast City Hall (26 June 2002)'.

Moore, M. 1999. 'Clonard: A Thirty Year History, [Belfast]'.

Murray, G. 2003a. 'Unveiling of Plaque in Memory of INLA Loughran, Campbell, McLarnon, McCann, Tumelty, Gallagher and Dornan, Divis, Belfast (6 April 2003)'. Access to speaker's notes granted by Gerard Murray of the IRSP/INLA Belfast Teach Na Fáilte Memorial Committee.

————. 2003b. 'On 11 May 2003, a Memorial to Four Martyrs of the Irish National Liberation Army Was Dedicated in the Markets Area of South Belfast. Chair's Opening Remarks, Belfast (11 May 2003)'. Retrieved 17 July 2013 from http://www.irsm.org/statements/irsp/current/030511.html.

———. 2003c. 'Unveiling of Plaque in Memory of INLA McNamee and Daly, Andersonstown, Belfast (6 July 2003)'. Access to speaker's notes granted by Gerard Murray of the IRSP/INLA Belfast Teach Na Fáilte Memorial Committee.

———. 2003d. 'Unveiling of Memorial in Memory of INLA Neil McMonigle, Derry (9 November 2003)'. Access to speaker's notes granted by Gerard Murray of the IRSP/INLA Belfast Teach Na Fáilte Memorial Committee.

———. 2006. 'Unveiling of INLA Mural in Memory of Patsy O'Hara, Derry (12 May 2006)'. Access to speaker's notes granted by Gerard Murray of the IRSP/INLA Belfast Teach Na Fáilte Memorial Committee.

———. 2007a. 'XX Anniversary of the Death of INLA Power, Power, O'Reilly and Gargan, Market, Belfast (21 January 2007)'. Access to speaker's notes granted by Gerard Murray of the IRSP/INLA Belfast Teach Na Fáilte Memorial Committee.

———. 2007b. 'Unveiling for INLA Colin Maguire, Glasnevin Cemetery, Dublin (4 February 2007)'. Access to speaker's notes granted by Gerard Murray of the IRSP/INLA Belfast Teach Na Fáilte Memorial Committee.

Republican Socialist Youth Movement. 2007. 'Easter Statement. The Following Speech Was Delivered by a Representative of the Republican Socialist Youth Movement Ard Comhairle at the National Republican Socialist Movement Easter Commemoration Held in Belfast on Easter Sunday, 2007', *The Blanket*, 10 April. Retrieved 17 July 2013 from http://indiamond6.ulib.iupui.edu:81/RSYM2230407.html.

Ruddy, G. 2003a. 'On 11 May 2003, a Memorial to Four Martyrs of the Irish National Liberation Army Was Dedicated in the Markets Area of South Belfast. Dedication Speech, Belfast (11 May 2003)'. Retrieved 17 July 2013 from http://www.irsm.org/statements/irsp/current/030511.html.

———. 2003b. 'Speech Delivered by IRSP AC Member Gerry Ruddy at Unveiling of Daly/McNamee Plaque, [Belfast], 22 June 2003 [sic – 6 July]'. Retrieved 17 July 2013 from http://www.irsm.org/statements/irsp/current/030622.html.

Ulster Defence Association. 2007. 'Ulster Defence Association Remembrance Day Statement, 11 November 2007'. Retrieved 17 July 2013 from http://cain.ulst.ac.uk/othelem/organ/uda/uda111107.htm.

Miscellaneous Sources

Belfast City Council. 2008. 'Freedom of Information Request: Sandy Row Redevelopment'. Freedom of Information Request E521/00, 27 August.

Murphy, Y., A. Leonard, G. Gillespie and K. Brown. 2001. *Troubled Images: Posters and Images of the Northern Ireland Conflict from the Linen Hall Library, Belfast*. CDROM. Belfast: Linen Hall Library.

Northern Ireland Divisional Planning Office. 2000–2008. 'Digital Records of Planning Permission Applications for Memorials: 2000–2008'.

Northern Ireland Housing Executive. 2006. 'Sectional Symbols Survey. Housing Executive Estates: [June?]'.

———. 2008a. Freedom of Information Request RFI/402, 17 June.

———. 2008b. Freedom of Information Request RFI/440, 27 August.

Northern Ireland Roads Service. 2006. 'List of Memorials, Southern Division, 19 May'.

———. 2008. 'Count of Illegally Erected Monuments/Memorials on Public Roads, 16 May'.

Teach na Fáilte Memorial Committee Belfast. 2002–2004. 'Minutes from Committee's Meetings: June 2002 – May 2004'.

Interviews and Correspondence

The author would like to thank the following people (in alphabetical order) who agreed to be interviewed and/or entered in correspondence with the author for the purpose of this book. Some interviewees did not wish to be identified and, therefore, their names have been omitted from the list below.

Chittick, George
Deighan, Anne
Devenny, Danny
Ekin, Tom
Ervine, Mark
Gibson, Mervyn
Haggan, Harry
Hartley, Tom
Hawthorne, Jennifer
Humphrey, William
Hutchinson, Billy
Jack, Daniel
Little, Paul
McCotter, Pádraic
McDonald, Jackie
McKeown, Laurence
McMichael, Gary
McMurray, Joe
McVeigh, Jim
Maginness, Alban
Maskey, Conor
Murray, Gerard
O'Doherty, Malachi
Smith, William
Smyth, Hugh
Stoker, Robert
Timmons, Lisa
Upritchard, Lynne
Warren, David

Secondary Sources

Academic Books, Book Chapters and Articles

Agar, M.H. 1980. *The Professional Stranger: An Informal Introduction to Ethnography*. New York: Academic Press.
Anderson, B. 1983. *Imagined Communities: Reflections on the Origin and Spread of Nationalism*. London: Verso.

Anderson, B. 2002. *Joe Cahill: A Life in the IRA*. Dublin: O'Brien Press.

Arensberg, C. 1968. *The Irish Countryman*. New York: Natural History Press.

Argenbright, R. 1999. 'Remaking Moscow: New Places, New Selves', *Geographical Review* 89(1): 1–22.

Ashplant, T.G., G. Dawson and M. Roper (eds). 2000. *The Politics of War Memory and Commemoration*. London: Routledge.

Assmann, J. 1995. 'Collective Memory and Cultural Identity', *New German Critique* 65: 125–35.

Atkinson, D., and D. Cosgrove. 1998. 'Urban Rhetoric and Embodied Identities: City, Nation, and Empire at the Vittorio Emanuele II Monument in Rome, 1870–1945', *Annals of the Association of American Geographers* 88: 28–49.

Azaryahu, M., and A. Kellerman. 1999. 'Symbolic Places of National History and Revival: A Study in Zionist Mythical Geography', *Transactions of the Institute of British Geographers* 24(1): 109–23.

Bar-Tal, D. 2003. 'Collective Memory of Physical Violence: Its Contribution to the Culture of Violence', in E. Cairns and M.D. Roe (eds), *The Role of Memory in Ethnic Conflict*. Houndmills: Palgrave Macmillan, pp. 77–93.

Bauman, Z. 2001. *Community: Seeking Safety in an Insecure World*. Cambridge: Polity Press.

Bean, K. 2007. *The New Politics of Sinn Féin*. Liverpool: Liverpool University Press.

Beiner, G. 2000. 'Negotiations of Memory: Rethinking 1798 Commemoration', *Irish Review* 26: 60–70.

Bell, C. 2003. 'Dealing with the Past in Northern Ireland', *Fordham International Law Journal* 26: 1095–145.

Bell, D. 1990. *Acts of Union: Youth Culture and Sectarianism in Northern Ireland*. Basingstoke: Macmillan Education.

Bell, J. 1999. 'Redefining National Identity in Uzbekistan: Symbolic Tensions in Tashkent's Official Public Landscape', *Ecumene* 6(2): 183–207.

Bet-El, I.R. 2002. 'Unimagined Communities: The Power of Memory and the Conflict in the Former Yugoslavia', in J.-W. Müller (ed.), *Memory and Power in Post-War Europe: Studies in the Presence of the Past*. Cambridge: Cambridge University Press, pp. 206–22.

Bew, P., P. Gibbon and H. Patterson. 2002. *Northern Ireland 1921–2001: Political Forces and Social Classes*. London: Serif.

Bew, P. and G. Gillespie. 1999. *Northern Ireland: A Chronology of the Troubles 1968–1999*. Dublin: Gill and Macmillan.

Boal, F.W. 1982. 'Segregating and Mixing: Space and Residence in Belfast', in F.W. Boal and J.H.N. Douglas (eds), *Integration and Division: Geographical Perspectives on the Northern Ireland Problem*. London: Academic Press, pp. 249–80.

Boal, F.W., and R.C. Murray. 1977. 'A City in Conflict', *Geographical Magazine* 44: 364–71.

Bodnar, J. 1994. *Remaking America: Public Memory, Commemoration and Patriotism in the Twentieth Century*. Princeton, NJ: Princeton University Press.

Borneman, J. 1997. *Settling Accounts: Violence, Justice, and Accountability in Post-socialist Europe*. Princeton, NJ: Princeton University Press.

Bort, E. (ed.). 2004. *Commemorating Ireland: History, Politics, Culture*. Dublin: Irish Academic Press.

Boulton, D. 1973. *The UVF, 1966–73: An Anatomy of Loyalist Rebellion*. Dublin: Torc Books.

Bourdieu, P. 1990. *The Logic of Practice*. Cambridge: Polity Press.

Bowyer Bell, J. 1996. *Back to the Future: The Protestants and a United Ireland*. Dublin: Poolbeg.

———. 2003. *The Secret Army: The IRA*, 3rd edn. New Brunswick, NJ: Transaction Publishers.

Boyle, K., R. Chesney and T. Hadden. 1976. 'Who Are the Terrorists?', *Fortnight* 126: 6–8.

Breen, R., and P. Devine. 1998. 'Segmentation and the Social Structure', in P. Mitchell and R. Wilford (eds), *Politics in Northern Ireland*. Boulder, CO: Westview Press, pp. 52–65.

Brewer, J.D., B. Lockhart and P. Rodgers. 1998. 'Informal Social Control and Crime Management in Belfast', *British Journal of Sociology* 49(4): 570–85.

Brown, K. 2006. 'Public Memorials and Post Conflict Northern Ireland'. Belfast: Unpublished paper.

———. 2007. '"Our Father Organization": The Cult of the Somme and the Unionist "Golden Age" in Modern Ulster Loyalist Commemoration', *The Round Table* 96(393): 707–23.

———. 2009. '"Ancestry of Resistance": The Political Use of Commemoration by Ulster Loyalists and Irish Republicans in a Post Conflict Setting', Transitional Justice Institute Research Paper No. 09-09 5: 1–47.

Brown, K., and R. MacGinty. 2003. 'Public Attitudes toward Partisan and Neutral Symbols in Post-Agreement Northern Ireland', *Identities: Global Studies in Culture and Power* 10: 83–108.

Brown, K., and E. Viggiani. 2009. 'Performing Provisionalism: Republican Commemorative Practice as Political Performance', in L. Fitzpatrick (ed.), *Performing Violence in Contemporary Ireland*. Dublin: Carysfort Press, pp. 225–48.

Bruce, S. 1992. *The Red Hand: Protestant Paramilitaries in Northern Ireland*. Oxford: Oxford University Press.

———. 1994. *The Edge of the Union: The Ulster Loyalist Political Vision*. Oxford: Oxford University Press.

Bryan, D. 2000. *Orange Parades: The Politics of Ritual, Tradition and Control*. London: Pluto.

———. 2006. 'The Politics of Community', *Critical Review of International Social and Political Philosophy* 9(4): 603–17.

———. 2010. 'Forget 1960, Remember the Somme: Ulster Loyalist Battles in the 21st Century', in O. Frawley (ed.), *Memory Ireland 1*. Syracuse, NY: Syracuse University Press.

Buckland, P. 1981. *A History of Northern Ireland*. New York: Holmes and Meier Publishers.

Burton, F. 1978. *The Politics of Legitimacy: Struggles in a Belfast Community*. London: Routledge and Kegan Paul.

Cairns, E., and M.D. Roe (eds). 2003. *The Role of Memory in Ethnic Conflict*. Houndmills: Palgrave Macmillan.

Cannadine, D. 1983. 'The Context, Performance and Meaning of Ritual: The British Monarchy and the "Invention of Tradition", c.1820–1977', in E. Hobsbawm and T. Ranger (eds), *The Invention of Tradition*. New York: Cambridge University Press, pp. 101–64.

Cavanaugh, K. 1997. 'Interpretations of Political Violence in Ethnically Divided Societies', *Terrorism and Political Violence* 9(3): 33–54.

Charlesworth, A. 1994. 'Contesting Places of Memory: The Case of Auschwitz', *Environment and Planning D* 12: 579–93.

Clarke, J. 2007. *Commemorating the Dead in Revolutionary France: Revolution and Remembrance, 1789–1799*. Cambridge: Cambridge University Press.

Cohen, A. 1974. *Two-Dimensional Man: An Essay on the Anthropology and Symbolism in Complex Society*. London: Routledge and Kegan Paul.

Cohen, A.P. 1985. *The Symbolic Construction of Community*. London: Routledge.

Collins, P. 2004. *Who Fears to Speak of '98? Commemoration and the Continuing Impact of the United Irishmen*. Belfast: Ulster Historical Foundation.

Confino, A. 1997. 'Collective Memory and Cultural History: Problems of Method', *The American Historical Review* 102(5): 1386–403.

Connelly, M. 2012. *The IRA on Film and Television: A History*. Jefferson, NC: McFarland.

Connerton, P. 1989. *How Societies Remember*. Cambridge: Cambridge University Press.

Coogan, T.P. 2002. *The IRA*, rev. edn. New York: Palgrave for St Martin's.

Cosgrove, D., and S. Daniels (eds). 1988. *The Iconography of Landscape*. Cambridge: Cambridge University Press.

Cusack, J., and H. McDonald. 1997. *UVF*. Dublin: Poolbeg.

Daly, M.E. and M. O'Callaghan. 2007. *1916 in 1966: Commemorating the Easter Rising*. Dublin: Royal Irish Academy.

Daniels, S. 1993. *Fields of Vision: Landscape, Imagery and National Identity in England and the United States*. Princeton, NJ: Princeton University Press.

Darby, J. 1986. *Intimidation and Conflict in Northern Ireland*. Dublin: Gill and Macmillan.

———. 1997. *Scorpions in a Bottle: Conflicting Cultures in Northern Ireland*. London: Minority Rights Group.

Dawson, G. 2005. 'Trauma, Place and the Politics of Memory: Bloody Sunday, Derry, 1972–2004', *History Workshop Journal* 59: 151–78.

Di Lellio, A., and S. Schwandner-Sievers. 2006a. 'The Legendary Commander: The Construction of an Albanian Master-narrative in Post-war Kosovo', *Nations and Nationalism* 12(3): 513–29.

———. 2006b. 'Sacred Journey to a Nation: The Construction of a Shrine in Postwar Kosovo', *Journeys* 7(1): a1–a23.

Dillon, M. 1989. *The Shankill Butchers: A Case Study of Mass Murder*. London: Hutchinson.

Doherty, G., and D. Keogh (eds). 1998. '"Sorrow but No Despair – The Road Is Marked": The Politics of Funerals in Post-1916 Ireland', in *Michael Collins and the Making of the Irish State*. Cork: Mercier, pp. 186–201.

——— (eds). 2007. *1916: The Long Revolution*. Cork: Mercier Press.

Doherty, P.M., and A. Poole. 1997. 'Ethnic Residential Segregation in Belfast, Northern Ireland, 1971–1991', *Geographical Review* 87: 520–36.

Donnan, H.. 2005. 'Material Identities: Fixing Ethnicity in the Irish Borderlands', *Identities: Global Studies in Culture and Power* 12: 69–105.

Duncan, J., and N. Duncan. 1988. '(Re)reading the Landscape', *Environment and Planning D* 6: 117–26.

Durkheim, É. 1948. *The Elementary Forms of the Religious Life*, trans. by J.W. Swain. Glencoe, IL: Free Press.

Ellen, R.F. 1984. *Ethnographic Research: A Guide to General Conduct*. London: Academic Press.

Elliott, M. 2000. *The Catholic of Ulster: A History*. London: Penguin.

———. (ed.). 2002. *The Long Road to Peace in Northern Ireland*. Liverpool: Liverpool University Press.

English, R. 2003. *Armed Struggle: The History of the IRA*. London: Macmillan.

———. 2006. *Irish Freedom: The History of Nationalism in Ireland*. London: Macmillan.

Fay, M.-T., M. Morrissey and M. Smyth. 1999. *Northern Ireland's Troubles: The Human Cost*. London: Pluto.

Feeney, B. 2003. *Sinn Féin: A Hundred Turbulent Years*. Madison, WI: University of Wisconsin Press.

Feldman, A. 1991. *Formations of Violence: The Narrative of the Body and Political Terror in Northern Ireland*. Chicago and London: University of Chicago Press.

———. 2000. 'Violence and Vision: The Prosthetics and Aesthetics of Terror', in V. Das, A. Kleinman, M. Ramphele and P. Reynolds (eds), *Violence and Subjectivity*. Berkeley: University of California Press, pp. 46–78.

Fentress, J., and C. Wickham. 1992. *Social Memory*. Oxford: Blackwell.

Foote, K.E., A. Tóth and A. Árvay. 2000. 'Hungary after 1989: Inscribing a New Past on Place', *Geographical Review* 90(3): 301–34.

Foucault, M. 1977. *Language, Counter-memory, Practice: Selected Essays and Interviews*, D.F. Bouchard and S. Simon (eds). Ithaca, NY: Cornell University Press.

Funkenstein, A. 1993. *Perceptions of Jewish History*. Berkeley, CA: University of California Press.

Geertz, C. 1973. *The Interpretation of Cultures*. New York: Basic Books.

Gormally, B. 2001. *Conversion from War to Peace: Reintegration of Ex-Prisoners in Northern Ireland*. Derry/Londonderry: INCORE.

Gough, P. 2000. 'From Heroes' Groves to Parks of Peace: Landscapes of Remembrance, Protest and Peace', *Landscape Research* 25(2): 213–28.

Graham, B. 2004. 'The Past in the Present: The Shaping of Identity in Loyalist Ulster', *Terrorism and Political Violence* 16(3): 483–500.

Graham, B., and P. Shirlow. 2002. 'The Battle of the Somme in Ulster Memory and Identity', *Political Geography* 21: 881–904.

Graham, B., and Y. Whelan. 2007. 'The Legacies of the Dead: Commemorating the Troubles in Northern Ireland', *Environment and Planning D* 25: 476–95.

Greenblatt, S., I. Rev and R. Starn. 1995. 'Introduction', *Representations* 49(Winter): 1–14.

Gregory, A. 1994. *The Silence of Memory: Armistice Day 1919–1946*. Oxford: Berg.

Halbwachs, M. 1925. *Les Cadres Sociaux de la Mémoire*. Paris: Alcan.

———. 1941. *La Topographie Légendaire des Évangiles en Terre Sainte. Étude de Mémoire Collective*. Paris: Presses Universitaires de France.

———. 1950. *La Mémoire Collective*. Paris: Presses Universitaires de France.

———. (1926) 1950. *The Collective Memory*, trans. F.J. and V.Y. Ditter. London: Harper Colophon Books.

———. (1950) 1980. *The Collective Memory*. New York: Harper and Row.

———. 1992. *On Collective Memory*. Chicago: University of Chicago Press.

Hamber, B., and R.A. Wilson. 2003. 'Symbolic Closure through Memory, Reparation and Revenge in Post-conflict Societies', in E. Cairns and M.D. Roe (eds), *The Role of Memory in Ethnic Conflict*. Houndmills: Palgrave Macmillan, pp. 144–68.

Harnden, T. 1999. *'Bandit Country': The IRA and South Armagh*. London: Hodder and Stoughton.

Harrison, S. 1995. 'Four Types of Symbolic Conflict', *Journal of the Royal Anthropological Institute* 1(2): 255–72.

Hartley, T. 2006. *Written in Stone: The History of Belfast City Cemetery*. Belfast: Brehon Press Ltd.

Hartman, G. 1994. *Holocaust Remembrance: The Shapes of Memory*. Oxford: Blackwell.

Harvey, D. 1989. 'Monument and Myth', in *The Urban Experience*. Baltimore, MD: Johns Hopkins University Press, pp. 200–28.

Hayward, K., and C. Mitchell. 2003. 'Discourses of Equality in Post-Agreement Northern Ireland', *Contemporary Politics* 9(3): 293–312.

Heller, A. 2001. 'A Tentative Answer to the Question: Has Civil Society Cultural Memory?', *Social Research* 68(4): 103–42.

Hennessey, T. 1997. *A History of Northern Ireland, 1920–96*. Houndmills: Palgrave Macmillan.

———. 2005. *Northern Ireland: The Origins of the Troubles*. Dublin: Gill and Macmillan.

Hewitt, C. 1981. 'Catholic Grievances, Catholic Nationalism and Violence in Northern Ireland during the Civil Rights Period: A Reconsideration', *British Journal of Sociology* 32(3): 362–80.

Higgins, R. 2012. *Transforming 1916: Meaning, Memory and the Fiftieth Anniversary of the Easter Rising*. Cork: Cork University Press.

Hobsbawm, E., and T. Ranger (eds). 1983. *The Invention of Tradition*. New York: Cambridge University Press.

Holland, J., and H. McDonald. 1994. *INLA: Deadly Divisions*. Dublin: Torc.

Humphrey, M. 2002. *The Politics of Atrocity and Reconciliation: From Terror to Trauma*. London: Routledge.

Hutchinson, J. 2007. 'Warfare, Remembrance and National Identity', in A.S. Leoussi and S. Grosby (eds), *Nationalism and Symbolism: History, Culture and Ethnicity in the Formation of Nations*. Edinburgh: Edinburgh University Press, pp. 42–52.

Huyssen, A. 1995. *Twilight Memories*. London: Routledge.

Ivory, J.D. 2007. 'Sneak Peeks at Insurrection: Portrayals of the Irish Republican Army in Film Trailers', *Atlantic Journal of Communication* 15(3): 214–29.

Jackson, P., and J. Penrose. 1993. *Constructions of Race, Place and Nation*. Minneapolis, MN: University of Minneapolis Press.

Jarman, N. 1992. 'Troubled Images: The Iconography of Loyalism', *Critique of Anthropology* 12(2): 133–65.

———. 1993. 'Intersecting Belfast', in B. Bender (ed.), *Landscape: Politics and Perspectives*. Oxford: Berg, pp. 107–38.

———. 1996a. 'The Ambiguities of Peace: Republican and Loyalist Ceasefire Murals', *Causeway* 3(1): 23–27.

———. 1996b 'Violent Men, Violent Land: Dramatizing the Troubles and the Landscape of Ulster', *Journal of Material Culture* 1(1): 39–61.

———. 1997. *Material Conflicts: Parades and Visual Displays in Northern Ireland*. Oxford: Berg.

———. 1998. 'Painting Landscapes: The Place of Murals in the Symbolic Construction of Urban Space', in A.D. Buckley (ed.), *Symbols in Northern Ireland*. Belfast: Institute of Irish Studies, Queen's University Belfast, pp. 81–98.

———. 1999. 'Commemorating 1916, Celebrating Difference: Parading and Painting in Belfast', in A. Forty and S. Küchler (eds), *The Art of Forgetting*. Oxford: Berg, pp. 171–95.

Jarman, N., and D. Bryan. 2000. 'Green Parades in an Orange State: Nationalist and Republican Commemorations and Demonstrations from Partition to the Troubles, 1920–1970', in T. Fraser (ed.), *The Irish Parading Tradition: Following the Drum*. Basingstoke: Macmillan, pp. 95–110.

Jenkins, R. 2004. *Social Identity*, 2nd edn. London: Routledge.

Johnson, N.C. 1994. 'Sculpting Heroic Histories: Celebrating the Centenary of the 1978 Rebellion in Ireland', *Transactions of the Institute of British Geographers* 19(1): 78–93.

———. 1995. 'Cast in Stone: Monuments, Geography, and Nationalism', *Environment and Planning D* 13: 51–65.

Kapferer, B. 1988. *Legends of People, Myths of State: Violence, Intolerance and Political Culture in Sri Lanka and Australia*. Washington, DC: Smithsonian Institution Press.

Kelly, W. 2001. *Murals: The Bogside Artists*. [Derry/Londonderry: The Bogside Artists].

Kennaway, B. 2006. *The Orange Order: A Tradition Betrayed*. London: Methuen.

Kerr, R. 2008. *Republican Belfast: A Political Tourist's Guide*. Belfast: MSF Press.

Kertzer, D.I. 1988. *Ritual, Politics and Power*. New Haven, CT: Yale University Press.

King, A. 1998. *Memorials of the Great War in Britain: The Symbolism and Politics of Remembrance*. Oxford: Berg.

Knox, C. 2002. '"See No Evil, Hear No Evil": Insidious Paramilitary Violence in Northern Ireland', *British Journal of Criminology* 42: 164–85.

Knox, C., and R. Monaghan. 2002. *Informal Justice in Divided Societies: Northern Ireland and South Africa*. Houndmills: Palgrave Macmillan.

Koonz, C. 1994. 'Between Memory and Oblivion: Concentration Camps in German Memory', in J.R. Gillis (ed.), *Commemorations: The Politics of National Identity*. Princeton, NJ: Princeton University Press, pp. 258–80.

Koshar, R.J. 1994. 'Building Pasts: Historic Preservation and Identity in Twentieth-century Germany', in J.R. Gillis (ed.), *Commemorations: The Politics of National Identity*. Princeton, NJ: Princeton University Press, pp. 215–38.

Lebovics, H. 1994. 'Creating the Authentic France: Struggles over French Identity in the First Half of the Twentieth Century', in J.R. Gillis (ed.), *Commemorations: The Politics of National Identity*. Princeton, NJ: Princeton University Press, pp. 239–57.

Leerssen, J. 2001. 'Monuments and Trauma: Varieties of Remembrance', in I. McBride (ed.), *History and Memory in Modern Ireland*. Cambridge: Cambridge University Press, pp. 204–22.

Leonard, J. 1997a. 'Facing "the Finger of Scorn": Veterans' Memories of Ireland after the Great War', in M. Evans and K. Lunn (eds.), *War and Memory in the XXth Century*. Oxford: Berg, pp. 59–72.

———. 1997b. *Memorials to the Casualties of Conflict: Northern Ireland 1969 to 1997*. Belfast: Northern Ireland Community Relations Council.

Lijphart, A. 1977. *Democracy in Plural Societies: A Comparative Exploration*. New Haven, CT and London: Yale University Press.

Lisle, D. 2006. 'Sublime Lessons: Education and Ambivalence in War Exhibitions', *Millennium: Journal of International Studies* 34(3): 185–206.

Longley, E. 1994. 'The Rising, the Somme and Irish Memory', in *The Living Stream: Literature and Revisionism in Ireland*. Newcastle-upon-Tyne: Bloodaxe Books, pp. 69–85.

———. 2001. 'Northern Ireland: Commemoration, Elegy, Forgetting', in I. McBride (ed.), *History and Memory in Modern Ireland*. Cambridge: Cambridge University Press, pp. 223–53.

Lowenthal, D. 1985. *The Past Is a Foreign Country*. Cambridge: Cambridge University Press.

Lukes, S. 1977. *Essays in Social Theory*. London: Macmillan.

Maier, C.S. 1988. *The Unmasterable Past: History, Holocaust, and German National Identity*. Cambridge, MA: Harvard University Press.

Maillot, A. 2004. *New Sinn Féin: Irish Republicanism in the Twenty-First Century*. London: Routledge.

Marx, K. 1852. 'The Eighteenth Brumaire of Louis Bonaparte', *Die Revolution* 1.

Mayo, J.M. 1988. 'War Memorials as Political Memory', *Geographical Review* 78(1): 62–75.

McAuley, J.W., and J. McCormack. 1990. 'The Hound of Ulster and the Re-writing of Irish History', Études Irlandaises 5(2): 149–64.

McBride, I. 1997. The Siege of Derry in Ulster Protestant Mythology. Dublin: Four Courts Press.

McDonald, H., and J. Cusack. 2004. UDA: Inside the Heart of Loyalist Terror. Dublin: Penguin.

McDowell, S. 1997. 'Armalite, the Ballot Box and Memorialization: Sinn Féin and the State in Post-conflict Northern Ireland', The Round Table 96(393): 725–38.

———. 2008a. 'Commemorating Dead "Men": Gendering the Past and Present in Post-conflict Northern Ireland', Gender, Place and Culture 15(4): 335–54.

———. 2008b. 'Selling Conflict Heritage through Tourism in Peacetime Northern Ireland: Transforming Conflict or Exacerbating Difference?', International Journal of Heritage Studies 14(5): 405–21.

McEvoy, K. 2001. Paramilitary Imprisonment in Northern Ireland: Resistance, Management and Release. Oxford: Oxford University Press.

McEvoy, K., and A. Eriksson. 2008. 'Who Owns Justice? Community, State and the Northern Ireland Transition', in J. Shapland (ed.), Justice, Community and Civil Society. Cullompton, Devon: Willan, pp. 157–89.

McEvoy, K., and H. Mika. 2001. 'Policing, Punishment and Praxis: Restorative Justice and Non-violent Alternatives to Paramilitary Punishments in Northern Ireland', Policing and Society 11(3/4): 259–382.

———. 2002. 'Restorative Justice and the Critique of Informalism in Northern Ireland', British Journal of Criminology 43(3): 534–63.

McGarry, J., and B. O'Leary. 1995. Explaining Northern Ireland: Broken Images. Oxford: Blackwell.

McIntosh, G. 1999. The Force of Culture: Unionist Identities in Twentieth-century Ireland. Cork: Cork University Press.

———. 2006. Belfast City Hall: One Hundred Years. Belfast: Blackstaff Press.

McKittrick, D., S. Kelters, B. Feeney and C. Thornton. 2007. Lost Lives: The Stories of the Men, Women and Children Who Died as a Result of the Northern Ireland Troubles. Edinburgh: Mainstream Publishing.

McKittrick, D., and D. McVea. 2001. Making Sense of the Troubles. London: Penguin.

Mesev, V., P. Shirlow and J. Downs. 2009. 'The Geography of Conflict and Death in Belfast, Northern Ireland', Annals of the Association of American Geographers 99(5): 893–903.

Metress, S., and E.K. Metress. 1993. 'The Communal Significance of the Irish Republican Army Funeral Ritual', Irish Studies Paper 1.

Misztal, B. 2003. Theories of Social Remembering. Maidenhead, Berkshire: McGraw-Hill Education.

Mitchell, C. 2003. 'From Victims to Equals? Catholic Responses to Political Change in Northern Ireland', Irish Political Studies 18(1): 51–71.

Moloney, E. 2002. A Secret History of the IRA. London: Allen Lane.

Monk, J. 1992. 'Gender in the Landscape: Expressions of Power and Meaning', in K. Anderson and F. Gale (eds), Inventing Places: Studies in Cultural Geography. Melbourne: Longman Cheshire, pp. 123–38.

Mosse, G.L. 1990. Fallen Soldiers: Reshaping the Memory of the World Wars. Oxford: Oxford University Press.

Mulholland, M. 2004. 'Why Did Unionists Discriminate?', in S. Wichert (ed.), From the United Irishmen to Twentieth Century Unionism: Essays in Honour of A.T.Q. Stewart. Dublin: Four Courts Press.

Müller, J.-W. (ed.). 2002. *Memory and Power in Post-war Europe: Studies in the Presence of the Past.* Cambridge: Cambridge University Press.

Nora, P. 1989. 'Between Memory and History: Les Lieux de Mémoire', *Representations* 26: 7–24.

Nussbaum, M.C. 2001. *Upheavals of Thought.* Cambridge: Cambridge University Press.

O'Doherty, M. 1998. *The Trouble with Guns: Republican Strategy and the Provisional IRA.* Belfast: Blackstaff.

Officer, D. 2001. '"For God and Ulster": The Ulsterman on the Somme', in I. McBride (ed.), *History and Memory in Modern Ireland.* Cambridge: Cambridge University Press, pp. 160–83.

O'Keefe, T.J. 1992. '"Who Fears to Speak of '98?"': The Rhetoric and Rituals of the United Irishmen Centennial, 1898', *Éire-Ireland* 27(3): 67–91.

O'Leary, B. 1999. 'The Nature of the British–Irish Agreement', *New Left Review* 233: 66–96.

O'Malley, P. 1990. *Biting at the Grave: The Irish Hunger Strikes and the Politics of Despair.* Belfast: Blackstaff.

Outhwaite, W., and T. Bottomore (eds). 1993. *The Blackwell Dictionary of Twentieth-century Social Thought.* Oxford: Blackwell.

Ozouf, M. 1988. *Festivals and the French Revolution.* Cambridge, MA: Harvard University Press.

Papadakis, Y. 1994. 'The National Struggle: Museums of a Divided City', *Ethnic and Racial Studies* 17(3): 400–19.

———. 2003. 'Nation, Narrative and Commemoration: Political Ritual in Divided Cyprus', *History and Anthropology* 14(3): 253–70.

Perks, R., and A. Thomson. 1998. *The Oral History Reader.* London: Routledge.

Picard, R.G. 1991. 'How Violence Is Justified: Sinn Fein's An Phoblacht', *Journal of Communication* 41(4): 90–103.

Prager, J. 1998. *Presenting the Past: Psychoanalysis and the Sociology of Misremembering.* Cambridge, MA: Harvard University Press.

Pringle, P., and P. Jacobson. 2000. *Those Are Real Bullets, Aren't They? Bloody Sunday, Derry, 30 January 1972.* London: Fourth Estate Limited.

Roche, R. 2008. *Sectarianism and Segregation in Urban Northern Ireland: Northern Irish Youth Post-Agreement.* Belfast: School of History and Anthropology, Queen's University Belfast.

Rolston, B. 1991. *Politics and Painting: Murals and Conflict in Northern Ireland.* Cranbury, NJ: Associated University Presses.

———. 1992. *Drawing Support: Murals in the North of Ireland.* Belfast: Beyond the Pale.

———. 1996. 'Culture, Conflict and Murals: The Irish Case', in T. Ziff (ed.), *Distant Relations: Chicano, Irish, Mexican Art and Critical Writing.* New York: Smart Art Press, pp. 191–99.

———. 1998a. *Drawing Support 2: Murals of War and Peace.* Belfast: Beyond the Pale.

———. 1998b. 'Culture as a Battlefield: Political Identity and the State in the North of Ireland', *Race and Class* 39(4): 23–35.

———. 2003a. *Drawing Support 3: Murals and Transition in the North of Ireland.* Belfast: Beyond the Pale.

———. 2003b. 'Changing the Political Landscape: Murals and Transition in Northern Ireland', *Irish Studies Review* 11(1): 3–16.

Rosenberg, T. 1995. *The Haunted Landscape: Facing Europe's Ghosts after Communism.* New York: Random House.

Ruane, J., and J. Todd. 1996. *The Dynamics of Conflict in Northern Ireland: Power, Conflict and Emancipation*. Cambridge: Cambridge University Press.

———. 1999. *After the Good Friday Agreement: Analysing Political Change in Northern Ireland*. Dublin: University College Dublin Press.

Russell, B. 1960. *Power: A New Social Analysis*. London: Allen and Unwin.

Said, E. 1978. *Orientalism*. London: Penguin.

Sanson, R. 1976. *Les 14 Juillet: Féte et Conscience Nationale, 1798–1975*. Paris: Flammarion.

Santino, J. 2004. *Signs of War and Peace: Social Conflict and the Use of Public Symbols in Northern Ireland*. New York: Palgrave.

Sauer, C. 1925. 'The Morphology of Landscape', *University of California Publications in Geography* 2: 19–54.

Schudson, M. 1997. 'Lives, Laws and Language: Commemorative versus Non-commemorative Forms of Effective Public Memory', *The Communication Review* 2(1): 3–17.

Schwartz, B. 1991. 'Social Change and Collective Memory: The Democratization of George Washington', *American Sociological Review* 56(2): 221–36.

Scott, J.C. 1990. *Domination and the Arts of Resistance: Hidden Transcripts*. New Haven, CT: Yale University Press.

Sherman, D.J. 1999. *The Construction of Memory in Interwar France*. Chicago: Chicago University Press.

Shils, E. 1981. *Tradition*. London: Faber.

Shirlow, P., and K. McEvoy. 2008. *Beyond the Wire: Former Prisoners and Conflict Transformation in Northern Ireland*. London: Pluto.

Shirlow, P., and B. Murtagh. 2006. *Belfast: Segregation, Violence and the City*. London: Pluto.

Sider, G., and G. Smith (eds). 1997. *Between History and Histories: The Making of Silences and Commemorations*. Toronto: University of Toronto Press.

Silke, A. 1998. 'The Lords of Discipline: The Methods and Motives of Paramilitary Vigilantism in Northern Ireland', *Low Intensity Conflict and Law Enforcement* 7(2): 121–56.

Sluka, J. 1989. *Hearts and Minds, Water and Fish: Support for the IRA and the INLA in a Northern Irish Ghetto*. Greenwich: JAI Press.

———. 1992. 'The Politics of Painting: Political Murals in Northern Ireland', in C. Nordstrom and J. Martin (eds), *The Paths to Domination, Resistance, and Terror*. Berkeley: University of California Press, pp. 190–216.

———. 1996. 'The Writing's on the Wall: Peace Process Images, Symbols and Murals in Northern Ireland', *Critique of Anthropology* 16(4): 381–94.

Smith, A.D. 1981a. *The Ethnic Revival*. Cambridge: Cambridge University Press.

———. 1981b. 'War and Ethnicity: The Role of Warfare in the Formation, Self-images, and Cohesion of Ethnic Communities', *Ethnic and Racial Studies* 4(4): 375–97.

———. 1996. 'LSE Centennial Lecture. The Resurgence of Nationalism? Myth and Memory in the Renewal of Nations', *British Journal of Sociology* 47(4): 575–98.

———. 1997. 'The "Golden Age" and National Renewal', in G. Hosking and G. Schöpflin (eds), *Myths and Nationhood*. London: Hurst and Co., pp. 36–59.

———. 2003. *Chosen People*. Oxford: Oxford University Press.

Smyth, M. 1998. *Half the Bottle: Understanding the Impact of the Troubles on Children and Young People in Northern Ireland*. Derry/Londonderry: INCORE/the United Nations University/University of Ulster.

Sperber, D. 1975. *Rethinking Symbolism*. Cambridge: Cambridge University Press.

Stevenson, C., S. Condor and J. Abell. 2007. 'The Minority–Majority Conundrum in Northern Ireland: An Orange Order Perspective', *Political Psychology* 28(1): 105–25.

Stewart, A.C.Q. 1967. *The Ulster Crisis: Resistance to Home Rule 1912–14*. London: Faber.

———. 1989. *The Narrow Ground: Roots of Conflict in Ulster*. London: Faber and Faber.

Stewart, P., and A. Strathern. 2003. 'Introduction', in *Landscape, Memory and History: Anthropological Perspectives*. London and Sterling, VA: Earthscan Publications.

Switzer, C. 2007. *Unionists and Great War Commemoration in the North of Ireland 1914–1939*. Dublin: Irish Academic Press.

Switzer, C. and S. McDowell. 2009. 'Redrawing Cognitive Maps of Conflict: Lost Spaces and Forgetting in the Centre of Belfast', *Memory Studies* 2(3): 337–53.

Szacka, B. 1997. 'Systematic Transformations and Memory of the Past', *Polish Sociological Review* 118(2): 199–232.

Taylor, P. 1997. *Provos: The IRA and Sinn Fein*. London: Bloomsbury.

Taylor, R. 1991. 'Northern Ireland and South Africa: A Consociational Path to Peace?', *First International Congress on Prejudice, Discrimination and Conflict, July 1991*. Jerusalem.

——— (ed.). 2009. *Consociational Theory: McGarry and O'Leary and the Northern Ireland Conflict*. London: Routledge.

Terdiman, R. 1993. *Present Past: Modernity and the Memory Crisis*. Ithaca, NY: Cornell University Press.

Thompson, W., and B. Mulholland. 1995. 'Paramilitary Punishments and Young People in West Belfast', in L. Kennedy (ed.), *Crime and Punishment in West Belfast*. Belfast: The Summer School, West Belfast.

Thomson, A. 1994. *Anzac Memories: Living with the Legend*. Melbourne: Oxford University Press.

Tonge, J. 2002. *Northern Ireland: Conflict and Change*, 2nd edn. Harlow: Pearson Education.

Vannais, J. 1999. 'Post Ceasefire Political Murals in Northern Ireland: A Process of Legitimisation', MA dissertation. Belfast: Queen's University Belfast.

———. 2000. 'Mainstreaming Murals', *Fortnight* 385: 21–22.

Verdery, K. 1999. *The Political Lives of Dead Bodies: Reburial and Post Socialist Change*. New York: Columbia University Press.

Wagner, P.L., and M.W. Mikesell (eds). 1962. *Readings in Cultural Geography*. Chicago: University of Chicago Press.

Walker, B. 1992. '1641, 1689, 1690 and All That: The Unionist Sense of History', *Irish Review* 12: 56–64.

———. 2000. *Past and Present: History, Identity and Politics in Ireland*. Belfast: Institute of Irish Studies, Queen's University Belfast.

Walker, G. 2004. *A History of the Ulster Unionist Party: Protest, Pragmatism and Pessimism*. Manchester: Manchester University Press.

Whelan, Y. 2003. *Reinventing Modern Dublin: Streetscape, Iconography and the Politics of Identity*. Dublin: UCD Press.

White, H. 1990a. 'The Value of Narrativity in the Representation of Reality', in *The Content of the Form*. Baltimore, MD and London: John Hopkins University Press, pp. 1–25.

———. 1990b. 'The Politics of Historical Interpretation: Discipline and De-sublimation', in *The Content of the Form*. Baltimore, MD and London: John Hopkins University Press, pp. 58–82.

White, R. 1989. 'From Peaceful Protest to Guerrilla War: Micromobilization of the Provisional Irish Republican Army', *American Journal of Sociology* 94(5): 1277–1302.

Whyte, J. 1983. 'How Much Discrimination Was there under the Unionist Regime, 1921–68?', in T. Gallagher and J. O'Connell (eds), *Contemporary Irish Studies*. Manchester: Manchester University Press, pp. 1–35.

———. 1990. *Interpreting Northern Ireland*. Oxford: Clarendon.

Williams, P. 2007. *Memorial Museums: The Global Rush to Commemorate Atrocities*. Oxford: Berg.

Winter, J.M. 1995. *Sites of Memory, Sites of Mourning: The Great War in European Cultural History*. Cambridge: Cambridge University Press.

Winter, J.M., and E. Sivan (eds). 1999. *War and Remembrance in the Twentieth Century*. Cambridge: Cambridge University Press.

Wood, I.S. 2006. *Crimes of Loyalty: A History of the UDA*. Edinburgh: Edinburgh University Press.

Zerubavel, E. 1997. *Social Mindscape: An Invitation to Cognitive Sociology*. Cambridge, MA: Harvard University Press.

Zerubavel, Y. 1995. *Recovered Roots: Collective Memory and the Making of Israeli National Tradition*. Chicago: University of Chicago Press.

INDEX

memory-making function of Unionist establishment in 4–5
Nationalism in 4
Orange Order 5, 10, 20, 23, 27, 33, 36, 39, 41, 45n10, 65n9, 132, 148–9n13, 149n15
public memorialization of past in 4
Troubles in, outbreak of (1969) 5
Twelfth of July celebrations 5
Ulster's Solemn League and Covenant 131–2
Unionism in 4
Northern Ireland Civil Rights Association (NICRA) 28
Northern Ireland Parades Commission 155
Northern Ireland Roads Service 51
Nussbaum, Martha C. 11

O'Doherty, M. 44n5
Officer, D. 25n3, 86n10, 132
official narratives 70, 80
O'Hanlon, Feargal 197
O'Hara, Patsy 113, 114, 115, 116, 127n4
O'Keefe, T.J. 25n3, 86n10
O'Leary, B. 45–6n17
Omagh bombing 60
O'Malley, P. 86n10
O'Neill, Hugh 123, 127n8
oral history
  memorial projects and 92–3
  projects concerning 42–3
Orange Order 5, 10, 20, 23, 27, 33, 36, 39, 41, 45n10, 65n9, 132, 148–9n13, 149n15
O'Reilly, John 127n8, 127n11
O'Riordan, Sean 105
O'Toole, Fintan 42
Outhwaite, W. and Bottomore, T. 85n2
Ozouf, M. 65n15

painted kerbstones 50, 51–2, 64, 181
Paisley, Ian 29, 136–7, 167
Papadakis, Y. 25n8, 71, 74–5, 84, 86n14
paramilitaries
  affiliations of interviewees 24
  casualties, Loyalist commemorations in memory of 142–3

combatants, memorials to 38–9
communal reactions to 177–8
cultures, commemorative forms relating to 20
groups and local communities, complex relationship between 177–80
narratives of, promotion of 195–6
paramilitary-related memorials, common occurrence of 47
Parnell, Charles Stewart 31
party offices, memorials in 40
past
  attitudes to past, changes in 13–14
  cherry-picking from history 73–80
  collective history vs individual stories 67–70
  collective narratives of 173
  contemporary political endorsement and selectivity in use of 196–7
  historical change 185, 187–9
  historical continuity, 'illusion' of 196
  historical selection, exercise of 101
  inspiration from historical events, properly understood 194
  public memorialization of past in Northern Ireland 4
  shared past
    opposing versions of 73–80
    selective versions of 17, 48, 80, 105, 197
patriotism and remembrance 16
peace memorials 43–4
peace process, memorialization and 199–200
Pearse, Padraig 83, 86n9, 100, 108n10, 120
Perks, R. and Thomson, A. 91
permanent memorials 38–41
An Phoblacht 86n14, 122
Picard, R.G. 86n14
Plunkett, Joseph 83
police service legitimacy 178
politicized memory 134–5
  power and 15–18
politico-idealism 185, 189–92
politics
  collective memory and politics of memorialization 5–6, 11–26
  of commemorations 80–85

www.ingramcontent.com/pod-product-compliance
Lightning Source LLC
Chambersburg PA
CBHW060030030426
42334CB00019B/2256